THEN AGAIN

Irma Kurtz writes a regular column for *Cosmopolitan*. Her most recent books are *Dear London* and *The Great American Bus Ride*. She was born in Jersey City, and is a graduate of Columbia University.

For more information on Irma Kurtz visit
www.4thestate.com/irmakurtz

THEN AGAIN

*Travels in search of
my younger self*

Irma Kurtz

FOURTH ESTATE • *London*

This paperback edition first published in 2004
First published in Great Britain in 2003 by
Fourth Estate
A Division of HarperCollins*Publishers*
77–85 Fulham Palace Road
London W6 8JB
www.4thestate.com

1 3 5 7 9 8 6 4 2

A catalogue record for this book is available from
the British Library

ISBN 1-84115-694-9

Typeset by Rowland Phototypesetting Ltd,
Bury St Edmunds, Suffolk
Printed in Great Britain by
Clays Ltd, St Ives plc

One

One way or another, the journey will end where it began. If the last stop does not return the traveller to the start, if it strands her somewhere strange, the beginning will come looking for her. And it will find her, too: in dreams, in madness, in rogue memories that thunder out of the blue, and in things. Individual memory tends to be a self-aggrandising, over-edited branch of the human imagination; those of us existentialists, however, whose nature is to live hard and fast in the here and now, are afflicted with gaping forgetfulness, recollection sieved, chronology all to pot. A small compensation for bad memory is an acute sensitivity to things. The walls of my flat are albums; my wardrobe is an archive; a ticket stub at the bottom of an old suitcase can stop my heart. Things more than aid my memories; things contain them. A name and number scribbled in the margin of a yellowing page; a hotel bill from years ago marking my place in an abandoned book, bronze iris or moss roses from the past blooming in a current garden; music, measurable too after all and a kind of thing; scents and flavour: these and countless other objects of virtue can return me instantly to points along the journey and where it all began.

I came across the old notebook on my last trip home. It is curious, after so much water under the bridge and so many keys on the ring, still to call the place I left three-quarters of my life ago 'home'. But home sticks to where the traveller leaves her mother and America must always be my homeland because it is my mother's land. I had no say in the matter. Practically every morning of my school years I stood shoulder to shoulder with others in my class and pledged allegiance to the flag and to the republic for which it stood, flapping in the dank breeze off the New Jersey marshland where we first- and second-generation Americans were growing up. And some of us, not many of the girls, outgrowing that place too, faster than we outgrew our patent-leather shoes called 'mary janes', gleaming under us like the hooves of circus ponies. You don't often see patent leather on the feet of children these days, only occasionally in Latin cities where families walk out together on Sundays; there are fewer and fewer of such cities and such families. Right, left-right, left: those shoes were made for skipping. In my case for skipping town. When the leather cracked over the toes it showed buckram underneath. What has become of buckram? And taffeta, and starched cotton and faille, and all the stiff fabrics of a post-war childhood? My old notebook too is not a thing found easily today. It has a hard cover bound in black library tape that has not yielded or split in the half-century since I bought it for a nickel. What a nickel bought in the early 1950s costs around $3 now. On the other hand, what was an hour then passes now in fifteen minutes: illogical sums of ageing that make old folks fumble at checkout counters and turn up way too early or too late for buses and trains.

Nearly thirty years ago, when my mother was almost the age I am now, my father twelve years older than she, they sold our holiday house in the country and the flat in Jersey City where my brother and I had grown up, and they moved to a sheltered community near Princeton, New Jersey. On one of my visits not long after they had settled in, my father strolled out with me to have a look around. Mother had long before stopped walking to no purpose or destination, but my father's body was strong and had outlived the full vigour of his mind by a decade or so; it was just the two of us trudging along side by side, more attuned in silence than conversation. Streets of the gated square mile were empty as usual, more or less identical cottages were laid out along them like pieces on a board game for players with fixed incomes and shrunken ambition. A few cars passed, driven slowly by white-haired women on their way to the community clubhouse or the cottage hospital or the shop; they put on speed in shows of bravado whenever they saw us trying to cross a street ahead of them. A group of chattering dowagers in shell-suits came towards us, a few of them were swinging mallets, apparently heading to the croquet green.

3

My father gripped my arm. 'Look, Irma, you see the kind of place this is,' he whispered in a kind of panic, 'only the men die here.'

It was the last walk he and I took together; not very long afterwards he went ahead to prove his point.

Once my mother arrived at an age when she could no longer reach or stoop to the top or bottom shelves of her cupboards, they remained crammed with things that provide poignant forage when I visit home. There is practically none of my father, no notes in his oddly dainty script, no letters, even the flyleaves have been torn out of books he inscribed to his then beloved when they were courting: *The Thoughts of Epictetus*, *The Rubáiyát of Omar Khayyám*. What mother has destroyed and thrown away, I imagine in a single vengeful frenzy, is evidence, too, of anger and disappointment as fierce as love. It was not a marriage made in heaven; it was made, in fact, in Indiana. They met there at university, the fatherless local girl and the handsome man from the east. A few photographs of him have escaped, but there are spaces, too, crusted with old library paste on the black pages of ancient albums where his image once was. Repudiated as husband, he incidentally became nobody's father.

It was at the bottom of one of mother's domestic oubliettes that I found my old notebook two years ago, languishing among curling papers and postcards in a cardboard box. The moment I saw it my breath caught and there I was again, eighteen, exultant and trembling on the deck of the Italian ship, *Castel Felice*, about to embark on a journey that was going to effect the romantic transformation of my life at last. Years earlier when I was ten or twelve I had started sometimes to feel a sense of something other ahead, something adventurous, something more than a future of prosperity, fidelity and motherhood for which I and every other girl in my class was being designed. It was no gift of birthright that animated my daydreams, I knew I was no changeling; I certainly had no outsized sense of self-importance. On the contrary, what excited me was the freedom that derives from knowing myself unimportant and without status: the freedom of invisibility. Perhaps my early diffidence is why age, which throws a shabby cloak over all women, has not descended on me as an ugly surprise. If anything, to know I am of no interest to those who interest me so I can see, unseen, has increased the fun of travelling. Occasionally, and never for long, I used to indulge in adolescent self-pity and pretend to envy Marie Caso, the fishmonger's daughter, and the other playmates of my street who were free of responsibility, free of the possibilities, free of the freedom that I felt myself stuck with. By the time I turned seventeen and left for university, Marie and I lost touch; probably, she was already engaged to a nice Italian boy. And two years later, in the spring of 1954, when I bought the notebook in which to keep a journal of my first trip to Europe, it is a safe guess she was pregnant with the first of three, maybe four, lovely children.

I wish I could walk around myself as I was on the deck

of the *Castel Felice* surrounded by college students from every state in America, hundreds of them, all on their dutiful six-week cultural European tours. My own group was called 'Study Abroad' and composed mainly of students from the Midwest and the east coast. I wish I could see the back of my head, watch it turn a face my way and hear my young voice answer when I ask her – you, myself – whether she suspects or hopes that she alone in the noisy crowd is bound to leave something of her very self on that other continent. And find something. And never quite come home again.

The journal of my first trip to Europe is a typical American kid's notebook of a design that continues to be produced, though modern taste prefers the cover soft and its traditional mottled pattern seems to me over the years to have become increasingly white. The cover of my old notebook is mostly classic black, giving the effect of water seen from above on a moonlit night. I wonder if the word 'Compositions' is still being set in elegant typeface over a white rectangle on the front? Probably not. Nowadays, all but doodles are undertaken by keyboard. On the line below, in the space after 'Name' is my own, written proudly and carefully as I used to sign it when I was eighteen. By the time a body turns sixty or so, her signature is required increasingly seldom; all important deliveries have been made, their receipt acknowledged; contracts, last wills and testaments, births and marriages have been put in order, and someone else will sign the death certificate. Aged signatures become impatient and jagged with hardly any delineation between the central letters as if to say: if you don't know who I am by this time, to hell with you. Besides, in modern life even the most intimate messages are sent electronically or by phone; not many cheques need to be filled in either, not since plastic came on the scene. The day lies not very far ahead when, as before the dawn of literacy, a thumbprint or an 'X' will see most people through a lifetime.

The way I wrote my name on the cover of the notebook, so dewy and guileless, makes my aged heart go out to the young me, unknowing of what an awful lot of promiscuous signing lay ahead of her, unaware that her virginal surname was bound to remain unchanged for ever. As I opened the old notebook and started to read, I wanted more than ever to go back and find her on deck among the other American youngsters outward bound for the first time.

'If I could tell you,' I would tell her, 'for a start, you will not be especially lucky. Don't count on anything heaven-sent to happen in your life. Expect no serious serendipity. No lottery wins for you, dear. In any case, as even the luckiest bastards grow old, serendipity gives way to mere coincidence. So expect only what you yourself make happen and allow. Nobody is going to do you any favours and in that way at least you'll be lucky. Because favours are an anchor; favours are a drag. Favours are power; kindness is strength. Got that? Don't do anyone any favours either, lest you bind him to you bitterly. Give and forget, no strings attached and nothing to call in. I wish you knew now, girl, how strong you are, so much stronger than you, or I, were led to believe. I wish you had the conviction of your courage. Are you listening to me? Time is short. Very, very short.

What more? Let's see. Stay away from handsome men this time; easy conquests make them slack. And beware of childless women over forty; they take up residence in their empty nurseries and behave accordingly. Ride a low horse and stable it away from high ones: the higher the horse the more stupid its rider. Cut your hair before you're forty. Any woman over thirty-five wearing a mane like yours is in trouble. Don't smoke. Nobody is going to tell the public for another couple of decades, but smoking kills unduly. Do stand up straight, can't you? There is much more, so much more! Oh, how I wish I could tell you. What can I tell you, after all? How can I tell you all you are going to forget? How can I tell you what I don't remember? How can I tell you all that has happened to me and must happen to you? Watch closely. It starts happening here. Look! The second gangway is being raised and when the anchor is weighed at last, a long, long time must pass before you reach a harbour to call home. You are eighteen on your maiden voyage and, appropriately, a maiden; you will return in only six weeks, changed and knowing, a maiden still; but that's a minor adjustment and it will take place on another journey out.'

Did it occur to you that half a century later you, as I, were going to study your primitive squiggles, looking for a map?

Not a map ahead, oh no; ahead is all too clear at our age. The path behind is what I want from you, the one that finally led a girl from Jersey City into residence beside the Thames, where to this day she continues to survive on your nerve and wits. How it would have annoyed you to feel me breathing down your neck as you stood on the deck. What fantasy of her own, you would wonder, did this old madwoman believe you were acting out? Why was she ogling you like an owl a mouse and threatening to touch you? Ugh! You were never going to let yourself be like that, were you? Dried up and past desiring. You intended to die young; most of us who were reading Eng. Lit. at Barnard College in Columbia meant to die young. Like Keats. Ever since you or I can remember, even as a child, we have been regularly buttonholed for reminiscences or warnings by garrulous grown-ups in the street, on buses, at drugstore lunch counters; they took advantage of your curiosity, later mine, combined with the unnatural self-effacement that was drummed into us practically from birth. Already, you knew how to back off, how to free yourself politely from the old bat, soon forgotten in the bustle of departure. The next time we met face to face – she and I, me and I, you and I – was nearly fifty years later when I rediscovered the notebook.

'Well, about time too,' cried the notebook, leaping into my hand. 'Fancy leaving me behind when you left! Letting them stash me here with worn shmottas and chipped cups, and crumbling paperbacks, and diplomas nobody has asked

to see since the ink was dry! Aren't you ashamed of yourself?
To forget about me! Me! Journal of your first trip to Europe,
though sporadically kept, may I say, and puerile, and sloppily
written back in the days when you were fool enough to think
you could trust your memory. Daft child! She who did not
intend to keep her journal should not have kept one in the
first place. What for? "For posterity?" Honey, in case you
ain't noticed, a whole lot of your posterity is behind you.
The pun implicit is all yours, by the by. I've had my fill of
puns thanks to your precocious appetite for the damn things
in your teens.'

Merely holding the journal in my hand, before I had read
a word of it, brought a vivid memory back to me: the ship
had started pulling away when I saw my father break free of
the crowd on shore. Alone, he walked the length of the dock
and stood for as long as I could see him, waving the ancient,
perplexed farewell of parents to their departing children.
Already he was barely in sight, a little figure at the perilous
end of the pier. A boy leaning next to me on the sticky rail
was whistling 'Jesu, Joy of Man's Desiring'. And I was swept
by a wild and paradoxical new feeling, comforting and scary,
sweet and painful, thrilling and melancholy: I thought it must
be loneliness. And I was right.

Two

From our arrival into life, a journey that frees the spirit must cross water. No matter how arduous and dangerous, overland travel leads logically from one foregone conclusion to the next on this mapped world. But on all the breadth of oceans there is no fixed logic, no still border, no language except the one you carry on board; in all the depths of oceans there is no history but prehistory. Time itself is adrift; clocks run down while terrestrial minutes give up their ground to a celestial measure. Somehow, I have conspired to spend more of my life at sea than any woman I know of similarly constrained upbringing. And when I say 'at sea', I do mean in fact as well as fancifully.

'1954: At sea! I have only ever been on the ocean before when Dad took me deep-sea fishing once in Florida. This is different; tonight for the first time ever I will sleep at sea! All at sea! It is divine to be alone. And it was divine to walk around the ship and learn it, all by myself.'

* * *

'All by myself': favourite words since the first time you tied your shoes all by yourself, and rode the bus all by yourself, and finally when you were fourteen or so stayed in the city sometimes all by yourself while your family went to the house in the country for weekends. Of course, dear child, one of the disadvantages of keeping any sort of journal is that it presupposes some sort of reader, even if it is only oneself years later. The moment pen is put to paper the writer ceases to be all by herself. Nor, strictly speaking, were you anything like alone on your first trip to Europe. The deck was crowded with young Americans, thirty or forty of them on the very same undergraduate tour as you. And even as the ship was leaving port, the suitcase in which you had packed your pristine journal was being tossed on an upper berth by one of four cabin mates you had yet to meet. You could be a snooty little Manhattan bitch on the quiet, by the by.

'July, 1954: They are dreadful girls from the Midwest, not with our group. We are called "Study Abroad", mostly from the east. One of them is with some sort of religious tour called "Faith Studies" and headed straight for Rome. She is called Sally or Jane or Mary. Possibly all three. She spent all the time we were pulling away playing solitaire hands of bridge. And while I was on deck, she was busy moving me out of my berth into a less desirable upper one. She had the nerve to say the steward assigned her to the lower bunk. According to the brochure, allocation of bunks is first come, first served, and Dad got us to the pier really early to secure a lower bunk for me. He was afraid when the sea was rough I might roll out of the top one. But what can I do? With a long journey ahead, I must let it pass. Hereafter, I will call her Ass-in-igned. The other two are Ruth and Ethel. They are with a group from their college. Hereafter I'll call them Nothing A and Nothing B. Sat out on deck with the Nothings until 2.30. They twittered nothingspeak about their boring college and their boring boyfriends. But my mind was somewhere else. I kept seeing the dear old Statue of Liberty and remembering how a few hours earlier she had reversed the welcome she had given Grandpa Joe and Grandma Ida half a century before into a *"bon voyage"* for me. How do you know when you leave home for the last time? How do you know when you are leaving home for ever?'

In spite of a nod to my paternal grandparents on departing, I was not looking for my roots or expecting to find them abroad. Student tours such as the one I was on went nowhere near the misty regions of Eastern Europe whence most of my people had fled their unplumbed villages besieged by dangers rarely spoken of to their well-nourished American grandchildren.

'But why, why do you want to live there?' my father cried years later when my schooling was finished and I announced my imminent expatriation to Europe. 'All of them want to come and live here!'

13

I come from a tribe of tumbleweed nature; we rolled up our roots in shawls and scrolls, and ran with them before the wind. No, I was not looking for roots; I took them with me. I was looking for the source of what I knew as culture – the places where words and art and music came from – and I was looking for a good time. My best friend and room-mate at university, Marjorie, had taken the Study Abroad tour the preceding year and she promised me I would certainly find the fun.

The upper berth I complained about was next to a port-hole, and it turned out to be wonderful. Movies were mainly in black and white back then. Without colour telly, without computers or computer games, our adventures were never virtual: they had to be the real thing or nothing. True enough, books have always been able to take an imaginative land-lubber out to sea, but they cannot keep her there when the ship is becalmed and she would rather be somewhere else. Besides, on a literary voyage the author has to tag along. But for one week every sunrise was all my own. Six times through the porthole with my own eyes I watched the new sun tenderly separate the infinite black round into sky and sea: six times I watched life being created again out of space and brine.

'July 1954: It is so very big. Every day or two the Captain tells us to set our watches up an hour. Columbus needed such a long time to cross the ocean going the other way, he must have accumulated hours much, much slower than we are losing them. Did he factor the slow gain into his navigation, I wonder? Did he expect to find a new time in the New World? Do I expect to find an Old Time in the Old World? What will I find there, I wonder?'

And I wonder now, deciphering my faded scrawl: did we have biros in 1953? If we did, they must have been newfangled and dear, for by the fourth day at sea I complain of losing my pen, and ink does not reappear in the journal until weeks later when the tour arrived in Venice. For all my importuning of solitude – 'O, to be alone!' I wrote near the end of the crossing, 'without another American sophomore always at my elbow!' – I have always been indiscriminately social, seeing all strangers as diminutive nations full of curiosities and odd customs. Only in middle age did I learn how to wriggle guiltlessly off the hook of my own conviviality and walk away alone; when I was younger and hopeful of soulmates, I often found myself in too deep. After merely one day at sea a potential best friend had arisen out of the welter of college students aboard. A best friend was necessary to a smart American college girl's life in the early 1950s, as a psychoanalyst was to become a few years later and her own credit card is now. Evelyn Esposito was majoring in Biology at I forget which state university and was on the same tour as I. She was a happy choice for temporary best friend: not only did she appear, at least in the beginning, to be laid back and cheerful, she also spoke a smattering of Italian and had relatives in Genoa who were going to welcome us into their home for a few happy hours off the itinerary. She and her tall, stringy and slightly dour travelling companion, Midge, were three years older than I. For a teenager in those days, and perhaps even now, three years separated underclassmen from seniors, garter belts from girdles, and virgins from women of the world.

'1953: Like others I have met, they are surprised at my extreme youth and great maturity. Must it always be like that?'

No, you little drip, believe me, some day it will be your great age and extreme silliness that surprise them. But I must not be too hard on myself then, for judging every word I wrote, even more tellingly those I didn't, was the phantom of my journal's only likely reader, my most severe critic, my mother. Moreover, I suffered from the inescapable pretensions of late teen years, as well as the darned and ravelling yet distinctly bluestocking standards of Barnard College.

In the days after my journal came to light I began to consider and finally to plan retracing the journey that changed me for keeps. During the more than thirty years I have lived in Europe, I have travelled out of my neighbourhood, England, occasionally and only for a purpose generally connected to my profession of jobbing journalist and writer. True enough, I often go to France, but it hardly counts as a journey for I have a small flat in the Pas de Calais; I call it the 'west wing' of my equally small flat in London. Italy? I have been only once or twice in all these decades to visit friends in Tuscany; I've been to Mexico many times more than to Holland, and to Africa twice as often as to Germany. Soon, the idea of repeating the Grand Tour of my youth started to become compelling. Now that I am coming to the end of most desires, would I rediscover the joyous excitement of my first journal? Now that I am catching up in years with the stones of Rome, would I find the same enchantment in antiquity? Now that American tourists are two a penny, not the rare birds we were in the 1950s, would there be the same dawning sense not only of discovery, also of being discovered? And with the guide and talisman of my old journal in hand could I perhaps reverse time for a moment? Could I meet myself as I was at eighteen, sitting in the Tuileries gardens in Paris, weeping because I did not want to leave? I wish I could have begun precisely as I did the first time, sailing away from Manhattan, a jagged comb on the beach, to embark on a long, slow voyage over what I hear Americans now refer to as 'the pond'. We did not take the Atlantic so lightly in those days. Many of us had living ancestors like mine who had crossed that great sea in terror and in hope. East-coast kids with itchy feet commonly undertook a pioneering trek into America's alien inner spaces where a lot of them settled to raise local standards and money and children. Fewer of

17

us, however, were called to a choppy crossing of the mighty ocean that separated us Americans from our history.

The *Castel Felice* was no insulated five-star liner, that's for sure.

'1954: We eat at long trestle tables. It looks like the set for a prison movie except it never stops moving and there are no attempted escapes. Where there is a strong breeze, hardly anyone turns up for meals. Ass-in-igned has hardly moved out of the lower berth and the Nothings are green. I haven't felt a twinge of seasickness yet. But I'd better not crow about that until the journey is over. The food is surprisingly awful. But the Italian stewards are delicious. While he was serving the awful soup, one of them whispered in English that he was very fond of me. Alas, I love another. The man who makes the crew announcements over the loudspeaker has stolen my heart. "*Subito, Adriano . . .*" he says three or four times a day. Evelyn says Adriano must be a real good-for-nothing as he is never where he ought to be. I don't know who Adriano is but isn't it a lovely name? And I envy him being summoned to that dreamy voice.'

The *Castel Felice* was, in fact, an endearing old tub; in timorous, litigious times like these she would certainly be retired as unseaworthy. Her sort of no-frills ship for students was going to be replaced by cheap charter flights that turn the sea lanes into freeways and their crossings into airborne traffic jams. But the 'Happy Castle' was small enough to let us feel the Atlantic through her hull and to transmit every trill and tremor of the deep for good or very, very ill. The last person I expected to see on board such a maritime flivver was a member of Barnard's exalted faculty, albeit a raffish one. Mr Sweet was the coach of our college drama society. I knew him on sight, of course, though he gave no sign of knowing me, or remembering my tremulous performance the previous semester when I read for Juliet. I have always been stage-struck; my main reason for choosing a Manhattan-based university was to stay near Broadway. From the time I had begun to know hazily that I had to escape the mild academic life followed by suburban domesticity on the cards for girls where I came from, the only way that presented itself as romantic, tragic, dramatic, sexy, comic, stand-up, bohemian, the only way to be all I dreamed of being without too much risk of dreaded parental disapproval, was to act the part. But I had neither the gift for acting nor the necessary determination, nor the required tolerance for repetition, and Mr Sweet gave Juliet to a more single-minded undergraduate.

Dolph Sweet still pops up occasionally on movies made for early TV. He plays craggy villains or policemen on the edge of retirement and his acting is a trifle too big to fit the small screen comfortably. He already seemed pretty old to us Barnard girls in those days, at least as old as Shelley when he gave up the ghost. Although Mr Sweet was affable on campus and as far as the young can ascribe emotions to old men he

19

seemed happy enough, I realise now that it was all an act. Barnard College was hell for a 'resting' thespian. The bargain-basement trip to Europe must have been a treat he promised himself after a year spent trying to persuade self-conscious scholarly young women to let their hair down and perform.

'1954: Odd to see Mr Sweet in the dining salon today. He was off to one side at one of the few small tables with a handsome Negro' (politically correct form of the day) 'who is *certainement pas sa femme!*'

The conclusion I jumped to that Mr Sweet was having an affair with his handsome dinner companion was understandable, I guess. Four kitchen chairs piled high had long before taken me to the top shelf of our bookcase at home where salacious literature was stashed optimistically beyond the reach of children. Teetering at that giddy height, I found sheet music for the 'Internationale', already in those pre-McCarthy days an inflammatory document, widely considered suitable for burning. It was crammed between Erskine Caldwell's *God's Little Acre* and Krafft-Ebing's immensely instructive *Psychopathia Sexualis*. Thanks to vertiginous curiosity and older friends, among them plenty of young men who were queer – a politically correct form of those days for the current 'gay' – my knowledge of other people's sexual conduct was as wide as experience of my own was narrow. Moreover, like many clever, liberal, passionate yet strangely virginal women, I was an incipient fag-hag. My assumption about the Sweet menage was pretty sophisticated, I must say, for the early 1950s; too sophisticated by half, as it turned out. That very afternoon the young man told me from a neighbouring deckchair that he was on his way to meet a girlfriend in Paris, not with Mr Sweet at all.

'*Quel dommage!*' wrote this little busybody.

Mr Sweet had his share of devotees among my classmates and an unorthodox liaison would have made resonant gossip in the halls of Academe. Also, my homosexual men friends were always thrilled, though they pretended not to be surprised, when any figure of even the slightest eminence was revealed to share their persuasion. Privately and in their cups they maintained that all interesting men – Shakespeare, Mozart, Da Vinci, Rock Hudson, only not Hitler, thank you very much, and who would have imagined J. Edgar Hoover? – were that way inclined. And the more butch a guy appeared to be, the more he was resisting the inclination. I have since observed that shoe fetishists, paedophiles, mild sado-masochists and practically all erotic minorities genuinely believe that if mankind were liberated from prejudice, it would choose their way, too, to a man. And to a woman, it follows; it never precedes. I know it has become unfashionable to the point of derision to say so, but the fact is when it comes to sex, we women have less time to fool around and more important things to do.

* * *

'July 1954: Bored! Bored! Bored! I went to sea to see the world, and what did I see? I saw the sea! Finished the book I brought with me: *The Greek Passion*. Nothing to read. Nothing to do. I guess I should have brought Boswell after all. Will these long days never end? Ass-in-igned moved out last night while the rest of us were having dinner. Where to? She hasn't jumped overboard, I guess. Maybe there is a first-class deck hidden on this ship where she's had herself ass-in-igned to live like a queen in clover.'

How I would relish days and nights at sea right now: no telephone, no television, no interruptions, no demands beyond breathing in and out the salty blue air. And now I have come to the age of rereading, how many more than one book would I pack for such a journey! What was tedious in the long, long days to spare of youth becomes on short time a welcome respite from work and a rehearsal for eternal rest.

Ass-in-igned's name was Barbara. She was from a small state college and had just turned nineteen. A pale girl, she was too plump and languid to have climbed comfortably to the upper berth. We learned later that while we were all at dinner on 7 July, the night before landfall, a steward found her in a diabetic coma. He carried her to the infirmary where she died a few hours later. Barbara's death was not announced publicly; we learned about it on the shipboard grapevine and, as the news spread, students gathered in mutinous groups on the decks. Damn it. Boredom is an affliction of youth;

death should rightly be an affliction of old age. Betrayal of that prevailing logic made us all furious at someone or something.

'1954: How could it have happened? They say the drug needed to save her was not on board because her parents had not informed the ship's doctor of her condition. How could it have happened? Because the family doctor had not told them how serious the condition was. Or so I have heard. And how the hell could it have happened? How, how, how the hell did any of it happen? Because. Because. Because. It is too stupid that she is dead.'

Only now, fifty years on and the mother of a child of my own, do I think of the dead girl with pain and melancholy instead of anger. Only now do I think of her at all. Perhaps we were less sensitive in the 1950s, before flying doctors and sophisticated medication and grief counsellors, when life was that much younger and closer to its primal cave. By the time we sighted land, the waters had closed over Barbara's memory as they have throughout the ages over graves of sailors lost at sea.

'Today is 8 July 1954. In one month, three weeks and five days I will be nineteen. Nineteen! Getting on a bit! We have been at sea for seven days and should see land any moment now. Days without end on the ocean are like long sentences with no punctuation. I told Evelyn that I thought days at sea were Henry James without commas! She didn't seem to get it. Maybe natural science majors don't have to read Henry James? Do they have to read anything? Maybe they do it all by touch.'

Ha! Very funny! Your brother became a doctor in the end, and is he not to this day the most avid reader I know, obsessive almost? He reads for the joy of acquiring information, the more recherché it is the more joyous is he, history and biography, rarely fiction, never poetry, or so I dare say. The tale of how my new baby brother and only sibling was introduced to me sixty-odd years ago is one of my cherished false memories. As I like to recall, they brought the bundle home from hospital, plunked him into the baby scales set up on the kitchen table and said: 'Irma, meet your seven-pound-brother-the-doctor. . . .' I was not yet four years old at the time and this had to be an invention of my later life. Nevertheless, there is no denying that conception is contaminated by preconception and parental love in general spoiled by ambition. Names given babies are tiny epitaphs in advance. My brother's name, for instance, Michael David, was a parental ploy; even after it was changed briefly to Michael Dean during an episode of Semitic collywobbles when American medical schools were rumoured to have begun imposing Jewish quotas, the poor little tyke remained stuck with the initials MD. As for me, my name, Irma, is practically an anagram of my mother's name: Myra. My middle name, Lois on my birth certificate but Louise or Leah depending on which member of my family I asked, provided the initials ILK as in: you will be of that ILK and you will like it. When it came to my own introduction to waiting family members, in one of my rummages I found and have kept in my possession a letter my mother sent to her mother, who was still back in Indiana, announcing my birth. 'It's a girl,' she wrote in her tight, controlled backhand. 'Drat it!'

Anger has not been one of my outstanding characteristics; the moment insult enters my system it encounters my grotesquely enlarged sense of responsibility and is converted immediately into guilt and hurt. As I grow older I understand and will at last accept that mine was the final generation of females in Western society to be born into an ancient tradition that found each newborn daughter a new burden. Love your little girl if you can, but above love and, over all, keep her safe for a stranger's pleasure and another family's benefit. To that end, let her possess beauty but only to a modest degree, so it shouldn't incite desire among the goyim. As for education, an adornment for girls of my ilk, may it be decorative yet not so flashy or deep that it threatens her good sense or the vanity of her future husband, not so costly that it subtracts one penny from the more important school fees of her brothers. Margaret Mead, eminent graduate of Barnard College for Women, in the address she delivered to my graduating class in 1956 congratulated us on having accumulated great words and thoughts and poems to mull over in the future while we prepared dinner for our families and washed dishes at our kitchen sinks. Many years later I realised the lady was being ironical and provocative. But her audience was too young for irony. Besides, we were American, weren't we? And thus we were indoctrinated from the cradle with characteristic literal thinking. At the time, her words made me unhappy and a little provoked, too. Oh, so few of us girls then became anthropologists or lawyers or doctors! Even fewer put out to sea.

The late teenager I used to be, I mean you there, intense and long-haired youngster leaning on the rail and eastward-bound, you are lacking in self-confidence, lacking in self-awareness and, to a great degree, lacking in self. I know, I remember, how you sometimes drift away to hover in a high corner of the room watching your family at dinner and hearing yourself ask, please, for the salt or water. You did not always feel all there; you don't now. But you had a strong sense that your self had not yet arrived, was waiting somewhere in the wings. The selfish years have ended now; your self dropped in, barely made herself known and is departing. I hardly knew anything about myself at all back then. I did not even realise, for example, that I was exhausting most of my lifetime's allowance of rage in battles with my father. They marked my adolescence, those screaming matches toe to toe with Daddy, and as long as each one lasted I felt an inkling of my own weight and stamina. Mother stood in the background during these struggles: has sly memory super-imposed a smile on her face? Her own father died when she was barely seven; is it possible she thought this late and agonising parturition was what fathers were for? No. It is more likely that my mother believed it was not my battle I fought with the man she regretted having married, but her own. And what were our endless screaming matches ostensibly about? About right and wrong, tolerance and intolerance, food, entertainment, what was safe and what was dangerous: all the murderous and petty strategies of revolution.

And yet, after the shouting, my father had himself to thank for my war of independence, and I thank him for it, too. When I was barely nine, and our bloodline had been mercilessly cauterised in the fascist camps of Europe, he used to take me to lectures at Cooper Union where lefties and crypto-anarchists still dared hold forth. At the end of the fiery screeds discussion was thrown open to the floor and my father glowed with pride when I stood up on a chair to squeal precocious questions at the speakers: from whom does an unenlightened, uneducated proletariat learn the precepts of self-government? How can killing people ever stop people from killing people? Is Russian a Western language? Suddenly and only now, recollecting his pride, his sorrow, his carpentry and his singing voice, I realise to what degree I trusted my father, more than I have trusted anyone. I trusted him enough to show him all my anger. And he, staunch in his love, was soon afraid: for me.

27

Intellectual parent-bashing was a relatively new sport in the 1950s, a kind of emotional lacrosse, played almost exclusively by girls. I was an enthusiastic amateur who never achieved the thrust and style of, say, my room-mate, Marjorie, or any other of the proto-analysands at my college. Those chicks blamed their daddies for crimes too subtle even for my imagining. But Marjorie herself, in spite of the coaching of a Park Avenue shrink, never attempted serious mama-bashing, a sophisticated permutation of the game. Blaming mama rose to a competitive level only after the daughters and grand-daughters of my generation were liberated to know that our own sex could be just as bullying, cruel, egotistical, possessive, venal and even more judgemental than men. No parent can ever get it just right or ever will. So what do you think about that, young one, squinting into the dawn for your first sight of land? Parents fuck us up from the moment we are born, it's in the nature of the beast: they are bigger than we are, they are older – our parents *have* us. You too, in your time, for all the love in the world will get it not just right. Hey, pay attention! This is you I'm talking about. It is you I am talking to. You'd like to tell me to mind my own business. I am. And we must be growing very old indeed to talk to ourself so shamelessly. Senility never lacks for company.

'1954: Land! This morning I saw land! Several rocks, beautiful, beautiful rocks, and an island called Wight that was once

a hideout for pirates, and a big, proud, lonely lighthouse.
Evelyn joined me and we watched the rocks slip by. English
rocks! Pointed white rocks! We waved to skinny soldiers
on a troopship behind us. English soldiers! Skinny English
soldiers! Evelyn said they looked more worried than pleased
to see us. I told her they've had a lot more to worry about
recently than we have in the States. I agree, though, they did
not look half as pleased at the sight of us as the Italian stewards
did every time they sauntered past while we were splashing
around the little swimming pool on deck, that's for sure! And
here we are! Here we are! And the formalities: my first ever
formalities! The first stamp in my passport! My heart is jump-
ing! The docks and countryside look neat, trimmed, pretty,
planned, charming. The people too, perhaps? My God!
They're English and in their own land. Not in a black-and-
white movie on television! The English in England, at last!
Through Customs. The officials are gentle and nice. The
trains! The people! Pale and small! Everyone not on this train
is riding a bike. No doubt there will be cars when we get to
London proper. Proper London! Headline on a newspaper:
CANDID ON THE DUCHESS OF WINDSOR. Outside a sign:
"Entry: frontal parking". "Mind the gap"! Mind the gap! I
thought of the Wife of Bath and her lecherous teeth! But
what does it mean? So many people look like Alec Guinness!'

Alec Guinness, yet! Where would a girl have been in those
days without exclamation marks! The pages of the notebook

are slit in places by the shrieking lead of my pencil! Old excitement is contagious; it was those noisy exclamation marks that made me decide one dull day only last week to go back to my European landfall. The Needles! The Isle of Wight! To see them again! From the other side and half a century later, to take a look at my first glimpse of Europe, and with luck to stumble into a glitch of time where the ghost of my ship is forever slipping into port so from the cliffs above I can look down and see the ghost of myself dancing on the deck. Would I know myself as I was then? What I did not know then, had never been told (for my own good) and could never allow anyone to tell me, what I can hear and admit only from the desiccation of age, and what is patently evident in the 'photograph of bearer' of my first passport, is that I was really quite beautiful. My face, a classic oval, showed fine cheekbones and a clear, balanced, starry gaze. As I recall, this old body wasn't all that bad either, toned by an energetic childhood, lots of swimming, rowing, hiking, as well as endless games of badminton in a homicidal version my brother and I invented that depended more on endurance than style. Had I known myself then to be good-looking, would it have made a great difference? Certainly, I would have expected more good things to come my way for free. Beautiful women are raised to expect a lot for nothing and to require very little of themselves, as nothing much more than beauty is required of them by others. Caretakers of the gift, vestal virgins, they soon learn to avoid hard travelling that makes squints, and hard work that makes wrinkles, and unguarded passion that makes shadows.

My first passport was not valid for travel to Albania, Bulgaria, China, Czhechoslovakia (correct spelling of the day), Hungary, Poland, Rumania or what was still the Union of Soviet Socialist Republics. I could not visit Egypt, Israel, Jordan and Syria, nor any portion of Korea or Viet-nam (hyphenated as it was then) under Communist control. Cuba, on the other hand, was hunky-dory. For my photo on page 4, and probably on the day of landing in England, I would have worn the usual dark-blue nylon trench coat and white turtleneck pullover probably over blue jeans as usual. The suitcase in my cabin was full of similar costumes suitable to the star of one of the classic romances of that time: the long-haired brunette of alien origin, fast-moving, intellectual, a little dangerous, no time for wimps. Incidentally, the brunette rarely got the man back then; in American movies she walked alone out of the last reel. Also, we American girls packed enough boxes of newfangled Tampax to see us through lest the Europeans hadn't caught up with American know-how. Those of us who were not yet convinced tampons did not compromise the maidenhead and were too timid to ask for sanitary napkins in foreign languages had to cram a bulk of sanitary napkins into their fake-leather suitcases. Whether a girl of my generation styled herself after Juliette Greco or June Allyson, each of us was the star, looking for her co-star, and at the bottom of her chest packed hopefully

31

lay the evangelical Hollywood-based tenet that one and only one true lover was out there, in search of her. And even though girls back then were shamelessly taught to tease and lead men on, she and he – he and I – were bound to know each other on sight and without brokering or pre-arrangement to make each other deliriously happy for ever after: Ginger and Fred, Katie and Spence, Bacall and Bogart. Always with parental approval, of course. Never mind the heresy we saw every day in the family home, true love was the distaff faith of my generation. I too was a believer. I knew I would find one true love, my mate and heart's twin. I was just as persuaded then I would end my life with a man whose mind and mine were one as I know now that I did not even come close. Even in my darkest days I never lapsed from the faith; I exhausted it.

Three

Nowadays, instead of Tampax I pack a small box of the hormone pill that slows down bone loss and enough calcium supplements to see me through. Half a century ago lipstick was all I wore for everyday appearances; I pack more make-up now, though far less than I did twenty or so years ago before libidinous hope had utterly expired. Only a small case slung over my shoulder, nevertheless, it would have been less problematical to take off impulsively to Calcutta than just down the road to the Isle of Wight. I have roamed around India without prior knowledge of train timetables, changed plans on the Australian hoof, and bussed all over the American vastness rarely choosing a destination more than a day in advance. In England, however, where I am at home yet not, I know too much, and for that very reason, because I know it almost all, before I set out I need to know more, particularly when travelling by rail. A national taste for convolution and a compulsion to fix what ain't broke, complicated by the greedy fragmentation of what used to be a premier railway system, means that irregular travellers must ask for help to make sense of British timetables and tickets. It vexes me after nearly forty years to be mistaken for an American tourist, but that's what happened as soon as I opened my mouth and asked about train and boat connections to the Isle of Wight, thanks to the sharpness of the British ear for accents, from which in part derives a marked gift for mimicry and theatre. In my long and footloose travelling life I regret not being a car driver only when I find myself in a London train station where architecture of imperial design is these days belied by avarice and confusion.

Many women of my generation learned late, as I did, to drive a car, or do not drive at all. Women drivers and mothers-in-law were comedy mainstays of my childhood. Mom-in-law stood for the viperine nesting instinct of the female and deflected the entrapped male's frustration away from his own mother and his wife to put it where it would do less harm. And the car was a symbol in the 1950s not so much of freedom as of power and capability: he who drove, chose his destination. She who drove, drove him to the station, the kids to school and the dog to the vet. My mother was born three years before Henry Ford began mass production of the automobile. Given her innate loathing of even the most innocuous machinery, it is understandable she never once in her more than ninety years sat in the driver's seat. My father, upright and tense, drove our Buick through the back roads of New Jersey as if it were a tetchy elephant with a basket on its back. I have a hunch my brother would rather not drive at all, only he lives in southern California where to be unable or unwilling to run a car relegates one to life on buses and pavements among the mad, the maimed and the destitute. I'd be surprised if more than a dozen girls at my urban university in the early 1950s were learning to drive; to be driven was part of the deal we were expected to make. When I was pushing fifty, I finally took driving lessons. To my surprise, I liked doing it and I got my licence first try. But it was too late. Not too late to acquire the skill or practice necessary to make me a good driver: it was too late to park a car in my imagination. 'My car': a tripping phrase now for women but one that I could find no space for in my mind – no more than I could 'my husband'.

'1954: Mooky (my pet name for my brother) would love the railroad train I am on as I write this. Evelyn and Midge and I are facing each other in high-backed seats in a small discrete area like an old stagecoach. There is a table between us to give us a place to take tea. Tea! I wish I liked tea!'

'You don't know what good is,' my maternal great-grandmother – I called her 'Gay Gammaw' – used to scold whenever I refused some gristly titbit considered a delicacy when she was a girl in what was then Ruthenia. At least, I think Ruthenia was her home before she emigrated and somehow washed up in Indiana where my grandmother and

35

mother were born. Our family's history has been mythol-ogised beyond tracing on my mother's side, and on my father's side despised and hidden as a contemptible secret from us who were learning to pledge allegiance to our Ameri-can flag. I was three or four when Gay Gammaw died. I seem to remember being lifted to look down and see her, pinch-nosed and powdery in her coffin. Her English was never fluent, nor was mine yet, so I never put to her questions I now wish I had. What was your name when you were little? I'd like to ask her. What did your house look like? What did you eat and sing and play? Who were you really? Where do you come from really? Do you know why some little girls have to leave home?

'1954: My first day in England! Everything is so small!'

Gay Gammaw was right: I did not always know what good was. We young Gullivers from the land of giants, when it came to war and bombs, painful separations and stringent rationing, did not know what bad was, either. But we sure as hell knew what big was. After so long in Lilliput, have its proportions begun to suit me? More likely, I am shrinking with age; getting on for fifty years later, outward bound via the very line on which once I had entered London for the first time, everything I saw through the train window looked of normal size. For a full ten minutes out of Waterloo Station on the first lap of my odyssey, two old dears who were no doubt taking advantage of the off-peak rate for old dears, as I was, did not stop complaining loudly to each other that the layout of the coach, even though the train was half empty, meant most passengers had to ride backwards. They sat in a double seat, one of the few, it so happened, that faced forward.

'A lot of people feel ill going backwards,' said the one who was boss.

'Too right. You'd think they'd do something about it,' piped her companion and glanced around for allies. Or a fight.

I looked away quickly because I was alone at a table yet nevertheless had wilfully chosen to face backwards. I knew how futile it would be to justify or defend my choice against two old ladies. Not many of us who are starting to crumble dare to risk being left without a leg to stand on. Challenge any of an aged person's long-held opinions, knock the existence of a higher power, say, or the efficacy of cod-liver oil, or even just suggest a need sometimes to ride a train backwards, and the whole delicately balanced construct must totter. The last thing a body past mid-life can do is change its mind. Particularly since the rise of youth as a dominant market and political force, it has become the genuine duty of the aged to object, to carp, to cavil, to kvetch, to dig in arthritic heels and act as a drag on gimcrackery and whiz-bang technology, to put the brake on whippersnappers who might otherwise hurl humanity into space, leaving behind a ruin of history. Little old ladies like those across the aisle, if they are doing their geriatric best, must right to the end remain a pain in youth's ass. No argument, OK? I know what I am talking about. Shut up and listen, child, who once upon a time rode that very rail in the opposite direction; let me tell you why you will always prefer to leave London backwards. Remember how you stood on the deck at the start of your journey watching America recede into a westernmost glow? Facing backwards is the right and proper way, the only way, to leave home. And facing backwards, it would surprise you to know, young I, is the way you will one day choose to leave London and only London: waving farewell.

'10 July 1954: My first full day in London! We started at 8 a.m. with a rise and shine from our leader, Tony. By 9.30 we hit the London streets. Scary at first because the cars go the wrong way. Then the Changing of the Guard: crowds of tourists peering at tall, wonderful men in red suits and fuzzy black hats. Company A's captain changes swords with Company B's captain, while all the men play instruments. Silly but awfully thrilling. The high spot of the day for me was the Tower of London. When I touched the rough wall I felt an electric connection with the past through my fingertips. I kept myself as far from the group as possible there. I feel things better on my own! I feel better on my own! The Tower where the two little princes were killed! The very spot where Henry VI was murdered at his prayers! It was real! It happened and not just in books! You can feel it thrumming in the stone! The day was overcast and there were ravens, black and proud and ugly and hopping awkwardly like Richard III! There seems to be a dry and constant flow of jokes everywhere in London but no loud laughter. The city is scarred and charred from the Blitz but not Tony or the guide, nobody referred to any of these black gaps in the London smile. We went to a buffet for tea. How the woman wrinkled her nose when I asked for coffee! (How I wrinkled my nose when I tasted it!) And we went to the theatre. The play! Wonderful! Bliss! Then we bought food for one shilling. Buses are two or three cents a ride. What a funny place this is, like looking-glass land. The smaller the sum, the larger the coin! God! I wish my room-mate would paint her damned toenails in silence and shut the hell up!'

And I wish you had thought to name the damned play you were all taken to see. Could you not foresee that such a detail would be important to you later? Shakespeare, I imagine, in aid of colonial improvement. Then again, our leader, Tony, could be a mischievous young chap, perhaps it amused him to take his little Yanks to something wild and racy. Noël Coward? Terence Rattigan? You had a crush on Tony, perforce. All the girls in the group did; your college room-mate and best friend, Marjorie, when she was on the Study Abroad tour the previous summer had loved him madly. His softly tailored summer suits, his plummy vowels, that thing he did

39

with his longish hair when it fell over his forehead: he had altered her criteria of the opposite sex for ever, she declared. Presumably, you thought you too would remember Tony always; is that why you left no physical description? Trying now to bring him back to my mind's eye, my impression is of an Oxbridge undergraduate, young, fair and willowy, with wit enough to make the way he patronised us smitten girls enchanting and more than forgivable. Although he laughed with us and gently laughed at us, too, during our long journeys by chartered coaches around England and later on the Continent, he could suddenly become reserved as Americans rarely are, as detached and cool and secretive as a spy, in a way that suggested much, much more than his own welfare alone depended upon his never spilling the English beans.

As for your annoying and nameless room-mate, it is good for a traveller to learn early that suffering and boredom are the price paid for company on the road, especially if it is female. You are going to know women, intelligent though they are at home, who as soon as they find themselves in the big abroad respond with tantrums to the least impediment or delay. To travel with any one of them is to travel with an immense spoiled three-year-old who must have the window seat or sulk; must eat when she's hungry or make a scene; must set the pace and call the shots or she'll kick her little feet. And, yes, your first night in a great new city, she will paint her nails while chattering on endlessly about her toys and boys at home, never mind that literature and history are crying to get a word in. Travelling companions in general are one of life's torments and especially for you, girl, because of your blasted diffidence bordering on servility, and your inability to rise to anger except on occasion with a man. After every trip with a woman friend, and quite a few with men, battered and shaking, you will cry with relief to be alone again.

Mind, young'un, there is all the difference in the world between a travelling companion and a fellow traveller. Observing strangers on a train, talking to them when you can, and parting in the natural course of the journey, will add depth and joy to every journey, and supply a reason beyond necessity for you always to prefer public transport. Of course, it used to be that strangers, usually men, talked to me; but that wench is dead. Now, I talk to strangers increasingly. Incessantly? And as often as not, they are women of around my own age. If you want to travel quietly and speak to nobody, the most dangerous person to sit near is an ageing woman on her own. Nothing important remains for her to lose, no beauty, no shame, few of the sad boasts that collect in failing men; all an old woman has left and is dying to share is her opinion. Or, as I have seen in my mother and catch glimpses of in myself, she suffers from residual and indiscriminate need to be admired left over from parties to which she is no longer invited and platforms she used to dominate.

The train to the coast and the Isle of Wight stopped at

an outlying London station where a young woman boarded and sat at the table across from me. I sized up the potential victim of my assault. In her low twenties, very slim and casually dressed in jeans, she took immediate and total possession of the table between us. Marjorie used to be equally cavalier when it came to shared space, and she had similarly tawny good looks, right down to the deep-auburn hair and full, slightly overhanging upper lip that gave them both a look of cultivated melancholy. Except that the girl across the table wore a mop of curls and Marjorie's hair was straight and long, the resemblance was uncanny: they could have been twins, separated, of course, by forty or fifty years. In the years to come of our best friendship, Marjorie was going to decide to major in Art History. A degree in Art History was of even less practical value and much easier to get than my own degree in English Literature. Not that Marjorie saw things that way. She was a serious girl, very serious, and like the rest of us very, very, quite terribly seriously devoted to The Arts. Marjorie's ruthless streak would have suited her for a degree in Business Studies had such a vulgar course been open to girls in those days. But it had to be Art History, a course tailor-made for the daughters of the very rich, of whom there were a great number at Barnard College. Among the many things that Marjorie's father owned was a bank. And needs must.

So close was Marjorie in my memory that when the young girl on the train began turning the pages of a large portfolio open in front of her, I was not in the least surprised to see it contained photographs and pencil sketches of classic statues. She studied them with critical intensity. She twiddled her hair as Marjorie used to do. Still does? I wondered if this one also had a room-mate who helped write her papers? Did she too play Scarlatti sonatas on a baby grand piano? Marjorie's father gave it her when we moved out of the dormitory at the start of our third year, right after my return from Europe, in fact, and became the first two Barnard girls ever to live off-campus nominally on their own; our flat was always full of company. After a year or so, inexplicably and I begin to think inevitably between youthful best girlfriends, coolness set in; we began to argue, for nearly the last time about a documentary film on the recent bombing of Hiroshima. Marjorie thought the pestilential cloud that rose, puffed up and proud as death, was beautiful; I said there could be no beauty that entailed human suffering. I was wrong. We were both wrong as I had to admit many years later under an airborne inferno in Vietnam, and later still when I sat by my ailing mother's bed in New Jersey and watched the televised image of a skyscraper down the road being violently converted into September dust.

The stranger turned a page to yet another naked male of marble and scribbled a few words in the margin. She raised her eyes; they were dark brown like Marjorie's, but lacked the interesting cruelty of my old friend's quest for beauty and nothing but beauty.

I nodded towards her sketches of male nudes in marble. 'Dirty pictures?' I asked.

Her face mimicked a crabby middle age ahead. 'These', she said, 'are not dirty pictures.'

We both sighed and I turned to the window.

Outside, April bullied the countryside. I have never loved early spring, it manages to be both mawkish and acidic, like the lime and lemon sweets my brother and I always left at the bottom of the bowl. Clumps of daffodils on the verge were practically indistinguishable from their plastic replicas. Bare, knuckled branches lay under a haze of sickly green; the sky threatened rain. I returned to the book I had grabbed from the pile at the side of my bed. When it comes to reading on the road I occasionally give in to a weakness for unlikely combinations and impulsively I had packed *The Bolivian Diary* of Ernesto Che Guevara as perfectly unsuited to the Isle of Wight. What a tender and likeable man was the young Argentinian who fussed over his hairy guerrillas as a father his difficult sons. Meanwhile, the girl across the table had returned to her portfolio. The next time she spoke it was to Daddy on her mobile phone to tell him we would be pulling into Southampton in twenty-five minutes; would he meet her at the station? As she was repeating her request, garbled under a bridge, I read how Che, while bivouacking in the Bolivian jungle, discovered that several tins had been stolen from supplies by one of his hungry men – he had a pretty good idea which one. I glanced at the portfolio on the table,

then reread his short sentence of rueful explanation and forgiveness. This time I had to laugh out loud. The few words
seemed to me to contain the fact of many matters, I cannot
say precisely which or why. But that doesn't mean I am
wrong. The moue across from me, silly moo, was cross and
fearful. She'd known it all along: I was a half-crazed old bat
who ought to be locked up.

'Tinned milk', Che had written, 'is a great corrupter.'

Four

On my fourth birthday France and Britain declared war on Germany at last, and ever since, my generation has stumbled from one crisis to the next, greater or smaller, always faster and closer as speed of communication puts the Middle East a block away and Africa on the local tramline. Youngsters quite enjoy a crisis because it seems to promise change. The world is always changing for the young. And the world is always ending for the old. The young are bored most of the time. As much as ambition or curiosity or lust, it is the need to outrun boredom that accounts for their frenetic style. As life unwinds behind us and its sheer weight starts to slow us down, we turn round to squint at our memories. Old people are never bored; they are much too busy remembering. To remember, more often than not incorrectly and fantastically, is the final industry of the decrepit imagination. During my father's terminal dementia, I sometimes sat with him in the day room of his nursing home. Well into his eighties, he still had his teeth and most of his hair; only his wits had left him.

He referred to my mother as 'the woman who brings me food' and he called me by his youngest sister's name, Sylvia, but I think he did not mind me there quietly beside him, watching him. I watched once how he ate an apple, chewing thoughtfully and slowly, and I followed the play of original memories behind his eyes. For him that apple was the only fruit. Its small crunch and pop in his mouth enthralled him; he was delighted by its flavour of ephemeral life and his mind was occupied by the hallucinatory images it summoned. Bored? Not on your life, sweetheart. Too busy sampling one more time and for ever the celebrated fruit of Eden.

When I set sail from Southampton for the Isle of Wight it was yet another critical time in British history. An epidemic of foot and mouth disease raged in the countryside. Unchecked by an urban government that models itself after the far reaches of upper management, the virus threatened an ancient agricultural society. A mist of anxiety rose from the pyres of burning carcasses and spread over the land, growing thicker and darker with every mile out of London. Crossings between Lymington and Yarmouth are short and frequent, and I had chosen to travel just before midday on Saturday. Many of the other passengers on the ferry were elderly couples for whom World War Two was only yesterday. They sat in the salon over cups of tea, looking into space, not reading newspapers or speaking very much. The underlying mood on board, deeper than palpable depression, was familiar to me from a ferry I take every year or so to visit an American friend on Martha's Vineyard; also, there was the weekly boat that used to be the only connection to Ibiza where I lived, once upon a time. This too was a home-going vessel. Most of my fellow passengers knew exactly where they were bound. Their glances at tourists like me were vague, patronising and a little superior. Despite the chilly breeze, several young couples with children gathered out on the forward deck as soon as we pulled away. They kept their backs to the forest of slender masts in Lymington harbour and faced the approaching shoreline where grandma and grandpa were waiting with cakes and a nice cup of tea.

Disembarking passengers walked across a mat soaked in disinfectant while cars and one or two half-empty tourist buses rolled through a trough of the stuff; everyone then disappeared purposefully. All except me. The pretty little town of Yarmouth lay snug behind bastions built by Henry VIII, more decorative than defensive now in this era of air-borne peril. Although I thought I had glimpsed the Needles far off to starboard as we were entering the port, I had no idea how to get to them over the rolling landscape, already greener than the mainland. I listened while the frazzled woman behind the desk in the tourist office warned a pair of young backpackers they were going to find some of the trails closed because of the crisis.

'But surely you don't have foot and mouth here! This is an island!' the girl cried. She could have made the same complaint anywhere in Britain, it seemed to me.

'Can I walk there?' I asked about the Needles.

She looked at me for a long moment, assessing and bemused, she herself no spring chicken. 'It is six miles. There's a bus,' she said.

The bus made a two- or three-hour circuit of the entire island. Theoretically, I should be able get off near the Needles, reminisce moodily for, say, half an hour or longer if the fine weather held, and then return to Yarmouth on a bus coming from the opposite way. I was pretty sure no more than two coastal buses were needed to service this island for retired gentlefolk, well-bred ramblers and mainland tourists who brought cars, bikes and buses of their own. At worst, I would have to wait an hour or so to pick up the same bus I had arrived on, and rejoin it for a round trip of the Isle of Wight, returning at last to Yarmouth from the other side. Browsing the bookshelf in the tourist office, while I pondered my choices, I realised with a start of recollection that the old and infamous Parkhurst Prison was on the Isle of Wight.

'1954: When we sailed past a pretty island, the Isle of Wight, white rocks stood like armed soldiers in the sea and a few people waved to us from high up on cliffs. And here we are! Here we are! We landed in Southampton! Southampton! I have seen liners sail into New York from Southampton. We didn't see much of it, just the docks and cranes of a working waterfront. The dashing Tony was waiting and hustled us

IRMA KURTZ

on a train to London. From here on in, he told us, we will
be travelling by bus: he called it "a coach". A coach! And
four! I feel like Cinderella. Everything is English! Men in
vests! Little houses with chimneys and no TV aerials!'

It never entered your young mind, did it, that the pretty
island gliding by as we made for Southampton was an
Alcatraz of chilly climes? Or that just beyond our vision was
justice, replete with her miscarriages, making all men equal
in suffering as they had not been in wickedness. You were
so young! You had periodic pimples; specks were forever
flying into your wide eyes; you regularly hit your funny bone
as children do, sending vibrations to your fingertips; and you
believed; you believed so many things. You believed there
was love enough to go round, you believed good prevailed
in the human heart and must triumph over evil in the last
reel; you believed greed was an aberration, and the English
were ever so well bred skinny people in vests they called
'waistcoats'. Home is reality for the young; everywhere else
they believe to be a set for make-believe so you could not
yet believe in crimes or punishments except those of your
homeland; no sirens portended misfortune or tragedy as far
as you could believe, except they were American. What one
believes, young Irma, is what one prefers to think: that's
what belief is – an extension of hope, and hope against hope.
To know, on the other hand, is to have no preference, no
choice. You knew so little then, young I. But you were keen

50

to learn, I'll give you that. And now? Now, my old darling, we know a thing or two. Now we know better.

In imitation of the what-the-hell way I used to up and go in my youth, I had made no hotel reservations on the Isle of Wight nor planned how long I'd stay. I packed my toothbrush and wore my hiking boots, and basking in the back of my mind was a dreamy open fire and a single-malt whisky after a day, perhaps two, spent strolling in the country to the sound of birdsong. Plastic in credit and a bank balance generally in the black have taken youthful what-the-hell out of travel and replaced it with a more mature and affluent version: faced with the complications of using the Isle of Wight bus system to get me to and from the Needles, I rang a local taxi company – what the hell? The driver kept me waiting outside the tourist office. He arrived at last, an unsmiling, affectedly busy man in his early fifties I guessed. Too big for the job, too broad and tall to spend his day comfortably in a car, he was solidly built in layers of compacted frustration and irritability: a smoker perhaps, not permitted by his employers to smoke at work? But no, it was evident in the brisk way he motioned me into the front seat this was no man to be bothered by the petty rules of overlords; more likely he was a once-prosperous self-employed businessman forced by adversity to drive a cab. Every third minicab in England is driven by one such. Would I be able to persuade a tough customer like this to wait quietly in the car some distance away while I stood in the shadow of the remembered rocks and all by myself tried to recollect myself?

The Isle of Wight was in much greater peril of infection than the tourist office had led me to believe. Among many closed roads was the one down to the coast and the Needles. 'Bloody typical!' the driver muttered when we were stopped by a red tape stretched across our road.

'Bloody typical!' he said again, though in all my decades in England there had only once before been such an outbreak, and it was typical of nothing.

When I told him in a burst of chronic loony loquacity that I was on a quest for memories, not only did he drive me to a vantage point atop a cliff, whence he said I could see the Needles, he even stayed behind in the car, I assumed to smoke a cigarette. I stepped alone into an old-fashioned amusement park for children overlooking Alum Bay. Not a child or grown-up was in sight. Salt-stung vacancy, cartoon artwork on empty stalls, and merry-go-round horses stalled in mid-leap conjured charm out of the air and stirred memories of childhood encounters with sleeping magic.

A few steps to the summit of the encircling cliffs and finally, there they were again: the Needles, dental white and small below me in the greenish water, as if seen from a low-flying plane. I waited for a moment, trying to recall the thrill of that sight all those years ago from the deck of the *Castel Felice*; instead I found myself wondering: wondering if someone had happened to be standing right there in that very place at 9 a.m. on 8 July 1954 – an English girl of eighteen, perhaps, whose dreams were travelling the opposite way. Had she by chance looked out to sea at the very moment our toy ship was sailing past, bound for Southampton? Was she one of the figures we saw waving at us on board? I wondered if the telescope put in that place for tourists swallowed her halfpenny as it did my twenty-pence piece and delivered no view but the very same big black 'O' it gave me. Soon she boarded her own *Castel Felice* and crossed the Atlantic to a whole New World. And in New York the young English rose met and fell in love with a dark American boy who grew up to become a shrink, say, or a book reviewer and professor of Russian Literature at City College of New York. After two children, now grown with children of their own, and thirty-three indigestible Seders with her alien in-laws, and the menopause, and years of increasing, wasteful fury, she divorced him. I don't blame her. It is precisely what I would have done in her place. He then married a secretary he'd been canoodling sporadically, or maybe a nurse. Clever old philanderers usually choose a nurse or secretary as their final helpmeet: to help them meet their makers and leave no mess behind.

The ashtray was clean when I returned to the car and there was no smell of smoke; the driver sat precisely as I had left him, sullen and massive behind the wheel. His introspective anger was too heavy to penetrate in any customary way; uncharacteristically, I never discovered his age, political affiliations, or even his name. Certainly in charge, every inch the driver, he said he had something for me to see, and before I could tell him I'd really rather not he'd turned off on to a bumpier road. En route he complained bitterly about the shortage of tourists, and the lack of civic concern shown by aged residents who had retired to his native island and who didn't give a damn what happened to it. A dilapidated fence appeared in the middle of nowhere beside our road; when he pulled to a stop in front of its gate the scrunching of our tyres sounded of dereliction and breakage. He did not bother to lock the door and I left my small overnight case on the front seat. When he led me through a space where the gate was off its hinges, I was dismayed to see a large sign claiming the area for 'Warner's'. I would have preferred the cause of his dark anger not to derive from an American company. In spite of coiled barbed wire here and there, the deserted compound was easily accessible. It had clearly once been a vast holiday camp for adults, another haunted place where the cool breeze seemed to carry echoes of past years' amusements. He referred to the rows of attached units as 'chalets'; I would have called them barracks. Smashed windows and unhinged doors gave on to small rooms with peeling wallpaper. A few torn mattresses and pieces of broken furniture were scattered around, but there was no wet mess, no drug paraphernalia and no sign of fire. Propriety in desuetude: further evidence the Isle of Wight belongs to the well-off aged. The smell of the sea was everywhere and its irrepressible sparkle was reflected against the sky; however, the buildings were tucked into a dip behind the cliffs as they were at the amusement park, out of sight of water, facing inwards and each other, designed for an island chastened by prevailing winds and by terrors that sailed in on ancient tides.

'1954: Pirate country!'

The driver led me from place to place feverishly, describing each landmark in its heyday: the naughty casino, the ballroom once so lively, the best chalets set apart from their neighbours in the camp and turned towards the sea that lay beyond a rise and out of sight. He was not animated by nostalgia but by rage and outrage: a rapacious invader had snatched all the gay days from him, from him alone, from him and nobody but him. He told me that in his youth he had worked here to earn extra money during the summer holidays from school.

In my day and my place, students on summer break used to work at hotels in a region of the Catskill Mountains known as the 'Borscht Belt'. On the wall of my London flat is a photograph of my father's first Buick with its long sleek running-board like a stowed gangplank, and me, about three, grinning out of the window. Behind us is one of the long white buildings that housed the busboys and waitresses at the Borscht Belt hotel where my grandparents spent the summer. Called 'hotels', most of them were in fact a collection of dedicated buildings older, prettier but along the same general lines as those at Warner's abandoned holiday camp on the

Isle of Wight. Nice old Jews from New York used to go to the Borscht Belt to escape summer in the city. They rocked on the porches while competitively enumerating symptoms of their ailments. They splashed in the pools awkwardly, not a generation of swimmers. Some of them remembered and would tell a visiting grandchild how more than half a century earlier when they were little they used to tremble in the dark pits full of stored potatoes where their parents hid them from Cossacks on the rampage. Of course, they did not yet know and could not imagine – who could? – that an infinitely more efficient machine was even then slipping into gear, preparing to exterminate friends and relatives left behind in the cities and shtetls of Europe.

'You'll find a nice Jewish boy some day, Irmele,' the old ladies used to say, stroking my hair, trying to console me for being born female.

Then the men maybe played pinochle, a card game incomprehensible to us little Americans raised on gin rummy and canasta, while the women boasted about sons and grandsons, and tried to arrange a few marriages: what's the harm? Big kosher meals were the main event of the day, and live entertainment in the evening featured sharp, satirical jesters in Yiddish and English, sentimental balladeers and, occasionally, a world-class violinist with a repertoire heavy on Brahms.

The driver was furiously trying to dismantle a barricade so he could show me the Olympic-sized swimming pool.

Empty swimming pools are creepy; they put me in mind of murder and accidental death. Besides, I had not packed my little bag and locked my door behind me to go out in search of his memories, thank you very much. Admittedly the Isle of Wight might seem an odd starting place for a repeat of my first journey to Europe; nevertheless, it had been our stunning landfall after many days at sea, and I hoped to find there a glimpse of myself and England as we were fifty years ago when the *Castel Felice* sailed by on its way to port.

'Please don't bother! Please don't!' I said twice as he beavered away at the fence, and once again before it got through to him. 'Please! Stop!'

He remembered that pool from the old days. Oh, the old days! Oh, what times they had! Oy, what times! Like the boys and girls employed at Borscht Belt hotels, he in his youth got up to no good at this holiday camp, you can be sure. Here he had probably loved for the first time. Was it the loss of innocence or the failure of love that fuelled his anger now? It is generally perceived failure that maddens men in middle age. And sexual menace attaches to a grown man's anger, be he lover or stranger, or father. Back when I was an urban kid with a developed alarm system, I would never so gormlessly have trailed any big, angry man into a lonely place. Not unless I trusted him. Or fancied him. Was the driver any threat to me now that I was old and of no account to questing males? Not unless he was crazy. Or I was. It struck me then, as I watched him fulminate, that the lust of strange men was going to be missing this time from my repeat odyssey. My years would protect me on the road even when I returned to sexy old Italy, the most overtly flirtatious country in Europe of my youth. The driver, shaking his head now, perplexed as a bull, would never have had the temerity to take a young woman to such a desolate location and show her the source of his anger. No adult male with half an ounce of sense would dare embrace such a dangerous test of his self-control with an inadvertent temptress looking on. So my age was going to protect men, too, on the journey to come. I was as near as a woman can be to absolutely safe. At last. Alas.

We stood side by side looking through an open door into a ruined bedroom full of erotic rustlings. All around us, fattening on silence, were memories: not the memories I had come for – not my own.

'You should write about what's happening here,' he said. 'The waste.'

'No, no. Not me, you,' I said and, sounding dismissive to my own ears, I added as gently as I could, 'They are your memories. You have to write them.'

We made two more stops on the short trip back to Yarmouth. The driver, apparently known locally and fearful of being recognised, stayed in the car and sent me out alone to scout functioning holiday camps, he said, and see for myself; I wasn't sure what or why. They were certainly underpopulated, but it was very early in the season, and even though the few guests in residence were pretty much of the Zimmer frame generation, the grounds were well equipped and well tended. Was it age itself and the ruination of all things that surprised and enraged him to such a degree?

On the outskirts of Yarmouth at last, we passed a number of little shops that were boarded up. 'Closed. Closed. Closed,' he hissed at each 'to let' sign.

His anger started to change its nature; no longer raw or personal, it slowly became political, until by the time we neared Yarmouth it was hardly more than pub moaning over beers with like-minded mates. His mobile rang once and he spoke to his wife about some necessary shopping on his way home. When he told her he had taken his big-city fare to observe the sorry state of the island, I matched her undoubted gaze heavenward. By the time he and I shook hands in Yarmouth my mind was practically made up to leave the Isle of Wight on an early boat. First, however, I wanted lunch.

And it was there, as the only customer in a café on a side street in Yarmouth, I found my own memories, and to spare. As memories often arrive and always will, they came in a bottle.

'9 July 1954: So this is England! London, at last! Englishmen walked by in black bowlers, even some old fellows with mutton chops. This evening the three of us went to Marble Arch, a corner of Hyde Park where complete freedom of speech is practised. Men on soapboxes were advocating points of view as disparate as misogyny is from Communism! There were some ferociously witty hecklers. The bobbies were strolling about but there were no disturbances. We met a wonderful Englishman who walked back with us and outlined an elaborate plan for the assassination of Senator McCarthy. I wish! He said everyone could tell we were American because of our trim clothes and sparkling eyes. But we heard some cruel things said about us, too: "Overlords of Western Europe . . ." Could that be right? Perhaps! I hope not. I want the lovely differences to last. Midge and Evelyn and I went out to eat. Most odd! There was something on my salad that was sticky and sweet and tasted like a big mistake. Why put sugar in salad dressing?'

Oh, so much to discover! Men of the far left, for example, were – still are? – more overtly male chauvinist pigs than pigs of the far right. In Communist households I visited hopefully when I was young in New York and later in Paris, the food was always prepared by silent women and dished up to voluble men who did not believe in enslaving women: not one at a time. Monogamy was a bourgeois concept except, apparently, in the kitchen. Communism lost me in the end for many reasons, among them because I have never been keen on the catering business. Neither was the young waitress on the Isle of Wight who brought me the scampi salad I had ordered wistfully, inspired by sea and salt in the air. Reconstituted, thawed, deep-fried, faintly fish-flavoured patties rested on a bed of undressed lettuce. Along with a cold doughy roll on a damp plate, she plunked a bottle of salad cream in front of me. And bang! A whiff of old smoke and river, and there was London as I had first encountered her in the 1950s, still a post-war city, showing the furtive appetites and cautious guilty reassembling of battered pride that a Yank from the unscarred land of plenty summed up in her journal as 'innate dignity'.

'July 1954: The city is big, bigger than New York but left-handed, much quieter. London has innate dignity. I like this city. I want to come back.'

Not long before setting out for the Isle of Wight, on a subsequent reconnoitre of mother's many stores of a lifetime's sweepings, I had come upon a box full of letters and postcards from different people and in no particular order. In the jumble was a postcard of London Bridge, dated July 1954: 'London is a wonderful city!' I had written. 'But somehow it feels weary. Only the flowers in the park are bright and velvety. It would be sad to live here.' An illustration of to what a great degree prophecy is based on experience and why the young for all their gifts cannot be trusted as oracles, for in time the fact turned out to be that I could live happily nowhere but in London.

I put a drop of gooey salad cream on my finger, tasted it, and instantly a misplaced memory fluttered back where it belonged. I was no stranger to the Isle of Wight. How could I have forgotten? In 1962 I gave up my wretched job at the Berlitz School in Paris and my poky room on the Left Bank, and came to live in Cowes for ten days aboard a twelve-metre yacht, *Stormsvalla*. Eight of us friends and crew provisioned her there, preparing to sail the Bay of Biscay to Gibraltar. On 11 June of that year we made a quick unscheduled sortie out of port, perhaps far enough to take us past the Needles, I don't remember. We were following an ocean liner westbound for New York. My parents were on board, though not on deck to watch us bravely tacking in their wake. Probably they were below in their cabin blaming each other for their only daughter's defection from all that was established and proper. Ostensibly on a European tour, they had in fact come to check up on me after more than four years. I am sure of the date because I also found a thin blue sixpenny air letter from me to them postmarked 'Cowes, Isle of Wight, 12 June 1962', the return address: care of Yacht *Stormsvalla*, Poste Restante, Gibraltar. 'If only you had been on deck yesterday, you would have seen me aboard *Stormy* waving goodbye. Tell me of your adventures after we parted in Paris. I am sorry I had to leave you there and go on to London. London is a nice place to visit.'

There is a reason beyond wear and tear for the blank space the Isle of Wight left in my memory. I was in love. Being in love changes the nature of an adventure; love on the road is like staying in five-star hotels, it irons out impressions and puts recollection to sleep on lavish cushions. What I remembered suddenly with the scampi salad was a threat made a few miles down the road and a few decades earlier by one of *Stormsvalla*'s crew, Martin W-T. The lean, likeable, daft Englishman swore he would mutiny if I, as chief galley slave, did not stow enough bottles of salad cream to see us to Gibraltar. Tinned milk, it turns out, is not the only great white corrupter.

Five

'13 July 1954: Yesterday it was Blenheim, Oxford and Stratford. Blenheim was nice. Stratford was ghastly. And Oxford was divine. We met some charming Oxford boys, friends of Tony, who joined us to see a not awfully good *Troilus and Cressida* at horrible Stratford. Shakespeare's glory is not in his birthplace, that's for sure. Tony snoozed next to me on the way back and woke to chat to me. To me! We all went to eat out in of all places a Chinese restaurant! The same menu as at the China Clipper in Jersey City! Is there any city on earth without a Chinese restaurant? Is China really a place or a world-dominating cuisine? Tony called me "My dear Irma"! I love him. And I love London. I do so hope I return some day. This is where the language comes from. This is where the books were written. We arrived in Holland yesterday. Holland is sweet.'

A few years before my grand tour with Study Abroad, when I was just turning fourteen, I was yanked out of my expensive private school and plunked into a third-rate state school. Ostensibly, it was because I had used a profanity at the dinner table. But the deeper truth was that my brother was just finishing his own elementary education and I was transferred to Henry Snyder Public School in Jersey City in order to spare the family two sets of crippling fees, one of them, in the opinion of that time and place, wasted on a girl. The four subsequent years would have been a dead loss intellectually were it not for one beautiful and discerning woman, my English teacher, Sybilla Farrell. Not only was Miss Farrell alert, vibrant and in love with her subject; she was also rumoured to be conducting an affair with a married naval officer. And she drank sherry. And she smoked like a chimney. I continued to see her after I entered university. She died of throat cancer two years after my return from the Study Abroad tour. On my shelves now, and always, I have a copy of Frank Swinnerton's *The Bookman's London*. Miss Farrell was not one to scribble on flyleaves; tucked into the book is a yellowing card, printed in raised letters, 'Miss Sybilla Farrell', and inside is her message dated June 1954.

Dear Irma [she wrote],

I saw this in my browsing and I couldn't resist sending it to you. Hardly a 'travel book' yet since you will soon be going to London some of its 'lit'ry' background may stand you in good stead and give you a bowing acquaintance with that great nation's most important past. I envy you your maiden voyage. May it be a *très bon voyage*.

Sincerely,

Sybilla Farrell

I must agree with you, young Irma, about Stratford. I have been there a few times in the course of my London life and like you I prefer Shakespeare on a stage, not in souvenir shops. As for Blenheim, and Hampton Court, the Tower, and all the other distinguished attractions you toured with Study Abroad, they are too near home, too familiar now; I have seen them too often with visiting Americans; after so many years in residence, I have no desire to see them again as a tourist. Forgive me, I don't care to try. In any case it is not among those courtly splendours I will find your trail. To this day, however, I still feel exactly as you did, moved and awestruck, whenever I glance up on a London street and discover a blue plaque in honour of Dickens, Blake, Hazlitt, H. G. Wells. You and I can thank Miss Farrell for that meeting of our minds.

The first school I attended from kindergarten through the sixth grade was the Demonstration School of New Jersey State Teachers' College. Commonly known as the 'Normal School' to protect us white, bright, middle-class kids from being considered or considering ourselves in any way out of the ordinary or so it generally believed. We were guinea-pigs for elementary-school teachers in training, nine out of ten of them young women. In those days, when teaching the under-twelves was a profession for women, the most embarrassing gaffe a child could commit in the classroom was accidentally to call a teacher 'mommy'. The trainees turned up regularly in groups of twenty or thirty to audit our classes from a platform that encircled the room, and occasionally one of them would be called upon to perform nervously a turn of her own in our little theatre-in-the-round under the critical eye of our teacher, Miss Carnes.

Miss Carnes embodied the very word 'spinster', its angularity and clump of sensible shoes, its suggestion of muddy colours, its industry, and selflessness, too, and purity, and devotion hardly seen these days; of course, she was also reactionary, and rigid of opinions. Decades later, when I learned that Miss Carnes, close to one hundred years old, was in a nursing home in California, I took my three-year-old son to visit the ancient teacher, who was drifting in and out of terminal fuddle. I must have turned away for a moment, for I did not see her slip him five crisp ten-dollar bills. He showed them to me later on the road home. 'The old lady told me', he said, 'that five times ten is fifty and I must count on that.'

Every Christmas Miss Carnes directed her 'Festival of Many Nations', a day-long shindig for which we were required to dress in costumes that reduced the ancient nations of Europe to their most adorable elements, never mind that vast chunks of them had been recently smashed to smithereens. Tiny Frenchmen in berets, lacking only miniature

67

Gauloises hanging from their lower lips, pretended to be painting canvases; diminutive señoritas clacked in circles swirling their mantillas; wee leprechauns leapt about, and infant Somethings in the City, wearing little bowler hats, served iced tea. Is memory being sardonic when it sends me the image of classmates in mini-lederhosen dishing out sausages and sauerkraut? There was no television yet to glue Americans to the screen as they would later weep and cheer over instalments of the war in Vietnam. Beyond our parroting of jingoistic folderol, we baby Yanks were absolutely uninformed about the storm across the water. Dutifully, we collected and flattened empty tins for the war effort, though precisely why was anybody's guess. Every once in a while sirens summoned us to air raid drills, practically indistinguishable from peacetime fire drills, and mild rationing was in place. Families who had city lots or summer-houses such as our own in nearby countryside were encouraged to cultivate 'Victory Gardens' and good little Americans ate every horrid boiled carrot put in front of us because children were starving in Europe.

'But that doesn't make any sense . . .'

'Don't argue. Clean your plate.'

A banner with a silver star hanging in the window meant a man from the household was overseas; a gold star meant he had been lost in action, so much we knew. How, or why, or even exactly where were our menfolk risking their bones and leaving them? Most of us little Americans were spared that knowledge. We Jewish children, girls in headscarves and boys in adorable little black hats standing behind our candles and twisted loaves at Miss Carnes's festival, knew a little more than the others. The unnatural tears of our grown-ups, their whispers, the anguish in their eyes when they watched us silently and didn't think we were noticing, told us something very, very bad was out there and aimed at us. But God forbid anyone should tell us precisely what was the snarling terror or how it had been unleashed, often with the acquiescence of neighbours, clients, tenants, patients and even old friends in the big and small places where our people had settled and lived for centuries. We were the lucky Jews, the safe Jews, American Jews, transplanted in the course of our race's history, always in the nick of time. We had not merely survived; we had thrived and we lived well.

Sure, anti-Semitism was abroad in the States. Where has it not been? It is the quintessential racial prejudice of the West. In certain universities, country clubs, on some American streets including my own we were excluded, taunted, on meaner streets than mine we were beaten up. My father carried visible and invisible scars from his childhood on Manhattan's lower East Side; mother would have been in greater danger still, her small town in Indiana supported an active branch of the Ku Klux Klan, except that her family was isolated and discreet about its origins, and besides, the Klansmen were too stupid out there to recognise a Jew who wasn't wearing horns and a tail. All in all, far and away the heaviest burden American Jewry has had to bear is the guilt accruing to good fortune.

'Hitler is a psychopathological maniac,' my mother coached me to say as a tautological party turn when I was barely four. He had a silly moustache, too, and, it was said, only one ball. Whatever *that* meant. My best friend, Judy Brenner, thought it probably meant that Hitler grew up poor without many toys. But salacious quivers wake early in bright children and something told us not to bother asking Miss Carnes or any other adult. By the time I was in the fifth grade and it was the turn of my class to present the Festival of all Nations, the Führer had been dead for eight months and the number of balls rotting in his grave was academic.

'So Hitler has killed himself. Folks, we gotta mourn the loss of a hero!' one of the Catskill comics started his shtick that year at the hotel where my grandparents used to holiday. 'If only a Jew had got him first!' he cried, and slapped his forehead. 'What a hero that Jew would have been!'

Children raised within hailing distance of New Amsterdam, in a city with its most posh street called Van Nostrand Avenue, in a nation headed for as long as they could remember by a man named Roosevelt could be expected to take Holland seriously. However, of the Normal School's fifth-grade cute displays, the cutest by far was Dutch. Wooden shoes and windmills and little white hats with turned-up flaps, tulips and round red Edam cheeses: how sweet!

*   *   *

'July 1954: The crossing to the Hook of Holland was quite rough. Poor Evelyn was sick for the entire journey. I never get seasick. The Dutch dockers were pink and well-scrubbed, and were real flirts.'

Under sail one dark and stormy night in the Bay of Biscay decades thereafter, foolhardy child, you will remember and regret your early hubris on open water. To boast about never being seasick is like saying 'I don't often lose my temper, but when I do . . .' or 'I'll see your twenty and raise you twenty . . .': commonplace pretensions that court disaster. Believe it or not, my little neo tar, I envy you the historical roll and pitch of your first Channel crossing. William the Conqueror's challenge, Napoleon's mistake, Hitler's hurdle has these days been Disneyfied into a sort of 'English Channel Experience': a penny-ante casino and aquatic mini-mall catered by McDonald's and Burger King. The monstrous cross-Channel vessel that carried me to the Netherlands offered but one outside deck and it was barely the size of an urban bathroom. Instead of sea air and billow we were given a choice of Hollywood movies people of taste would cross water to avoid.

While the graceful masts of Harwich were receding into our widening wake, I found a seat in one of the bars near a porthole blurred by salt spray and tried to read, for once a book most apposite: *Embarrassment of Riches*. Simon Schama's dissertation on Holland is brilliant, but awfully heavy in the literal sense, a kilo at least. Announcements were being made in English and in Dutch, an incomprehensible language for me except I recognise its tone of common sense and cajolery: 'Please listen – to know the location of life preservers is for your own good. You can understand that, can't you?' At a table nearby a bunch of balding cockneys were getting drunk, shouting and laughing in the early afternoon. Behind them a couple of young Goths, pierced, tattooed, both with heads half shaven and dressed in black leather, held hands and gazed into each other's eyes. Television screens suspended overhead showered us with rubbish and bad music. Screaming, hyperactive children thundered past, trailing mothers behind them like limp security blankets. Evenly spaced on the far horizon five container ships processed at a stately speed towards the English coast, and watching them through a porthole, I gave in to a melancholy that had been threatening me since my departure from Liverpool Station. Why does an old woman travel? No change will ever again be for the better.

The big blonde next to me in the shuffling queue of disembarking foot passengers introduced herself as Chrissie from Liverpool. Without preamble, as if continuing a weathered conversation, she told me she'd had her first baby at fourteen, a girl, who at sixteen is now pregnant.

'Are you pleased?'

She shrugged.

'She's awfully young,' I said.

'So was I. And I survived.'

Chrissie could never travel alone like me; she said she'd be too scared.

'Of what?'

'Dunno. Just scared.'

Her sister, who was waiting for her in the port, had lived in the Netherlands for twenty years. As a woman grows old, her intuition becomes more and more difficult to distinguish from experience: one or both – call it wisdom – told me not to ask why her sister had become an expatriate; it was not an edifying story, I was sure, and nothing I needed to know. Chrissie was on her way to meet a Turkish boyfriend, also a Dutch resident, whom she expected to make husband number three. A few months earlier Chrissie had been in a serious car accident; she told me that she'd nearly died. Suddenly her face knotted and she drew back, as confessional Englishwomen almost always do sooner or later. Why was she telling this nosy American her life's story? It had to be the strong painkillers; she'd been taking them ever since the car crash and they'd loosened her tongue.

'You're not supposed to mix that stuff with drink,' I said.

She held her paper cup under my nose as we shuffled towards the exit: 'It's only lemonade! Smell it!' she said so aggressively that I figured the contrary must be true and the lemonade I was reluctantly smelling was mixed with odourless vodka.

*　　*　　*

73

'July 1954: From first sight, Holland was neat and clean.'

Prodigal child, those few words are pretty much all you left as your first impression of the Netherlands. Too young to step away from the mirror's view of yourself, were you? Still too scared to look around and see more than what lay directly behind you. Or were you saving adjectives for the more vivid Latin sites ahead on your itinerary? Fair enough, an ignorant kid could not mark the quirks of topography reclaimed from the sea by the blistered hands of men, or note the way birds fly a long straight line against a horizon made abstract by flatness of the land. But how could you fail to comment on the curious liquidity of daylight in Holland? The way it flows around every tree and steeple, and makes even industrial cranes and chimneys stand as proud as dry things at sea. Except for Rotterdam, reconstructed after the war in sky-scraping canyons of glass and steel, thanks to its unearthly levelling and light Holland offers few places to lurk even in built-up areas. Alleys are plentiful and give a special charm to strolling in Dutch cities, rather like the lure of footpaths in a forest; the narrow ways are far from sinister, however, they are too well peopled by pedestrians trying to avoid the wider streets and boulevards hectic with trams and cyclists.

Eye contact with passing strangers in the streets of Amsterdam lacks the edgy side of glancing contact in London, or the quick assessment and totalling of sum parts that happens in Paris and New York. Even-handedness and limpidity seem to have entered the very bones of Netherlanders. The shock of a European political assassination soon after my journey was compounded for the world because it took place in Holland, of all places! And though the victim, Pim Fortuyn, stood to the far right in that level land, anywhere else in the world his tenets would barely have tipped the ideological see-saw.

Whatever nastiness Netherlanders got up to in the days of their mercantile empire, these days at home they show tolerance that is benignly totalitarian: it allows no rebellion. Against what? Legislation is designed to accommodate and control rather than outlaw. Kids smoking pot? Let them. That way you can keep an eye on them and track infiltrations of hard drugs. Bicycle theft on the increase? Try putting licensed state-owned bicycles into circulation, to be borrowed then left outside unlocked for the next needy passer-by to borrow and leave unlocked, and so on. Squatters squat. Why not? Allow the terminally ill and incurably sad to pass away in peace. And give minority groups time and space in media to put across their messages, or semblance of messages; is there a more sensible way to keep quiet in the streets than to credit the metropolis with the principled friendliness of smaller communities? Contrary to most cosmopolites who boast of their urban roots, it is very hard to find a Netherlander even in Amsterdam or skyscraping Rotterdam who does not proudly claim to have come originally from a small town. As refreshing as Amsterdam is in many ways, it is too even-minded, too upfront, too downright wholesome to be sexy. Darker, madder cities are sexier.

'Guys always end up at the Banana Bar. The strippers there do something weird with bananas,' said Flavia, a young Italian woman also a guest at my bed and breakfast. Flavia had been resident there for many months: postcards were pinned up on the wall of her little room, her toiletries were permanently installed on the shelf in the communal bathroom, and she sat down for her evening meals in the kitchen with the Indonesian Buddhist couple who owned the place. They seemed bewildered, not to say a little frightened, by a guest who took 'family run' so literally. It was early morning, our quiet home on a residential street near the Museumplein had just been descended upon by eight tough, streetwise Glaswegians on a weekend stag party in the charge of a frantic and despairing older man, the father of the groom-to-be, and Flavia was explaining to me why Amsterdam was the destination of stags' choice. Strong beer and marijuana aside, I had seen the strip clubs and red-light district of Amsterdam where prostitutes are proudly displayed in every window, like butterflies in cases. Flavia's whispered disquisition on Amsterdam's clean-shaven underbelly was interrupted by the arrival of eight well-dressed young women, who turned out to be medical interns from London on a hen party. Stags and hens commingled for a while at the hotel reception.

Humankind does not merely eat; we restaurate, marinate, celebrate. Other creatures drink, we ferment and inebriate.

Breathe? Certainly. Of course. But first, aerate and fumigate, if you please. Right to the end we decorate, complicate and obfuscate animal functions. Die? If we must. But let us obliterate with dignity and incinerate in style. As for the way we fuck, in default of automatic lust and a regular mating season, we alone among animals have contrived institutions, aids, agencies, fashions, fantasies, romance, big, big business, even so-called experts to keep us at it. What a song and dance to renew our tribe's residency on earth! Necessity no longer pertains. We do it for love, for fun, for money, for vengeance and for fame. Procreation? Not right now, thanks. We prefer recreation. Sometimes with bananas. Only late that night when I was awakened by a loud knock on my door and a slurred drunken voice said, 'Let me in. It's the Scottish man . . .' did the sheer, exuberant absurdity of human sexual appetite manifest itself to me in Amsterdam.

'Oh, go away!' I told the befuddled stag.

Vaguely wondering for which roost the jerk had mistaken my room and which posh hen was going to miss out on her bit of rough, I went straight back to sleep.

'July 1954: I'm surprised to see so many women out scrubbing their front stoops! Is it a kind of community service, I wonder, or are the Dutch terribly house-proud? And every window has something interesting in it so they look like framed pictures along the street. Walking around Amsterdam without the rest of the mob, Ev and Midge and I went in

77

and out of enticing little shops on pretty shady streets with bridges and canals looking for a gift for Ev's mother. In one shop window she saw a teapot she said her mother would like. The door was standing open so we went in to browse around. Only it turned out not to be a shop! We had wandered into someone's house! The woman was very understanding when she found us in her living room, picking up her candlesticks and saucers, looking for price tags! She laughed when we made her understand our mistake. In New York she would have called the cops.'

Enticing shops are thin on the ground everywhere in Europe nowadays. They have been overtaken by souvenir shops stocked for a Normal School sensibility, in Amsterdam with tulip bulbs and wooden shoes. And, of course, everywhere are installations of the huge chain stores that are strangling self-expression in low- to middle-income shoppers and preempting the inspiration of artisans everywhere in the swelling Western world. Arise, prisoners of obesity, conformity and insecurity! You have nothing to lose but your chains! Not that having lots of money encourages originality or taste. Like every other city, Amsterdam has a few streets where toffee-nosed salesgirls purvey trademarks just as banal as the others, only they are pricier and harder to pronounce. At least the domestic windows of Holland continue to frame verve and style that misled Evelyn and Midge and me all those years ago. Set out on practically every ledge are prize pieces of china, oriental gewgaws, carvings, dolls, toys and flowers in beautiful vases, all arranged with taste that transforms residential streets into galleries. If there turns out one day to be a painterly gene, then it will be found in abundance among the Dutch.

'1954: Amsterdam – Marjorie always says I don't know how to look at paintings. Maybe she's right. I am looking for a glimpse into another life or way of life. I want a painting to tell me a story. Will the sick child survive? Will the cat have that cloth off the table? Why is one man scowling at another? What games could children play, wearing such clothes? For me, paintings are like windows or open doors. Marjorie says that's all wrong. I am supposed to feel things about a painting, not think about its content. She says I think too much. I say there is no such thing. But in the Rijksmuseum today, I sort of knew what she meant. Looking at paintings feels more like reading stories than looking at pictures.'

You and me both, young I; we are not connoisseurs but voyeurs in the galleries. I remain as deficient as you were in whatever is the quality that makes a great viewer of great pictures, and thus the classic Dutch painters have always pleased us both simply because their greatest pictures are as scenes glimpsed through a stranger's door. In the 1970s my son's father, a painter of Dutch extraction as it happens, used to take me along to exhibitions of art that was modern then.

I wasn't sure how to respond to what I was seeing except for thinking that somehow, like going to the ballet, it must be doing me good and making me more sensitive to subtle and sensuous levels of beauty. Thinking about it now, I wonder if I was right. About art exhibitions, not about ballet. I continue actively to dislike the athletic posturing and the thump of stubby feet off the beat, mucking up music. But it would surprise you, child, as it surprised me to find myself equally delighted in Amsterdam by Malevich, Newman, Stella, especially Rothko, and others at the Stedelijk Museum of Modern Art as I was by the tale-telling paintings of the Rijksmuseum. Have we grown up at last, you and I, and learned to look through image to meaning? Past signs to significance?

'July, 1954: I can see why rich men hire art thieves to steal masterpieces for them. There are always so many people surrounding me at museums. I'd love to know how it feels to stand in front of a Vermeer or a Rembrandt all by myself.'

Sweetheart, I am glad to tell you that by a fluke of demographics you will be privileged one future day – just the other day – to stand alone, all by yourself, for a full three minutes in front of the self-portrait of young Rembrandt at the Rijksmuseum. What fun! I took out my pad and pen to jot down a few words about his eyes, evenly spaced, ever so slightly Mongoloid, and the tussling copper filaments of his hair.

'Excuse me,' hissed an angry American woman's voice behind me. 'Do you speak English?'

'Yes, I speak English. Can I help you?'

'Your bag is open,' she snapped, outraged that an Anglophone tourist could so let the side down as to tempt foreign pickpockets.

'And so is your mouth,' I thought. But I said 'Thank you', slipped the pad back into my bag, zipped up and hurried away from young Rembrandt's seeing face.

Every city is big to itself. As impressive as the unfolded street map of Amsterdam may be, practically everything I wanted to see was in easy walking distance for someone used to London's patchwork sprawl, and that was as well because I could not get my head around the ticket system for local trams. The way Flavia's fine English dissolved when she tried to explain the routine made me think the problem was not just due to my own senile obtusity; she herself did not seem all that sure just how to fold the travel card over to the correct date and distance before inserting it into the franking machine. Transport police frequently board trams to parade down the aisle imposing stiff and immediate fines, generally on hapless tourists. I felt safer entering by the front and paying the driver directly with coins.

'But that works out much more expensive than a travel card,' said my Dutch friend, Annette, who had travelled in from the country to lunch with me in Amsterdam. 'It's a waste of money.'

I pointed to what was translated into English on the menu

as 'Dutch Pee Soup'. 'In for a penny, Annette,' I said, taking advantage of an earlier observation that the Dutch are so pleased to laugh that even the feeblest joke or most glancing innuendo is hilariously received.

Four days alone in a strange city is a little lifetime. Patterns are formed, routines established. Within an hour or so I had sniffed out my Amsterdam bar, a big one with a terrace, and my restaurant, a small one with seafood on the menu and windows on the street. My hotel room was so narrow I could span it with outspread arms; it was soon familiar, even welcoming, to return to Simon Schama and the absence of a TV set after sightseeing and an early dinner. Every morning before going down to breakfast I stood at my window to watch the woman across the street see her boy off to school on his bike; I knew – I remembered – how she was going to wait in her doorway, looking in his direction for a few minutes after he was out of sight. My penultimate morning in Amsterdam I awoke from a dream of comfort and found a phone number, 743–3874, floating at the front of my mind. It took a moment to recollect that it belonged to the first home I had owned in London, a terraced house in Shepherd's Bush I sold nearly twenty years ago and the place where my son grew up. Then I made the daily walk to the underground supermarket at the Museumplein to buy my usual bottle of chilled water. Around me Dutch women shopped briskly, from memory. Outside, clouds, rain, faint sun and bright shifted constantly over the Museumplein so the vast plain seemed to unroll through several seasons in the twenty minutes it took to stroll across it.

On my last full day in Amsterdam, returning to the hotel in the late afternoon, I stopped on a bench to watch Dutch children at play. Some of them showed ethereal beauty that would be swallowed by adolescence. A little boy, whose mother was not in evidence, danced in and out of the fountain oblivious to the chilly north breeze; he was laughing and water was pouring from the yellow sleeves of his jacket. Tourists from Japan took pictures of him, others carrying ubiquitous bags and boxes decorated with Van Gogh's sunflowers stopped to smile. Earlier while rambling around town near the station I had come upon a street redolent of marijuana where someone was singing 'I'd rather be a hammer than a nail . . .' I could not stop humming the silly tune softly. On a bench near me sat a woman dressed in flowing layers of thin weave, mainly salmon pink. She wore strings of beads, her grey hair was straggling out of a tousled chignon. Now, there was a gal who could explain why it was better to be a hammer than a nail, a preference that has always eluded me. The sun came out and suddenly I remembered an outing to Amsterdam more than thirty years ago with Tony.

'July 1954: After lunch today Tony gave me a gin. It was vile but I pretended to like it. I love Tony. In an English sort of way . . .'

* * *

No. No. Not *that* Tony. You will discover, child, there are many more than one Tony on earth. I am referring to another sort of English Tony who was going to be our son's father. I'll confess to you that on our trip to Amsterdam he and I were caught and fined for inadvertently fare-dodging on the very first tram we took. Otherwise, I could not recollect that we did anything special except be in love. And Tony bought himself a black leather coat at the market in Rembrandtplein. That must have been at the end of the 1960s; it remains a jolly street market. I had browsed it that very morning on my way to the Jewish Museum, chosen over the Anne Frank House with its discouraging queue of tourists, including many nuns and clerics. The house where that poor child suffered has become a big, glossy memorial to her martyrdom that simplifies the event and makes it too sentimental for my taste. An image that kept returning on the boat bus back from the Jewish Museum and for hours thereafter was of two yellow stars of cloth exhibited in a cabinet; why was one bright and unused, the other ragged and faded? Had one belonged to a father and the other to his child? A woman, laughing and scolding, appeared at last to pull the little boy out of the fountain. He was drenched to his skin and left wet footprints on the path when she dragged him away. I tried to feel in love again, I knew the words; I could not remember the tune. Clearer, sharper, I remembered Tony's coat. My son's father is not a Jew: had he been one in the open season, however, it would have been awfully hard to stitch a yellow star on to a garment as tough as that coat. I wondered if he still had it. A coat like that was made to last a lifetime.

Before returning for the last time to my little hotel in Amsterdam, I raised a glass of thick red wine to you, my younger version, in a café on Museumplein where you too once watched the children flying wonderful kites like giant dragonflies against the sky. Next to me a Japanese girl who was on her own bravely attacked a platter of gummy Dutch sushi. In the ladies' room of the café was a feature new to me: each cubicle had a see-through glass door. Inside was a small sign with a message in English that immediately entered my small collection of *pensées trouvées*. 'Transparency goes', it read, 'as soon as you lock the door.'

Six

The journey from Amsterdam to Utrecht is not long and the train hardly more than a commuters' urban tram. Being one of the few passengers encumbered with a suitcase, I took the first available seat, on the aisle near the door, backwards out of Amsterdam, it so happened.

Between the window and me sat a tall, long-legged man with white hair, not young any more, not yet as old as I. 'You are English?' he said, glancing at Schama's epic work, open on my lap.

Sometimes I do not feel up to the sort of conversation that follows an explanation of American roots and British residency, so I opt for the easy: 'Yes.' And I asked, 'Dutch?' 'Yes.'

I commented on how welcoming and friendly looked the small villages we were speeding through.

'Not so friendly,' he said. 'Notice how in every town there are two church spires? They are not always getting along as well as you would believe. Like your Northern Ireland.' It is a human characteristic to dramatise one's own troubles, superstitiously, I think, so as to shield fortune from the evil eye and discourage the envy of mischievous gods. Amsterdammers, and their country cousins like my friend Annette, snug in their employed and integrated society, were still boasting about the terrible riot at that year's Queen's Day celebrations months after it had happened. My son, who had been in Amsterdam at the time, told me the riot amounted to a rush on the station when the word got out that late trains were going to be cancelled precisely, if ill-advisedly, to avoid a rush on the station.

'Only science has facts,' I said to the man on the train, distilling from aqueous thoughts about church spires and urban riots. 'Otherwise, my guess is that all the rest of us have are opinions and everything we know is relative to all we don't know.'

'So what makes you sure science has facts? Maybe their facts are only opinions with circumstantial evidence.'

We looked straight at each other for the first time. Under layers of volcanic ash stirred the fossil: the Dutchman was a handsome example of what used to be my type, back when I had a type. 'Do you live in Utrecht?'

'No. No. No,' he said, 'I come from the country. I am going to Utrecht to see a friend.' He frowned, sudden alarm in his crisp northern eyes. 'A lady friend.'

After that I read and he seemed to doze. As we were pulling into the station, he slipped past me and disappeared quickly, before there was any question of offering to help me off the train with my suitcase.

Amsterdam, for all its charm and wealth of art and history, has some of the elements of an international airport, organised for expediency and catering to strangers who are passing through. Utrecht is less prepossessing, not so eager to pacify or please, more self-involved; it is a competitive university town with edge. I could live in Utrecht. I have no intention of living there, of course. I have no intention of living in the Netherlands, or anywhere other than where I am living now. But we expatriates grow up – possibly we are born – looking for somewhere else. In whatever flat or house or castle, on whatever sea, in whatever desert, farm or forest, city or nation, the question arises automatically: could I live in this place? For us old hands who have spent most of our lives not quite here nor there, neither lemon nor limey, the question is more wistful: if I had it to do again, could it be here? When I was young I brushed off Utrecht with barely half a page of my journal. When I was young it was another story: the young want heat and colours. But now? Now, I could live in Utrecht. I could live, could have lived, and could die in Utrecht. I would say the same for Fargo, North Dakota. Aberdeen in Scotland. And a few other cool, chaste, stone-coloured cities I have seen.

'July 1954: This evening in Utrecht Ev and Midge and I went to a carnival. We had to draw pictures of clowns and ferris wheels for people on the street to get directions: clowns and ferris wheels transcend mere language! We walk along saying ridiculous things in English and nobody understands us! It is fascinating and powerful speaking a language nobody else speaks. The carnival was gay and noisy, filled with boys who kept pinching us. Stop it! We're real! Everything in the flat, flat fields and towns in this country is spotless. But in Utrecht the people smell! I refuse to play shocked American tourist. One of our boys, Earl, is a strict Roman Catholic from somewhere in the middle of America. When we mentioned the carnival was across the street from a church he said "disgusting" and "a slap in the face". He is amusing and exasperating. So many of us forget to exchange petty standards for broader ones or, better still, drop standards altogether. Yippee! I start clean!'

Sorry to tell you, honey, nobody but nobody starts clean. We are born in bloody muck, our noses wrinkled. Whew! What a stink! We are delivered on earth as tourists kitted out with a few basic life-saving instincts and some prejudices that might have been life-savers too in their time, but mostly have outlived their purpose. What you sniffed with Yankee distaste in Utrecht, for example, was probably not unwashed people but a harmless whiff of medieval fetor trapped in sewers that have been around as long as local history. You will grow up to tolerate and even appreciate such low, sweet wafts of pestilence that make some old, old cities museums for the nose.

Every Dutch resident I met on this, your hoary-headed future journey, spoke fair to fine English. You and your cronies, Midge and Ev, would be stunned to eavesdrop as I did on a pair of well-dressed young beauties punctuating their conversations in Dutch with the shrill exclamation 'shit, man!' in English. They took to the phrase so eagerly, my guess is it corresponds in rhythm and tone to a local expletive, a kind of Dutch *'Zut, alors!'*. And I imagine it made them feel 'fascinating and powerful' to say 'shit, man!' in public. In your lifetime, demotic English has been growing steadily into the nearest Europe has had to a lingua franca since the triumphs of Rome; it features more or less grammatically in high street ads and shop names everywhere; it runs computers and dominates popular music; at least a broad smattering of English is spoken by practically everyone on the Continent who has anything to sell and almost everyone, even old ladies on trains, who has anything to say.

French will hold out, protected by law and in exclusivity. Spanish will live, transplanted in the New World. Italian will continue to squabble among its selves. Dutch and Scandinavian tongues will probably in the end be exclusively in-house and art-house languages. As for German, to put the verb at the end of the sentence requires a speaker to know precisely where he is going when he begins to speak, accommodating pedagogues – demagogues too, I dare say – but otherwise restrictive and stultifying. The conquest of Western Europe by English has been bloodless, too, accomplished through

film and microphones and cyberspace, and all the sophisticated technology of an undercover operation rather than
weaponry of open warfare. Until a better, looser, happier
tongue comes along, English rules. OK?

Can you and I celebrate the empire of English while despis-
ing McDonald's and Burger King, and deploring the tidal
wave of Anglophone trivia sweeping over Europe? Shit, man!
You bet we can. Because essentially this language is strong
and beautiful; because it nourishes; because it steals and
borrows and adapts to itself whatever the liberal laws of its
grammar allow; because it is a joker, a gamester, an actor, a
poet, a revolutionary, a mother, and because it can leap from
deepest anguish of the soul to lean and curious concepts
without losing the beat. Prejudiced? *Moi*? Certainly I am. I
am a fan of my native tongue. And so, smug little missy,
were you. Why else do you think you end up as an expatriate
to the land where your language came from? Sorry, I forget
all you do not yet know: I forget myself – you do not know,
for example, or even imagine, that England will one day be
your chosen home.

By the by, Earl's people travelled too far into the territory
of American puritans; they broke the classic tie of carnival
to the rites of their own Roman church. To this day, carnivals
and funfairs of Europe pitch their tents close to cathedrals
because that's where they originated a thousand years ago
and more as sanctioned revelry before the austere period of
Lent. Sure, the crime rate goes up when the carnival comes

91

to town, so does the birth rate; it is on the earthy side a carnival is connected and connects Christians to their God-fearing history. Poor Earl, pity him. He doesn't know what he's missing. An annual carnival used to pitch up for a fort-night every July on a hillside near the lake where our parents had the country house. Do you remember? Of course you do. For you, only a few summers have passed since the long warm days of childhood and the thrill of the carnival. You and your brother liked to sneak under the flaps of the empty tents early in the morning while the carnie people still slept in their caravans and see all the painted wheels standing still and the big soft toys waiting, unguarded by man or dog in those days of innocence, until sunset when the raucous whirli-gig slipped into gear again. Nearly fifty years later, as I found myself ostentatiously out of place in a group of Japanese tourists being conducted through Utrecht's 'National Museum from Musical Clock to Street Organ', the carnival came rolling back on a full blast of honky-tonk music that set the palms to tingling again and made the feet to itch.

'July 1954: I sent the family another postcard, this one of tulips. Last time it was of windmills. Nothing if not original! Tony says it could take a week or more for our cards to arrive in the States and we would be better off sending air letters that you buy at the post office, already stamped and ready to fold for mailing. But we haven't time for letter writing!'

*   *   *

Postcards? How quaint! In some ways, my dear, you are the senior of us two. Only fogeys send postcards these days or suburbanites holidaying someplace exotic who want to make their neighbours envious. Not many letters are written now, either. Modern people who are the age you were then prefer to carry small phones around with them wherever they go now; they have all become so very much more important than you used to be, don't you know. Who knows what urgent decisions of state may be required from them while they are abroad? If writing must take place between them and friends or family members, it is transmitted electronically with a speed you could not imagine, dear little old-fashioned girl. You will communicate that way too in due course, when you are I. In the vast and entertaining but stupendously ugly Hoog Catherine Market, I waited in a short queue for ice creams next to a boy who was rolling a spliff. He lit up, happened to exhale just as I happened to inhale, and the day took a hip and rosy turn. I found myself at last hurrying along to an Internet café to check my e-mail. My Buddhist hosts in Amsterdam made their computer generously open to me so I had never before needed to avail myself of this new urban service.

'Your first time?' asked the boy at the desk.

It is daunting for anyone much over the age of thirty to show ignorance before their juniors. Blushing, I confessed that yes it was. What would you have made of it, little techno-primitive? You had barely accustomed yourself to a portable typewriter. Your family had not long before watched black-and-white television through a big magnifying glass in a frame on the floor in front of the set: I remembered it, and LP records, and portable hairdryers, and similar technological wizardry of your day while the courteous youngster was showing me the drill. Could I nip back in time and bring you bodily forward to watch how I access messages from friends as well as unsolicited pornography and other opportunistic garbage waiting for me in cyberspace, could I import you merely long enough to watch sixty seconds of an animated commercial on twenty-first-century television, or to hear domestic music on a compact disc, it would leave you gibbering, half crazed with delight, envy and horror.

Some of the kids in the Internet café must have been Dutch, most of them were from abroad and quite a few were beautiful. Side by side they sat at long tables, not looking at each other, faces to their screens, backs to the outside world. They were not all there: they were fragmented, elsewhere. Of the places where youth congregates, there could not be one less heated by flirtation and sexual surmise than an Internet café. In staid silence, they tap in questions, information, greetings, and they renew vows to family and lovers in distant places and different time zones. They play naughty games; they ask for money. Yes, their invention is stupendous. But invention at what cost to discovery, I wonder? I am not a Luddite. I am grateful to be still flexible enough to squeeze in under the barrier; word-processing has saved a forest of wasted paper and without e-mail I would be deprived of many friendships, some of them made on recent journeys through Europe. True enough, these young people glued to their screens are probably being spared the agonising loneliness and penury that await you, tearaway child of the 1950s, when you leave home again a few years later and for good. But to sail away will always require slipping anchor, and all in all, I am glad there was no quick, mechanical way for you to turn your back on the huge, unformed future and face a tidy image of home and safety on a screen. Had there been a cheap system to keep in touch when you were in your darkest, weakest hour – in 1960, say, as you struggled to survive in Paris – had you been able then to transmit an immediate cry home for help, you could well now be the predestined ex-wife of that psychiatrist in Scarsdale. Or, wizened and boozy, living in the West Village, teaching occasionally at City College of New York, and writing what we Barnard College literary snobs used to call 'romantic friction'. I hope you have taken notes, child, and take note always to think twice before you push the 'send' button. There ends granny's diatribe. You will be quizzed later when you are old on the spiritual and psychological effects of advanced technology. Quizzed and puzzled.

The only evidence of rush hour in Utrecht was a throng of bicycles, as noisy as an invasion of locusts in the streets. A dejected bunch of juniper and potato peel drunks were swilling on a bench not far from my hotel and silently watching the well-wheeled swarm past. A few blocks further along I had already staked out my supermarket and across the street my restaurant, small and bar-centred, where I chose to sit outside on the pavement in spite of the cool evenings. To wait on table in the Netherlands applies especially to the customer. I had finished reading my incredibly expensive day-old English newspaper and was starting to wonder if the young waitress had understood my dinner order. I looked around. Behind me two young Russians, one drinking beer and the other a Coke, were speaking to their Dutch companion in English. They must have just emerged from one of the many employment agencies in the neighbourhood; they were discussing offers of 'fool time work'.

Whether the young woman at the table nearby on my left was a natural redhead was doubtful; pink, orange and maroon hair was noticeably in fashion at that moment among the young women of Holland. She was a bottled carrot-top, big and gleeful, overflowing with life force and very loud. The older man she had been roaring at was her father; she turned to let me know this as soon as he went inside to fetch more beers. 'You have to serve yourself, otherwise you could die thirsty!' she cried, with a laugh that challenged the rising moon.

When I asked if she wanted my newspaper, as her English was so good, she tore it out of my offering hand. Her every movement had evolved from a race of giants; her gratitude was like the open door of an oven.

'Are you travelling alone?' she asked.

'Yes.'

'I could not do that! Never. Never. I cannot be travelling alone.'

'Why not?'

'I'd be afraid.'

'Of what?'

For an instant she was quiet: a tornado in thought. 'I'd be afraid. Afraid that with nobody to watch out for me, I would just disappear! Poof!' She threw her arms wide, all but grazing a spry octogenarian who had wheeled up and was leaning her bike against the fence next to us. 'One minute here, one minute gone!'

At that moment her father appeared, followed closely by the waitress bringing my dinner. The way the girl watched her father's approach told me somehow that they did not often meet. To intrude on their high-decibel tête-à-tête would have been thoughtless. Also, I was starving, a condition which enables the relishing of Dutch cuisine. So I let them be and merely jotted down what she'd said. It was an interesting reply to the familiar question, especially from someone so eminently visible.

'July 1954: Dutch breakfasts are frightening . . .'

I was referring in my journal to the mass of meats, cheeses, bread, pastries and fruits on offer, a Dutch culinary extravagance that continues now, only my capacity has diminished. My hotel in Utrecht was pleasant, inexpensive and appeared to be staffed by university students who served up a breakfast that was frightening this time mainly for the eldritch silence in which it was taken. A couple with nothing to say to each other sat near the window, the crunch and grind of toast between their teeth was audible around the room. As close as she could be to the exit was a solitary woman about my age, her yellow hair dry as straw and in her eyes wild terror. Of disappearing, perhaps? Her lips began moving in inward dialogue and a language unknown to me that struck my ear as a heartbreaking hum. I recollected how our guide at the museum of mechanical instruments told us that sad songs bring in more money than happy ones for street musicians. Surreptitiously, the unhappy woman wrapped three rolls and a few slices of cheese in a paper napkin and slipped them into her bag, then darted out through the door so quickly she upset her chair.

'Is it a soft egg?' The ringing question came in an American accent from a man seated alone, diagonally in front of me.

'I don't know,' the boy waiter said. 'You will have to look.'

There was the sharp tap of a spoon on eggshell. 'I prefer it softer.'

'How many minutes?' asked the boy.

'That depends. What is the temperature of the water?'

'Boiling.'

'In that case, two and a half minutes.'

Half an hour later the egg man and I bumped into each other at the desk and while we waited for a sudden downpour to pass, we undertook a conversation in which a triple pun was perpetrated within moments upon the words 'bread', 'breadth' and 'breath'. He was a mathematician from Chicago, he told me, visiting the university in Utrecht. I guessed his age to be in the late fifties; his machinations to find out mine before committing himself and asking me out for a drink later that evening were endearing. Instead of putting him out of his arithmetical misery, however, pretending not to hear his question as to whether I really thought Technicolor movies were an improvement on black and white, and before he asked what year I graduated from Columbia, I opened my umbrella and left him guessing. A few minutes later, as I was coming out of the post office, where I had gone to mail the heavyweight Schama back to myself in London, a young man pulled up on a bike and asked me directions in a mix of languages. As soon as I realised he too was an American I asked, as Yanks always do, where from in the States.

'Chicago,' he said.

'Really! There's a coincidence! I've just met another Chicagoan. What do you do?'

'Oh,' he said over his shoulder as he cycled off, 'I'm a mathematician.'

Two mathematicians from Chicago in one Dutch hour! What are the odds?

In Utrecht bells in the great steeple rang out the theme from *The Sound of Music* three minutes after every hour according to my infallible Swiss watch. That no two municipal clocks agreed and I found none accurate anywhere in the Netherlands increased the impression of everything and time itself bending to the force of light at liberty in a flat, unshadowed land. On my way out of town, I stopped in the cloistered herb garden. As I was emerging into the environs of the cathedral, suddenly across the garden there was the man from the train. He saw me, too. We started towards each other, just a step. Next to him was a woman a month or two more than half my age. She had russet curls, like the young Rembrandt. I looked at her, she at me. She narrowed her eyes, linked her arm to his and leaned her head against his shoulder. He and I exchanged a sketchy half-wave, before he disappeared with his rusty hoyden. I continued towards the station and the train to Germany. All by myself.

Seven

'16 July 1954: Even Tony was quiet on the bus today. (Maybe that's because when I woke up in Utrecht around 5 a.m. I saw him just creeping back into our hotel!) But we are all confused. Germany produces mixed feelings. Mainly they are bad feelings. The Germans stare solemnly at the bus as we pass, a few of them wave. The ones we meet seem friendly enough but we only meet people who depend on the tourist trade. Our German bus driver, Fritz, is silent, distant. I don't think he likes us. One of the boys was saying it was good they lost the war, and Earl started going on about "loving your enemy" and "turning cheeks" and "all men are brothers" until Tony told him to bottle it. Earl is a pain. Dad was worried when he saw Germany on the Students Abroad itinerary. Why am I scared?'

You're scared for more than one reason. Because you figure that barely ten years earlier Fritz – he would have to be called Fritz, wouldn't he? – would probably not have thought twice about the murder of your family. And because it will take more than one generation or two to make it safe again to breathe in Germany for those who until so recently had no immunity or mask against its poisonous gases. And you're scared because you are flirting with the other four-letter emotion that requires surrender of control, sense, balance, self and sanity: you are in danger of falling madly in hate. You toyed with it earlier in childhood, remember? Capital punishment must work as a deterrent; at least it deters little girls who hate their grannies, for intemperate hatred must lead logically to killing its object and when you were seven or eight not long after your maternal granny had moved in with your family, you decided against murdering her only because you figured you would be caught and electrocuted. Why did you hate her so murderously? She preferred your brother, of course, hardly a cause for hatred in a girl-child of your generation. Love gives life and cherishes it, and mankind could not have got very far without loving; hate too has probably been a life-saver in its way, uniting and making fierce against threats. But love is its own reason; hate wants a reason and thus it makes suckers for the arguments and propaganda of cynics and plausible lunatics. Love is happiest in the company of its object or all alone, basking in its own warmth. Hate is a cockroach that finds significance in the company of fellows; let it be defeated in one place, its progeny will survive in crevices. The cockroach dies hard. It will see us all out. That's why it is wise to be on your guard when you cross certain borders into lands where hate is known to have swarmed not that long ago. And if you think I am being sententious, remember that I'm nearly four times your age, baby. So mind your manners: I minded mine when I was young – when I was you.

Germany is a profound motif in the weave of Europe's east and west; to refuse to visit the place, as some Jews and others do to this day, is to be dictated to by one's resident vermin. Some of my friends were doubly scandalised a few years ago when I planned to visit not just Germany but Bayreuth to hear the work of a self-avowed anti-Semite and Hitler's inspirational composer. 'How can you?'

How could I not? It is precisely to hear the music of others that we are blessed with ears and wanderlust. True enough, the man's opinions were deplorable, and the genius of Shosta-kovich alone proves that opinions and political fervour can be transmitted through sounds. Yes, there is genuine danger in some music, certainly for the composer. But homicidal impulses roused in sane members of Wagner's audience could be directed only against sopranos. And Wagnerian sopranos can take care of themselves. When his noise man-ages to steer clear of bombast, boot tap and schmaltz, it has undeniable power and beauty.

'July 1954: I know all men are brothers. I know it, but I cannot bring myself to believe it. Not really. When Earl was going on and on about the brotherhood of man and how we are our brothers' keeper, I wanted to shout: I <u>am</u> my brother's keeper. And my brother's name is Michael!'

If you go in for brothers in grand metaphysical style, then Earl and Fritz the driver are your brothers. Shall we underline the verb the way you did back then, so it scratches three pages deep? They *are* your brothers! But you don't believe that for a minute, do you? Belief is what each prefers, remember? Belief is a choice. Who would choose a small-minded fundamentalist like Earl to be her brother? Who would choose a possible fratricide like Fritz? Accept them as cousins distantly removed by all means, to be treated with courtesy and charity, but brothers? No. Your brother is Michael. Your father, my father – our father – was the first of seven brothers: Irving, Abraham, Aaron, Max, Jerry, Milton and baby Simon who died in infancy. Not a Cain in the bunch. Brothers are not chosen. They evolve from the same place and pace, and run a practically identical course of hazards to ours.

In the early 1960s, not long after my third and what was to be my final assault on Europe, my parents left America for the first time in their lives and crossed the Atlantic on the *Queen Mary* to check up on me. I met them in Paris and guided them from one tourist attraction to the next, trying to keep them too busy, and too public, to ask what the hell I was doing with my life. It was a question to which I had absolutely no answer at that time. I still don't, even now that life has started having done with me. Mother was girlish and enthusiastic, seduced by the glamour of Paris. My father, however, was dumbfounded and concerned to his very heart that I had decided to live on the war-torn side of an ocean his parents had risked their lives to cross. We were walking through the old Jewish quarter of the Marais – my mother exclaiming; my father worried and brooding as usual – when suddenly he fell a few paces behind us. I turned and saw him captivated at last by a little grocery store. We followed him past a wooden barrel of pickles on the pavement, into a small space caving in under cluttered shelves and redolent with earthy odours. The bearded proprietor came from behind the oaken counter and greeted us in French; before I could reply in the same language my father said something in Yiddish. Suddenly both men were laughing, slapping their hands together and all but dancing. Until that moment I had not known my father to be fluent; on the contrary, the lacunae and solecisms of his English used to embarrass me in front of friends, beastly child. But here he was voluble and articulate; here he was speaking his mother's tongue; here was someone who knew what he was talking about with a *Landsmann*, a fellow, a brother. We don't have to love our brothers and sisters; we don't have to like them. But if we fail to keep them then we lose our selves within the vast, muddled history of the human mass.

Paternal Kurtzes, though I believe their origins to have been further east, ended up around the Black Forest; they and maternal Auerbachs are buried all over Germany. In the mid-1990s I was invited to Hamburg and installed by the professors of English in a small flat near the university where I was to speak to their students the next day. Tea and coffee were neatly stowed in my kitchen but thanks to a lapse of my hosts' vaunted efficiency, I had to go out in search of milk. That was how I happened to discover evidence of Auerbachs, four of them inscribed on a plaque naming the bodies disinterred when a Jewish cemetery was razed only a few years earlier to make way for a shopping mall. Insensitivity is not yet a capital crime. Nevertheless, leaving Holland on the train to Cologne, I felt wary and heavy with foreboding; increasingly victimised too, as it happened, by hoots of boyish American laughter and the groin-driven thump-thump of pop music behind me in the compartment.

Ten minutes out of Utrecht, the Dutch countryside opened around us like an ironed banknote. A young man wearing a huge T-shirt and long, baggy American shorts broke away from the bunch huddled over the dreadful noise and slid into the seat next to me. He tucked his rucksack into the space at his feet just as a voice behind us spat out a mess of gibberish from which the word 'motherfucka . . .' jumped like a poisonous toad.

'You know, someone ought to tell those inconsiderate boobies to turn the bloody sound down,' I said to the kid in my best old-lady fashion and nodded towards his companions.

All three were fair-skinned; the boy next to me was of

Mexican origin. 'That's why I came to sit here, Ma'am,' he said. 'That DVD is all those guys have been into ever since we left LA. Like. They don't know what they're missing. Like. This is so cool.' His glance shifted to the window where right on cue appeared a windmill.

His name was José: call him Joe. He spoke in the limp West Coast accent that had not existed when I was young, before California spawned its native generations. Husky, headed for the American body shape that seeks to conform loosely to a car's front seat, Joe lived in a grim, low-rent suburb of Los Angeles, notable for the density of graffiti on the walls. I pass through it on the train from the airport every year or so when I visit my brother, who lives near San Diego. One of Joe's co-workers – they were all baggage handlers at LA International airport – had won a free four-day trip to Amsterdam for himself and three of his mates.

'A guy dropped out at the last minute, so he asked me. I've never been to Europe before. Like. Europe is so cool,' Joe said.

They were on the train because their flight home out of Amsterdam that night had been abruptly rescheduled out of Frankfurt.

'I wish you had time to see Italy and France, too, Joe, and Spain. You'd . . . like, like them a lot.'

'Oh, I'm coming back most definitely, Ma'am. I wanna see it all. Like. Europe is so, like, awesome. Old buildings are so cool.'

I could have hugged him for his enthusiasm; I offered him my window seat.

'No Ma'am, I'm fine, thank you,' he said, a Latin American lilt for the first time loud and clear. And then, after a moment: 'I wish I could bring my mom here. Like. She'd flip out for the churches and the flowers.'

The image came to mind of a poor Hispanic woman in the middle of her hard life, a devout, industrious peasant woman, widowed and worn down by perils on the gringos' streets. I wondered if my son's eyes were as moist and proud as Joe's when he talked about me.

'My mom's cool,' Joe said. 'She rides a Harley Davidson.'

The noise, yclept music, from the rear of our compartment stopped suddenly. Three German border guards, wearing what appeared to be mufti tailored for respect, were moving forward at a steady pace, checking passports. 'Together?' asked the one who stood before us. He held a passport in each hand and compared the photos with our faces. Was it hateful fancy? Or was that disgust in his close-set icy eyes at the very idea that male and female, young and old, dark and white, might be travelling together?

'No, no,' Joe and I said in unison.

Whereupon the guard handed me back my passport. But he looked once more at Joe's photo, at his face, and then of forty-odd passengers in the compartment it had to be Joe, Joe alone, only Joe, he ordered to open his luggage. After going through the rucksack diligently, he moved off without another word.

'Well, Joe,' I said, embarrassed and angry, 'I guess this isn't the Netherlands any more.'

'Oh, like. That's OK,' Joe replied.

He was zipping up his rucksack, his eyes when he looked up and smiled at me were the colour of wet obsidian. How many times had he crossed the border back into the States from Mexico? And probably every time been turned over by American border guards. When it comes to being a current object of suspicion and contempt, Joe is a lot more experienced and better prepared than I, for all my years and travels.

'July 1954: The driver, Fritz, is old, over forty at least. I told Midge that every time we board the bus and I see him I wonder again: "Where were you?" She looked puzzled and then she said, "Oh, I get it. You mean the war." Am I the only one in the group who keeps thinking: "Where were you?"'

And where were you, smarty-pants? Tucked up safe and sound in your wee American bed and not yet too old for fairy tales. A few years after the war ended, Mother told you that when she and Dad learned about the death camps, they procured poison to do us all in fast and painlessly if, as certainly seemed likely in my father's congenitally paranoid fancies, the Nazis invaded America. By that time it was widely understood the Nazi Utopia was not absolutely German; it was, however, clear of every last Jew. Unlike subsequent programmes of organised murder and genocide

109

now called 'ethnic cleansing', they intended to make not simply their own territories but also neutral and puppet states completely 'Jew-free' as fast as they could. I recollect to this day Mother's proud and solemn tone when she told me about the poison. It was early evening, we were in the kitchen; there was corn on the cob on the hob. My brother has no memory of hearing about hidden poison. But Mom has always been an entertainer of panache, devoted to the higher drama life really ought to be to merit a star of her gifts. There is a good chance she made up the poison story on the spur of the moment; it was not a lie precisely, but like one of the wonderful stories she used to make up to entertain us and our friends, it was an event and drama of significance for her audience – me – and for herself.

'Where were you?' Ignoble and intrusive question – it would keep popping up again, just as it did for you. Did you leave it there beside the Rhine for me to find while I walked the well-appointed streets of Cologne?

On the terrace of an Italian restaurant sat five old nuns in habits, drinking beer, looking very like a row of dunking birds on the back shelf of a car. 'Where were you?' I whispered.

'Where were you?' asked my inner voice after the old man next to me on a park bench by the side of the Rhine offered me a mint. He turned out to be Swiss.

'Where were you?' I thought when a shrivelled bohemian shocker of the 1920s, a woman wearing trousers, a mannish jacket and a tie, brushed against me in the crowd on the pedestrianised shopping street, Hohe Strasse, where the usual stateless fashions and brand names are in evidence.

'Where were you?' I asked myself of the clerk in his early sixties who sat in state behind the desk at my hotel, receiving guests as a billionaire would suitors for the hand in marriage of his only daughter.

'And where were both of you?' I asked almost aloud of two old heads, one bald the other white, coming towards me on the river walk. Long-time marching companions moving at precisely the same pace, the men drew near. Litmus could not have passed between their shoulders. The taller one said a few words to which the other replied with the brevity of code. Then I saw that they were holding hands. Wherever they had been during the empire of hatred, they were in hiding.

'16 July 1954: A woman guide in her late thirties, I guess, took us around Cologne. In the ruins of what was the ancient Roman town by the big square she said, "This used to be a cathedral of world renown before it was bombed." After that every sentence ended with "before it was bombed . . ." She collected the sugar cubes at lunch to take home to her family. She says she and her husband have university degrees but they can afford meat only once a month. She was becoming more and more upset. Everyone on the tour was muttering, "They asked for it. They started it." But of all the things I'll never know, how wars get started is top of the list.'

*   *   *

Believe it or not, baby sister, some day you will know everything. You will know, for example, that from boyhood all
games males play will be war games; war itself is football
with guns, a mortal game fuelled by testosterone. Between
the age of about thirty-five and forty-five most women know
everything, absolutely everything, and all they ever need to
know. Throughout the 1970s, along with knowing what's
wrong with all your friends and what they should do about
it, as they will know and be quick to tell what is wrong with
you and how to put it right, you will know masses of other
stuff. Childless women often continue to know it all until
the day they die. Fortunately, by the time you are fifty, you
will have forgotten most of what you would have staked your
life on during the decade of female omniscience. And now?
Now that women clamour to be just as big, butch and bad
as men, now that the warrior has been outmoded by his
weaponry, all you know now about war is that hunger
attaches to it and in every war zone sugar and meat will be
at a premium.

Hunger is not a concept that sticks around for mulling
over in Cologne. Except for New York, I cannot think of
another city where food is so much in evidence everywhere,
in the eating of it on the hoof, at table and at all hours,
and also in prevailing sweet and frying smells. Food, food
everywhere but not a crumb to eat! Not with delight, not for
those of us who dislike chunks of briny meat or sausages and
who prefer our green salads not always pickled in vinegar,

barely an hour away from qualifying as bona fide sauerkraut. Why has Germany cultivated a cuisine suited to Arctic winters or to siege? Possible explanations occurred to me later when my lone sightseeing descended from bright day into a vast, unexpected subterranean labyrinth of shops and restaurants dressed in artificial light. Hibernal intimations? Memories of bombardment? Or simply a drive towards efficient conservation of urban space in one case and of calories in the matter of cuisine? Could there be another city on earth as august and ancient as Cologne to include a Museum of Chocolate on its must-see list for tourists? Many of the visitors the day I was there were tourists from other regions of Germany. Aside from the museum's nautical architecture, which makes it appear to be just passing through and lightly moored to its bank of the Rhine, and in spite of a gift shop designed for international chocoholics, it is a wash-out for visitors like me hoping to view perhaps a cup still marked with dregs of Charlemagne's morning beverage, or at least a petrified sweet from the vanity case of a Roman camp follower.

In a land where I have little of the language and where the man behind the window marked '*Renseignements*', 'Information', '*Informazioni*' at one train station, when I asked if I might speak English replied with a curt 'No', I was pretty much deprived of my addictive fix of strangers to talk to, overhear and annoy. *The Autobiography of Mark Twain* turned out to be just the ticket under these circumstances.

113

'For good or for evil,' wrote the prescient Yank in 1906, 'we continue to educate Europe . . . Steadily, continuously, persistently, we are Americanizing Europe, and all in good time we shall get the job perfected.'

Twain was a wry, observant companion, and whenever a fleeting envious whinge of ego threatened his native charm, he could be literally shut up as it is famously impossible to do with male writers in the flesh, or travelling companions of either sex.

I put my book aside and looked out over my coffee cup at the magnificent dark filigree of the Dom, its cornerstone laid in 1248. The bells were wildly, crazily ringing the afternoon hour.

'What a carry on!' I whispered to you, my younger version, bound to laugh at my worst punning jokes lest I disown you; they stem after all from a bad habit you instigated. The café terrace was across from the Romano-German Museum where I had just taken in as much as I could of the immense collection of mosaics, domestic utensils and jewellery. Exquisite glass vessels excavated from nearby Roman tombs were especially miraculous things, to have been created in a medium more fragile than flesh or bone and then to endure for centuries, impervious to corruption and worms. The plaza was crowded in late afternoon. Boys on rollerblades and skateboards raced each other across the big central space with a gladiatorial intensity, as if their lives depended on winning. Off to one side, behind a bowl that lay out to collect coins, a jester on stilts juggled flaming torches. Couples of all ages passed by, holding hands much more often than is seen in most modern European cities. A woman pushed her twin babies in a pram constructed so they faced each other and could see nobody but each other. A big boy, upright and head high, rode a wheelie on his bike across my line of vision, his right arm was raised as if it held a standard or a whip. Was it a perceptible self-containment and prosperity about so many in the crowd? Perhaps it was due to the treasures I'd just seen, or maybe there was ancient dust drifting back on the riverine air, all of it – something – made me feel as close as any modern man can come to touching down in ancient Rome. With a small shock I realised that it was on more or less that very spot I had stood with my Study Abroad group nearly fifty years ago and first looked upon the Dom, or what remained of it. Of course, the cafés were not there then, nor the frivolous yellow tram to take tourists sightseeing along the Rhine, nor the museum, nor much of anything but stumps and rubble in those days, before the ravaged city was completely rebuilt.

'July 1954: At one point the guide looked right at me and said, "Why did you have to bomb Cologne?" It gave me a chill and a sort of sick feeling. When she left us she was crying. I had to look away because tears are like yawns; whenever I see someone crying, I start to cry, too.'

*   *   *

The memory of her face resounded as a cry. Jaw-heavy, pale and boxy, with narrowed eyes that for a moment hooked mine painfully. And suddenly there was the skitter of hatred again exactly as it had been all those years before, hollow hatred, hatred without heat or effect except a sickly lurch in my stomach. Why had the Allies bombed Cologne and Dresden, and other places of no particular strategic importance? Why destroy cathedrals and monuments and historic sites of unique importance and renown? Why massacre civilian women and children? Partly because orders came down from ageing men who were sick to death of making war with Germany and wanted it done, this time once and for ever. Sometimes, given the relative imprecision of pinpointing targets in those days, it was accidental. And, damn it, because their airmen had killed our civilians, too, and pulverised landmarks as ancient as their own. They started it, for crying out loud. They asked for it. They deserved it. Hell, we're only as inhuman as the next guy. We barely know our own capacity for inhumanity; in living memory our hatred has never been as exercised or exalted and organised as that of the Germans by Hitler and the Third Reich.

A dark-green saloon car pulled into the plaza that was otherwise free of motor traffic. It parked in front of the cathedral; the driver and two others sat inside, making no effort to get out. Between the car and where I sat, a group of people had been for some time putting up trestle tables and posters on easels. Now they started distributing leaflets,

116

and two shaggy, bearded men holding clipboards solicited signatures from passers-by, very few of whom seemed interested. I finished my coffee and made my way over to them. A scrubbed blonde, wearing a floor-length skirt and dangling earrings, stood under a hand-lettered banner on which the word '*Rassismus*' was written in big red letters. She was buttonholing people and doling out leaflets. When I asked her if she could tell me in English what was going on, she called out to another woman, much older, who had been hidden from my view. The younger woman hurried away, glad to have us old girls busy and out of her hair while she herself got on with the evangelical work.

The figure before me was as stocky as a barrel and precisely my own height, so I looked into her eyes as into a mirror, except hers were blue. She was bundled into cardigans and skirts, not quite brown, not altogether green, not exactly navy, and too warm for the day. The jaunty tilt of her knitted cap on the back of her head suggested that once upon a time before her hair lost lustre and pigment, she had been as vain as all young women are entitled to be. Youth is beautiful. Eight or nine years my senior, she was old in ways I will never be. Disappointment can do it, stall a woman's spiritual growth so she develops no style for ageing and instead hangs on for dear life to one or two unrealised youthful characteristics. Flirtatiousness unsatisfied, thwarted lubricity, unproductive physical vanity, or, as in this case, hopelessly crusading hope can, like even just too much rouge and

117

lipstick, perversely make an old woman appear older than she is. I had time to think about this while she was unable to speak, too busy finishing off a triangle of cheesecake held daintily between thumb and all but the pinkie of her right hand. At last she swallowed hastily, wiped her fingers on her skirt, adding to its dull sheen, and smiled in a genuine, open way that I immediately realised I had been missing for the past few days. I liked her.

'Look,' she said, nodding with her chin towards the green car I had noticed in front of the cathedral; its passengers were still inside, still as still as stone. 'Policemen, you know. They watch us wherever we go. Oh yes, they watch us. Once, you know, they twisted my arm behind my back and pushed me into the car. Look.' From a sheaf of pictures in a folder under her arm she pulled a photo, not of herself but of one of the shaggy men collecting signatures nearby. He was face down on the ground in the photo, a police officer's knee in the small of his back. 'Because we want an end to racism in Germany and in the world. Of course we do. Will you sign?'

After some shuffling in the dirty blue folder, she brought out a petition. I cannot read German; however, I knew I could take her word for its anti-racist content. 'But I live in London.'

'So much the better,' she said.

Had I licked the pen she handed me, it would have tasted like cheesecake.

'Let me tell you, you know. I was a Pathfinder when Hitler

came to power. You know what that is? Like a Girl Guide, you call it. We went out one morning as Pathfinders and when we came home, we were no longer Pathfinders. We were Hitler Youth. Our leader, she is wearing this little insignia on her lapel and we are Hitler Youth. What did we know? You think we knew? But my grandmother was Jewish. I loved my grandmother very much. But I could not be a Pathfinder or Hitler Youth any more. I was so, what do you say? All alone. Lonesome. Lonely, you say? I don't blame the others. They were eleven years old then, and for the next twelve years they were raised like that. My childhood was murdered. Their childhood was murdered. I was alone. I was so unhappy. Now, it must not ever happen again. We go everywhere in Germany to the big squares like this to tell everyone it must not happen again. Sometimes there is some trouble. But there are other times . . .'

Her smile was youthful and radiant. 'Yesterday, you know, an Indian woman wearing, you call it a sari? She stopped and took my hand and said, "Madame, I want to thank you for what you are doing." That was so good. To know someone thanks us.'

I felt a little dizzy. Suddenly something eating me was loose. I heard myself saying the words that swim and circle in my head every time I cross the German border: 'I am a Jew.'

She gasped as if I had hit her. She grabbed my hand, her own was sticky from cheesecake, and mine looked bony and brown against her paler skin.

119

'If only . . .' I began, with not the slightest idea of what should come next.

'If only . . .' she said.

All these years later in the same city and standing on almost the identical spot where I had stood in 1954 with the weeping tour guide, once again pale-blue eyes inches from my own filled, then flooded, with tears. This time I did not turn away.

Cologne was handsome in the late afternoon sunlight. The constant rumble of trains over the great swoop of a bridge made a nice background for the Strauss waltzes a street performer of high ambition was playing on a baby grand piano he had somehow wheeled on to the pavement along the Rhine. At the riverside café where I stopped for a glass of wine, I was lucky to find a table. I said to the young Spanish waiter that the place seemed understaffed for such a vast crowd, there must have been three hundred people wanting drinks.

'No, Madame,' he said. 'We are five waiters.'

Time passed pleasantly after I invited a young couple waiting for a drink to share my little table. They were medical students from Düsseldorf, the girl was planning to be a plastic surgeon. 'My mother is very pleased,' she said to me, 'because now she will never have to grow old.'

The boy was going to be a dermatologist.

'Ah yes,' said I, waxing gnomic as old-timers will do over their wine, 'the envelope on which is scribbled a person's derivation and destination!'

He shrugged and winked at his girlfriend. 'Dermatologists never starve,' he said.

And I smiled too, even though avarice in the young is grotesque, like baby beauty queens and little boys smoking cigarettes.

'July 1954: Following the orders of a madman must be hard and soul-destroying. Building your own ethics and ideology around the ideology and ethics of a homicidal maniac and then having the rug suddenly pulled out from under everything you were hypnotised to believe must leave you feeling too tired to start a new pattern of living. Losing a war the way they did and knowing you are despised everywhere in the world must be demoralising, and a hard lesson to pass on to children. The children will be better for what happened. Maybe we will be better? I know we must not do unto others as they have done unto us, even if it is tempting. Oh dear! Am I actually trying to understand the Germans? Even feel sorry for them? I better not tell Dad!'

Your father was an emotional man who lived at one small remove from terror of the goyim, the Christians, the native-born, those others whose ways you threatened to embrace. As it happens you were perfectly correct to think the surviving followers of a dark power are its victims, too. From the ashes of evil's lost causes there emerge no winners, no losers, only survivors and, down to the last man, woman and child, survivors are victims too, marked for life with visible symptoms that usually include thin skin and a malignant chip on the shoulder. The unhappy condition is passed down through more than one generation until it is attenuated by passing years and subsides, probably to flare up again before the end, perhaps in another form. I am more pessimistic than you. I have lost your faith, little girl, in cures for the worst of what ails human beings.

The breakfast room at my hotel was immaculate and before seven in the morning it was empty of any semblance of life except for an infestation of six-inch-high plastic ladybirds grinning from the windowsills and three Donald Ducks ornamenting the buffet table. All in all, the little anthropomorphisms were preferable to the gigantic stuffed wild boar's head over the bar in the restaurant where I'd had dinner the night before. While I struggled in its shadow to get myself around a platter of creamed pickled herring and home-fried potatoes, a couple seated on a raised deck at the rear of the restaurant was necking so passionately they threatened to fuse. The only other customers were four German tourists. The two men were wearing jokey braces; they sat in a booth across from their wives, all ruddy, big and blonde. I did not need the language to translate their disapproval of the lovers trying to disappear down each other's throats. And then I saw reflected in the mirror behind the bar how they were struck as dumb as unstrung puppets, how their eyes bulged, how their jaws dropped, when the two slender figures finally disentwined and left the restaurant, passing their table slowly with calculated impudence and showing themselves to be a pair of beautiful young men.

The waitress at breakfast was an Iranian in her late thirties; in this and my subsequent journey to Germany I was not once in a café or restaurant waited on by a German national. She told me she was lucky, the elderly man who ran the hotel wasn't so bad. 'He doesn't make too many rules,' she said.

In Iran – she called it Persia – she had been studying to be a teacher but now she was raising her two children on the salary of a waitress. 'I am worried that all my sons think about is money, money, money. That's how all the young people are these days in Germany. Money, money, money. At least racism is not bad here in Cologne. Not like Hamburg and Berlin. Only money, money, money!'

On my last night in Cologne I took myself to a concert by Pinchas Zukerman playing Mozart with the Cologne Symphony Orchestra. Although I was high up and behind Zukerman, who was also conducting, brilliant engineering has achieved a sound quality so fine it requires immense control of stray coughs and pins in the audience. The young man in the ticket office told me I was lucky to get one of the last seats in the house. I felt lucky. As universal and transcendent music rose from beautiful instruments, I felt perilously close to perfectly happy.

And, budding young liberal of 1954, you would have been proud. As I was entering the concert hall, a man in his

123

well-preserved seventies stopped me and asked politely if I had a spare ticket for sale. His English was BBC circa 1940 with Teutonic shading around the consonants. He was very straight and well dressed; he had a patch on his right eye, under his cheekbone was a thin white scar. I barely gave myself time to wonder 'Where were you?'. Just told him, sorry, I had only one ticket, my own, and it was not for sale.

You see? I had a chance to scalp one of them. A reconstructed angel, I let it pass.

Eight

On the rails again, south to Koblenz. The compartment contained a dozen women around my own age, travelling off-peak in the parallel world of pensioners on the move. They sat alone or two by two and did not have much to say to each other: an occasional question, a short reply in German that sounded crisper than the local dialect. Those who were not looking out of the window bleakly, having seen it all before, turned the pages of glossy travel brochures. They were similarly dressed in matched hats and coats: women who had conferred in the preceding days on what to wear – women growing old together; widows on a day trip was my guess, bound for the castles and ruins of the Rhine. Their dry sorority brought to my mind my last and only visit to Berlin. It was May 1971 – I am sure of the date because I was five months pregnant and nothing sets a woman's chronology as straight as pregnancy. I had a few days to spend in Berlin on my way to Poland and the site of Auschwitz. I was following the trail of a leftover war criminal whose trial I had just attended in Hamburg on behalf of an English magazine. The defendant was scruffy, beaky, a decrepit vulture with dewlaps and small red eyes. His reply to every question he was asked was '*Ich weiss nicht!*'. And I thought, 'You and me both, brother.'

Sprays of withered flowers reminiscent of those on the hats of lonely old women were pinned over pictures of re-membered faces in the gallery of victims that lined the entrance hall of Auschwitz. Entrance? No. No entrance there. No welcome: a machine designed for departure only – stained and stinking from the effluence of panic and despair. Irrevocable evil, I sensed it or smelled it again on a small island in Senegal where, I was not surprised to learn later, captives had been penned to await the slave ships that carried them away for ever, dispossessing them of a home and history. I left the site of Auschwitz, numb beyond feeling except for the flicker of indomitable new life in my belly. It was only late that night in a comfortable Warsaw hotel room that I woke sweating, and weeping, and all but bleeding tears. At that time, before the wall came down, Berlin was a city of widows as old as those riding with me on the train to Koblenz, but less evidently affluent. They were everywhere, the wives of dead men, in parks, at the zoo, in every street, the widows of the widow-makers, sometimes two by two, usually alone, wearing plastic raincoats, moving at a stiff quick pace through air still quivering from bombardment and defeat.

The woman across the aisle from me wore pale beige, a rich woman's colour that requires dry-cleaning after every outing. Was her ramrod posture, her slivered mouth, to show her pique at travelling second class? Knee to knee with her sat a companion in washable blue who had never been her equal in birth or beauty. Approaching the end of a life with less to lose, Blue stooped a little and looked able to smile. Beige removed her velour flowerpot hat, Blue removed her cheap knitted version. Beige took off her camel-hair coat, then Blue her shabbier one. Beige was first at everything until spectacles came out of bags; in this concession to frailty Blue led by a minute or two. Before they noticed my curiosity, I turned quickly to the window just in time to see a passing hill, the first since my arrival at the Hook of Holland – a hill, a genuine hill at last! – it made the thirsty eye rejoice. A little further down the line in Königswinter hills began to lollop around us in earnest, and verges bristling with wild roses sprang up beside the rails; their shaggy tumult was heartening and friendly. Also, our German train was running twenty minutes late and that was endearing, too, in the land of mechanical perfection. Taking advantage of an unscheduled halt outside Bad Hönningen, Beige reached into her beige bag, removed from it a single beige glove of soft leather and tugged it carefully over her right hand. Lowering neither her gaze nor her chin, she stood and using but thumb and forefinger of her gloved hand, she opened the door leading to the next compartment and the WC. Had her companion in blue held my gaze a second longer, had we not turned tact-fully to our opposing windows, shared laughter would have made us friends.

'July 1954: Koblenz. We were not supposed to spend the night here, but I'm glad we did. Something went wrong with the bus and we were too late to catch our boat on the Rhine to Rüdesheim. Tony had to make lots of telephone calls. I don't think his German is very good.

"Who would want to be a leader?" Ev said. "Not me!"

"Who would want to be a follower?" I said.

The truth is that I don't want to be either. I want to be an explorer. There is something about Koblenz I like. But we won't be staying long enough for me to find out what it is. Tony got us all into a kind of hotel. It's more like a dormitory with double- and triple-decker beds. I am sharing with Ev and Midge, and a couple of other girls. The city is full of American soldiers and that led to a funny thing. No time and not important enough to write about here.'

Perhaps not important enough to write about in a journal that might be seen by Mom and Dad, important enough to remember, however, all these decades later and a lot better than you will remember, say, Tony's surname, the colour of Midge's eyes, or the names or faces of anyone else in your group of thirty-odd. You had already gone to bed, as ever on the top bunk, of three this time. Lights were still on and the other girls were talking, about Tony, I guess. Our leader and guide was the object of universal romantic conjecture, especially among those girls who had steady boyfriends at home. 'Going steady', as infant monogamy was known in the 1950s, did not make a girl sophisticated. On the contrary, she was probably an even more overheated devotee of true and eternal love than we unsteady singletons, while generally remaining technically a virgin just like us. When I try to recollect precisely our girl talk that night, all that comes back to me is the high perfume of cold cream we applied to remove make-up as our mothers had before us. In the 1950s, glamour still attached to older generations.

Suddenly, the door flew open and there stood a fair young American in uniform, hatless, breathless, clearly in trouble. 'Hide me, please!'

Ev and Midge, who were already in bed like me, pulled their blankets up to their chins and gaped, the other girls froze, one brushing her hair and the other brushing her teeth at the tiny basin, both just a heartbeat away from screaming. The room was small and except for the bunk beds, contained not so much as a chest of drawers let alone a cupboard big enough to hide a man. From somewhere down the long corridor came shouts and thundering boots. Without a thought in my head or a moment's hesitation I squeezed to the edge of my narrow bunk and held the blankets up to make a cave for the runaway boy. 'Come on! Quick!'

What possessed you, child? Were you ahead of your time

or behind it? Your generation produced no fashionable style of rebellion, beatniks were older and hippies yet to come. Obviously, the man was in flight from the Military Police. Every good girl in that room was prepared to turn him away or turn him in. Yet, before the coin had landed, you staked your life on the toss: on tails. The boy lay trembling in your bed; you could smell pomade on his hair, his uniform was rough against your silky gown and your skin: *that* you remember, strumpet! The MPs glanced in at the open door, barely paused to say 'Sorry, girls' and thudded on. Compromised by your recklessness, the other girls stayed in place for a few moments to be sure the cops had well and truly gone. And the boy remembered he had hands. You remember them too even now, little animals nuzzling in the blanket cave. There was stirring and grumbling as the reluctant accomplices came back to their senses. The boy took his leave with a bare thank you and a thoughtful backward glance my way. Midge looked at me in a funny way, too; Ev said nothing, but she shook her head several times: 'no'. Eventually, lights were turned out. A few hesitant conjectures in the dark were soon followed by the forgetfulness and silence of sleeping children. Only I for the first time in my life lay awake as an adult, worrying, repeating, rehearsing and trying to make sense. I wasn't sure I would recognise the young soldier if we passed in the street; yet whatever had happened or almost happened between us was indisputably related to love though a million miles from my chaste daydreams about

Tony. What electric force came from inside and outside at the same time? What heat left a body shivering?

Barnard College is near the banks of the Hudson, a location my classmates and I used to celebrate in free verse à la our hero, e. e. cummings. That overworked river cried tears for us literary Barnard sophomores of the dot ... dot ... dot persuasion ... cried buckets ... cried mercy ... cried '*Gardez l'eau*', all the while spooling its naiad threads around our mudstuck lives. And so on and endlessly, earnestly on ... 'bright young hudson ...' I recently found scribbled in my own hand inside the flyleaf of an old copy of *The Enormous Room*, '... running away from home again ... nobody pats your head and says ... "there, there, you're a good little river ... a god's little river ..."'

The Moselle and the Rhine make a corner for Koblenz, reason enough to enchant any river lover. Towards the end of a long walk through the pleasant, confluent city I found myself magnetised and drawn to the very bar my inner self always craves: longer than wide, darker than bright, tobacco brown, no terrace, no food, no music or semblance of it. A contingent of lithe androgynes from a ballet company performing at a nearby theatre graced a table in the rear, otherwise the place was empty. I climbed up on a high stool and found myself face to face with a muscular woman of around my own age. She wore remnants of unearthly beauty; her eyes were turquoises, her hair an ash-blonde tumble that looked eccentric and witchy, as flowing hair always does on women of our age. The keen interest of her appraisal as good as said she owned the place.

'The Valkyrie's eyrie,' I whispered to you, my invisible young sidekick and soulmate.

'Gudrun,' said the barkeeper.

'Irma.'

'Speak German?'

A logical expectation when Irmgard and Gundrun meet on the banks of the Rhine.

'Very little. Speak French?'

Everyone to whom I had previously put this question in Holland and Germany preferred to speak English if they could. But Gudrun told me in French more idiomatic than my own that when she was eighteen she had lived for a long time in Montpellier. What had taken a German girl to such a place in the 1950s or early 1960s, I wondered? It had to have been a man. Probably not a Frenchman; the woman towering before me must always have been too big and her beauty too untamed and flamboyant for French taste.

'There was an old man who lived near me in Montpellier. He used to flirt with me every day,' said Gudrun. 'He changed money. A money-changer, you know? One time I took him Deutschmarks to change for me. And he spat at them. Spat at them! Spat at me! He said if he had known I was German he would never have spoken to me.'

Was Gudrun asking me to believe, as she herself remembered, that a man who had known her well enough to flirt with her frequently had not divined her origins or enquired after them? Even my ear, tuned to English, discerned the trace of a German accent in her French. It is futile to expect anyone else's distant recollection to be more foolproof than one's own. Memory is the child of necessity. Nevertheless, let any long-held recollection be full of holes, there is always gristle at the centre of the invention. Gudrun's feelings had genuinely been hurt all those decades earlier, badly hurt, if not precisely how her memory came to explain it. Suddenly, she was peering at me, studying my olive skin, the length of my nose, and something in my manner: eagerness to please? Obsequious caution? And seeing the way she was seeing me, I understood and accepted the real point of the story. The money-changer in Montpellier was a Jew. Her memory was helping her stake a small claim to innocence by casting herself as a victim, too.

Gudrun told me she wanted to go to England some day to hunt for fossils around Lyme Regis. 'Fossils and certain rocks have healing properties,' she said, 'like crystals.' When she was not keeping her bar, she told me, she hunted wild herbs and collected magic crystals to dish out to friends and others who consulted her.

'These doctors! They know so little. What do they know? They are plumbers, they are chemists, they are butchers; they have no gift. One does not cure the body if the soul is sick. One cannot change karma with a knife,' she said, and I nodded even though I wasn't so sure. 'You know' – she spoke while topping up my glass of white wine on the house – 'two Americans both wanted to marry me back when the place was full of them. But I said no, America is not for me. Too materialistic, you know.'

Again I nodded agreement, though honestly? It would be hard to come up with an activity more materialistic than trolling in the mud for weeds and stones. Old stunners when they are starting to lose it often turn to half-baked mysticism; it is a simulacrum of the learning they were too busy to acquire in youth and too pretty to need. Versions of Gudrun's mumbo-jumbo are found everywhere; they transcend borders and work as a sort of Esperanto of the universal anima. There is no harm in it. All told, spiritual gobbledegook is a lot less debilitating to faded beauty than booze or drugs, and probably not so hard on the personality as serial facelifts.

'Corn-mother or not,' I scribbled in my notebook as I was polishing off my wine and my hostess was momentarily busy with the toe dancers, 'Gudrun is one great gal. If I were staying in town, this place would be my hang-out.'

As I settled my small bill, I mentioned that some alternative treatments were already being allowed on British National Health schemes.

'Who cares about governments?' cried Gudrun. 'Governments have no soul. Governments are not important. Who gives a damn for what the government tells us to do!'

'Oh Gudrun,' I thought as I walked out into the new

evening, 'what were your father and mother not doing? Were
they not giving a damn?'

'17 July 1954: The day was dark and grey. Solemn castles
stood on every mountain. We sailed past Lorelei Rock and
the sites of many Rhine legends. What did the siren sing?
Something big and Wagnerian, I guess. The title "Baron"
suits the mood of this river. The words: "baronial" and
"medieval" keep going through my head. I keep imagining
baronesses dying in childbirth in those high, dark places.
The vineyards are planted in vertical and horizontal lines on
the hills, it gives the effect of a rug drawn up around the
knees of towns and battlements. Truly lovely! But spooky!
Every building even in the quaint towns we pass looks solitary
and independent of the others. I want to see this all again. I
must come back and see it on a sunny day. Even in sunlight,
the Rhine would be a little creepy.'

Fifty years later not much had changed on that great river
with hardly any bridges. The sun shone this time, its radiance
was swallowed by the dark water and left no sparkle on the
surface. I had forgotten how the Rhine travels back into
legends so the next castle, the next ruin and the next painted
village is always more isolated, more distantly familiar than
the last. The river became ever more picturesque, only two
hours out of Koblenz, still far from Rüdesheim where I
intended to disembark, and I had already snapped so many

pictures of its dark unfolding fairy tale that I ran out of film. None of us with Study Abroad had a camera. Cameras in the 1950s were cumbersome and fiddly, not part of every tourist's equipage. Even nowadays my trim little camera can turn into a bossy plodder. It looks at, not around; it freezes images into souvenirs and discourages imagination from its creative duty: to turn brute recollections into mutable truths – to make living memories. I put away my camera and let go the urge to share every stone and hillock with the folks at home. Seated right at the prow of the little cruise ship while all my mainly German fellow passengers were in at lunch, I relaxed and felt myself visited by the old desire, increasingly rare, to go on and on, whim-driven, to travel without strings or anchors, provisioned only with curiosity and hope.

Dutch barges sailed by, in every helmsman's window were statuettes and plants and all the cosy adornments of lowland ledges. As we glided past a long cruise ship, the *Ste Odile* out of Strasbourg, a middle-aged French couple at lunch under an outsized porthole happened to look up from their laden plates with expressions of dismay; they caught my eye and we exchanged shrugs. Feathery willows swept the water's edge, silver birches streaked through foliage to the crests of hills where stood the watchful conifers.

Vineyards were woven here and there around crags and ruins, but there were no flowers blooming in Niebelung country that season. The defined interlocking of trunks and branches and gripping roots, the increasing complexity of patterns and the upper trill of birdsong make the Rhine linger in the mind as a leitmotif, heard rather than seen. A village hove into view on the right bank, at its watery edge was a huge tasselled tent of orange and blue; just as we were sailing by there arose from it a heartbreaking bellow of homesickness and misery, and two befuddled camels loped through the beaded swag, then stood still, looking in confusion at the river. Monkeys, tigers, even elephants would have appeared less outlandish beside the busy Rhine than those poor cruisers of the arid, empty quarters. Camels! What the blazes were camels doing there? Alligators would have been more at home in that green habitat for birds and short-legged river animals. The unfortunate creatures turned their long beseeching heads to watch us pass. I looked around for someone else to back up the mirage I was seeing; fellow passengers emerging from lunch were occupied with digestion and not aware of the Saharan visitation already disappearing in our wake. The witness I wanted so keenly that I almost saw her and almost heard her surprised laugh was you, my own self at eighteen on your first journey to the land of the Brothers Grimm. Camels on the Rhine? Oh yes, of course, darling. Once upon a time.

'I feel like totally, I feel like I learned a lot about myself,' said a voice behind me in the nasal whine of modern young American womanhood, so self-conscious and cute and anorexic, so distinct from man's speech that it is virtually a phonetic purdah. 'And I'm glad I didn't figure it out, like, six months from now when I'd be totally hurt, you know? Totally weird.'

'Here she comes,' warned another similar voice.

The Midwestern twang of an earlier generation approached, scolding the girls for not even looking at the pretty castles and the 'runes'.

'Honestly, Mom, like, we saw all that stuff already from the train. We are, like, totally tired of runes.'

The older voice overrode the others and complained that all her two girls wanted to do was find Internet cafés so they could talk to boyfriends back home.

'Whatever!' drawled the girls in unison.

You wondered a while ago what songs the Lorelei siren sang to reel in passing sailors? No soul-soaring arias, no subtle, seductive lieder: she warbled pop ephemera of the day, bet on it, backed by a thumping honky-tonk beat.

'July 1954. Some day I want to come back. Alone! Alone! Ev sat next to me on the bus today on the way to Bonn. She took the window seat, of course. Whenever someone sits with me on the bus, they get the seat next to the window. Why do I always let them take it? I want to complain, even to fight. It's just not fair. But I just can't. I cannot. Some day I'll do this whole trip again and I'll do it alone.'

From your mouth to my ear, baby. Returning to Koblenz alone – alone! – by train from Rüdesheim I watched the

138

Rhine from backstage passing in reverse, laundry hanging on lines behind oh-so-adorable villages, TV aerials tacked to the outbuildings of castles, vineyards giving way to motor traffic. Back in town, the restaurant I chose for an early dinner was upstairs on a busy corner. The waiter showed me to a table overlooking the street and I settled in to observe the locals streaming home from work. Pedestrians of Koblenz are orderly and obedient; they do not make foolhardy London-style dashes into traffic or inch forward like New Yorkers to catch stoplights on the turn. The restaurant was empty except for a party of couples at the far side of the vast room and one other solitary, a man about five years my senior who was already installed at a table diagonally across from mine and facing me with only a narrow aisle between us.

Apparently, he was a regular; his menu lay unopened and the waiter, an imperturbable Serb, brought him a glass of wine without any exchange of words. The diner wore glittering spectacles; he was conventionally and rather primly turned out, greyish from head to toe, unremarkable in any way except that it soon became apparent the man was dying. Hacking, coughing, rumbling, spitting into a big sodden handkerchief, his tattered lungs finally lapsed into a rattle before rising again to another hideous crescendo. When he began horribly to snort I pushed away my salad plate with its limp slivers of phlegm-coloured peppers. Was this terrible dry gasping his terminal agony at last? No. No, he had breath enough to wind a huge forkful of pasta and lift it to his

139

mouth. As long as he was chewing, he stopped dying, but when the hawking returned it was accompanied by ghastly whistling from a thorax evidently so deeply decayed and so far gone it must put paid to him. He was finished, on his way out; he was going fast. Very fast. Not fast enough. I pushed fried fish around my plate and fought a sudden tide of rage. Thoughtless pig, how dared he subject me to his gruesome demise? Was he not a suitable case for takeaway? Waiter, take that dumb animal away and put him out of my misery. And yes, OK, all right; to be candid? Yes, OK, in spite of trying not to, I had to wonder if an equally crude display could transpire publicly anywhere else in the civilised world. America might conceivably spawn a son or daughter as selfish. But other Americans, real Americans, normal Americans, would never sit still for such a noisy display of mortality, not while they were eating, for crissake. So why could I not signal the waiter, why could I not ask for another table, why could I not demand to be moved away from the strangulated diner in his death throes? What was my problem? It's just not fair. But you can't, you just cannot, my girl. You will never, never, not once in your life know how it feels to believe yourself entitled to the window seat. I hid my dinner under lettuce leaves, then peered at my watch and grimaced as if I had just recollected a pressing engagement. I called for the reckoning and paid quickly, included a tip and left the restaurant and in due course Koblenz, hungry.

*   *   *

'July 1954: Bonn and Beethoven's ear-trumpet!'

Thus was my entry in its entirety for our breeze through the new temporary capital of the nation. And this time too I stormed into the now ex-capital as if to colonise it. In fact, I was in a hurry. The season and I had both turned a corner in Koblenz; summer was setting in. No longer the inexhaustible fledgling of the Fifties and Sixties, nor the overworked woman of the Seventies and Eighties, I was nevertheless not yet defunct and besides, jobbing journalism is a profession from which a practitioner does not retire. Deadlines were goading me in London, an aged parent in New Jersey and a son who no longer needs me but whom I needed to see before he took off on the next of his life's journeys. It was time to think about heading home for a while to take care of business before setting out again on the second lap of my original journey.

There were only two other visitors to Beethoven's house, an American mother and son both so immense I feared for the floorboards. The creak of the wood was ancient, born in the tree and loud enough to penetrate the composer's early deafness; I made a note to listen for creaks in his string quartets. Nearby, mixing with the crowd in the market square and coldly watching the girls, were fit, lean young soldiers in showy camouflage gear. In front of the café where I took my coffee a handsome old man went suddenly almost mad when a cyclist brushed against him. He shook his stick after the departing boy and shouted in a passion of fury so strong it seemed levelled against youth itself. Behind his back a fearsome mime in white face parodied him and beat the air maniacally with an outsize stage prop banana.

'He got me once,' a French businessman sitting nearby said to his companion. He nodded towards the street performer who was now capering and waving his banana obscenely at an unwary girl. 'Afterwards one jokes about it. But at the time . . .'

Later, on my way back to a hotel chosen mischievously in Beethoven's old stamping grounds for its location on the corner of Bachstrasse and Mozartstrasse, I saw the mime again. He must have been on his way home. His face was washed and smeared, he slumped in a suit two sizes too big for him and he looked exhausted, poor soul. Mimes only do what they must. There is no past tense for 'must'. 'Had to' is not the same. 'Had to' suggests constraint and cowardice, and not a bidding of the soul.

To call the area around my hotel in Bonn 'residential' hardly does justice to the kind of stolid, leafy tranquillity only money can buy. Heavy houses set back from the street seem more than just residences; they are embodiments of middle-class prosperity and of the intention to preserve and increase it. In fact, sitting over a beer at a small café near my hotel in Bonn, I felt my surroundings to be more like London's NW postcode area than anything I have come across on the Continent. And also, it was my impression that as in many similar sections of London, the kind of gentility expressed in the architecture was on its way out and the big houses being broken into smaller units to accommodate students, wage slaves and greedy landlords. A young woman coming home from work hesitated on the front steps of her house for a last puff on her cigarette before she stamped on it and kicked it away. She wore no wedding ring and it was my guess she shared with a flatmate, or flatmates, who did not allow smoking inside. I watched her hesitate, eyes closed and lips moving in what could have been prayer, before she took out a key and opened the postbox, set like a safe in the outer wall. Carefully, she examined a few envelopes she found there; her shoulders lifted, then dropped before she stuffed them in her bag. She looked up and down the empty street, shaking her head: the expected cheque or love letter had not arrived. At that moment, somewhere in town church bells rang the hour and I felt myself suddenly suffused with forgiveness, almost affection, as the bells counselled me to let go of all blood grudges in spite of what the German kinsmen had long ago perpetrated against my own, one of whom, incidentally, is pinned on the wall over their altars.

In the compartment on the train to Venlo and the Dutch border I was by myself again except for a mother and her little boy who sat behind me. With an empty carriage that gave me choice, I chose to sit facing forward with Germany behind me and home ahead. While waiting on the platform the toddler had scaled all that was scaleable, touched all that was touchable, tasted all that was tasteable, be it inedible or not. I had been impressed by his mother's delight in his hyperactive curiosity; her patience was so rare, so cherishing, it made me wonder if she had perhaps once nearly lost her baby. Looking out at the passing villages of granite and gingerbread, I let myself revel in being en route again, free of current effect on anyone or anything: passing through and all by myself – at the window seat, observing from a rare position of power and innocence. The revel soon was ended, however, by the collision of a small powerful body with my knee; I looked down and had to smile. He was not at all a cute toddler; his expression was too keen and already adult, even his eagerness to move and touch and gabble seemed to belong to someone older, someone making up for lost time, a former patient or prisoner bursting with life restored. His mother told me his name was Lukas. Before Lukas was born she had lived for twelve years in Texas where her now ex-husband worked for a German company, whence her fluent English. Indulgent and proud, she watched Lukas fish the camera out of my bag.

'Photo!' he commanded.

Thanking goodness for the new roll of film I bought before leaving Bonn, I loaded the camera and raised it.

'Technically,' his mother said, 'Lukas is blind.'

So that was it. The wide blue eyes before me, sparkling with burgeoning intelligence, were all but sightless.

'He's a splendid little boy,' I said. 'And he has a terrific mother.'

I lifted Lukas up on my knee; he stroked my face. *'Oma,'* he sang out.

'He is calling you granny,' his mother told me.

'I am honoured, Lukas,' I told him.

'Oma! Oma!'

When my own son was not much older than Lukas, I had to go to Israel for two weeks to work on a documentary film. We needed the money. It was our first separation. The Hebrew for mother is *'Ima'*. Hearing myself called from knee height everywhere caused an ache in my mid-section that was not to end until I was home and hugging my boy again.

'Oma,' said Lukas.

There is no embrace in a lifetime as purely wonderful as the hug of a child who has made himself your own. The first time my son smiled and raised his arms up to me, all clocks and calendars changed: life became waiting time before him, and fuller, richer time after his arrival. The maternal urge is old hat; an urgent craving for solace from it plagued me off and on for most of my adult life. But nobody ever warned me and who ever talks about the grandmaternal urge? The force of my sudden longing to hug again and hold to my heart a small body packed with life came as a surprise on that German train.

'Oma!'

We threw our arms round each other. The baby sighed in my ear and I gave thanks to have been born a woman.

*   *   *

'July 1954: I feel on the edge of understanding German. The sounds and cadence are so like English, so familiar. But when I concentrate all I hear is nonsense. Here are some examples: "Ish has been on the Sliding Bard! The Sliding Bard." "Ah, oh, hiss is full of dark." "Yah! I am not in accord with the analogue." "But there is also a fumfummerie." "You can't go sliding with a banner!" I tried to say thank you very much politely in German to the bus driver, Fritz, and it came out: "Dunk you, field mouse."'

The train filled up at the station where Lukas and his mother left me and the air was thick with sounds I almost understood. Suddenly, youth was on the move, every local under thirty seemed to be heading for the Dutch border. Mobile phones chirruped like crickets on dope. A sulky sylph with pink dreadlocks and long eyelashes slid into a double seat across the aisle. The place next to her was soon filled by a tall, well-built young priest who took one look at his neighbour and got stuck into his breviary fast; she pulled as close as she could to the window, while mutual disapproval, attraction and fear rose palpably around them. Opposite me a young man opened his Dutch paper, was it actually called *Donderdag Spits*? The photo on the front page was of a bad train wreck outside Utrecht. Selfish as any other human animal in the face of someone else's disaster, my first reaction was relief it had not happened while I was on that very train with José from California; a rail crash might have spoiled his enthusiasm for all things European. The girl in the Information booth at Bonn had warned me that as there were but five minutes to spare between trains in Venlo, I had better ask the conductor on the way to the border from which track the Rotterdam train would be leaving.

'How would I know?' he said, when I tugged at his sleeve. 'Holland is a foreign country.'

As it turned out, we were ten minutes late so I would have missed my connection in any case. I didn't mind. The sun was shining on Venlo café terraces and the coffee was delicious. According to a report I had seen in Bonn on an English-language news channel, local citizenry was in ferment over the regular rowdy influx of pot-smoking youngsters from over the German border, but I saw only the cheerful mêlée of a Dutch town during my hour there before going on to lunch in Rotterdam. 'Lunch in Rotterdam': there is a glamour about northern cities I was too young to appreciate in 1954. 'Lunch in Rotterdam': now it suggests infidelity and betrayal and blackmail. 'Lunch in Rotterdam': it ought to be the scene for adventures of a mature order. Disappointingly, the station in Rotterdam was in a state of schoolyard pandemonium. An electrical storm the previous night had produced the wrong kind of lightning; trains were all off schedule and there were many cancellations. I needed to find out whether it was feasible to spend a night in Delft before going on the next day to the Hook of Holland. And home. The long queue at the information window was made longer by an American woman in front of me who chose this day of tumult to ask the girl behind the window about hotel rates and the availability of vegetarian food.

'I'm only supposed to know about trains,' the harassed girl complained when the American moved on at last and I stood before her. 'You all think I know it all. You all think I have the answers to everything,' she said and, looking at me, she sighed. 'So, now what do you want to know?'

'Tell me,' I said, giving in to ineluctable compulsion, 'is there a God?'

Life is performance. Sometimes the audience is invisible, supernal. This time, thank heavens, she laughed.

They were digging up part of the busy road into the old town of Delft so we pedestrians had to pick our way carefully or I would not have been looking down and found the seashell I am holding now. No bigger than a pampered woman's fingernail, domed and black with white striations, it has preserved its drop of original music under centuries of urban traffic. In New Church on the stone set into the floor to commemorate Johannes Vermeer someone had left a bouquet of yellow roses freshly picked from a country garden. Their simplicity and homeliness made me smile and rub my eyes. Since I graduated from university, poems comprise the extra book, not the primary one I take on a journey. John Donne was a fortuitous choice, so suited is he to the pellucid lowland light and the witty arrangements of canals and bridges in an urban setting.

. . . Here I bequeath
Mine eyes to Argus, if mine eyes can see,
If they be blinde, then Love, I give them thee . . .

When I looked up for a moment from the great poet's 'Will' to watch a pregnant woman cycle past the bench where I was sitting, the book on my lap fell back to its flyleaf. 'A slightly early birthday gift for Irma at Barnard, 1954' was written there. 'I love you . . .' and then a signature beginning with 'T', otherwise completely illegible.

I closed my eyes and tried to remember my friends of 1954: your friends, I mean, young I. Riffling through your address book in my mind, I could not come up with a single loving 'T'. There was 'M' for Marjorie who suffered for art and owned her own Kandinsky. And Judy B who wrote us others into a cocked hat when it came to river poems. Judy R, E. B. White's god-daughter, who nearly electrocuted herself once before your eyes when she grabbed a metal doorknob with one wet hand while the other held a hairdryer. Piri H became an art historian and will flicker pleasantly through your London life forty years after your graduation ceremony on the steps of Butler Library. Liana S gave you a copy of Johnson's *Table Talk* on that day inscribed 'We have endured . . .'; she subsequently married a Park Avenue gynaecologist. The Roosevelt girl went mad; she crawled along a sixth-floor ledge of the dormitory miaowing like a cat. Mary-J, daughter of the president of one of America's first black colleges, will commit suicide the very summer you are swanning around Europe with Study Abroad. There was Ronnie W, unbelievably rich, never known to carry a penny in her purse, and Rhoda B, who despised the use of a typewriter and thought the sun shone out of Virginia Woolf's every orifice. There was Rhoda E, who purported to be scandalised when she learned who had been pinning scurrilous anonymous verse up every Thursday on the English Department's bulletin board (it was you, naughty girl!). Binda M was a Nepalese princess for whom recent history has given grave reason for concern.

Not a 'T' among them. Oh, yes, there was Toby, but Toby was no giver and besides, she didn't love you. You had men friends too – Don-Don, Willy D, Jack R, Michael C, Michael H, Donald M – all but one were gay and none would bluntly dare 'I love you'. The blank following 'T' in memory was despicable. Who on earth had loved you in 1954? Who had ever loved you enough to warrant an almost new Herbert Grierson edition of John Donne's *Collected Poems*? If only you had been beside me there in Delft – beside myself in Delft? – just long enough to collect the name and gather it into my memory where by rights it ought to be. Or if I could go back and whisper 'Who is "T"?' to you, when all you had to say about the lovely city on a postcard of tulips again that I found in one of mother's boxes was 'Vermeer was here. But there are no Vermeers here to be seen. Instead, we had to look at loads of china. V. boring!'

A suntanned Englishman homeward bound from holiday was the only other passenger who chose to stand out on the ship's diminutive open deck during our departure from the Netherlands. He and I turned to each other with a laugh when the gangway released us from the dock with a clang and a big kiss. Impedimenta of the shipping industry rose as strange trees out of the flatland; a vast sandbar gave way to the North Sea, and I gave myself over to the melting joy of coming home: to my house, to my friends, to my son, to my language. East Anglia was a sharp green and flat. Holland and Britain appear much more compatible at their edges in spite of water between than, say, the Côte d'Opale of northern France with the White Cliffs of Dover.

It was a Saturday and the train to London was filling up at every stop. British youth, I noted, wears more daytime black than the continentals and tends to a more Gothic style, otherwise, same headsets, same mobile phones and a similar affectation of sophisticated indifference to each other. A middle-aged couple took the recently vacated table across from mine. The woman poured the dregs of soft drinks left behind by four departing travellers into one plastic glass; she handed it to her husband to chuck in the small bin halfway down the car. Then, as I had known she would, she wiped the table with a tissue out of her bag.

To this day, shopping and packing remain women's work derived, no doubt, from gathering seeds and berries, and making the pots to store them in. Now, how's that as a paper for an earnest sociologist to research? Primitive distaff gathering and stowing as they relate to modern shopping and packing, with a long footnote on female eating disorders. The human psyche is not designed for affluence; we are staunch against famine, at our sharpest and most industrious when we're just a little hungry. When hard times call atavism back into play, men primarily set out to hunt the perishable. But we women collect staple commodities, horde them, and even when things are looking good we tend to pack stuff in as if lives depended on it. We do not travel light. Modern mothers of none and mothers of few often anyway shop and pack for the string of kiddies they are plumbed in to nourish and nurture; in the Western world they often eat for them, too.

As I watched my neighbour unpack containers, cutlery, grapes, plastic plates and store-bought sandwiches out of her bag, I resolved to take less on the next lap of my journey. No need to squeeze in an extra pair of shoes with heels or, for that matter, a skirt; never again would I pack any garment that could not at a pinch be washed out in a hotel basin. Next time I was not going to bother with a travelling clock, either, as all hotel rooms except fleapits have bedside clock radios these days. I wish instead they continued to provide guests with local telephone directories; I used to enjoy checking out the number of local Quakers, synagogues, concert halls, psychiatric clinics, Auerbachs and Kurtzes before I went out to stroll around a new city. Next time I would not bother to pack aspirin or any over-the-counter medication that is the same in every language. Next time I would not pack a solitary thing prefixed by 'just in case'. Next time I resolved that my packing was going to be like the statement of a hunting male: a statement of intent.

Thanks to plans better laid than my own, 'next time' was not to be as soon as I, or anyone, expected.

Nine

'1 August 1954: Today Evelyn was sneezing on the bus and Tony asked her if she was "sickening for something". It turns out to be English-English, like pining for something, only it refers to illness. "I wouldn't be sickening for anything, not for a million dollars!" I told him. Gosh, it's swell to make him laugh. He wrinkles his nose and pushes back the hair that flops over his forehead. A friend of Tony's called Jeremy is tagging along with us for the trip to Italy. I don't think he's supposed to but who cares? In one month and two days I will be nineteen and, barring storms at sea, I ought to be home in time for my birthday. If not, it will be the first birthday I have ever spent away from home. What does that matter? Celebrations and anniversaries are unimportant as long as there is love.'

Please, child, you're too young to be a pretentious twit; leave pretensions to me and the rest of the superannuated crowd. To mark birthdays, anniversaries and other days special to the people we love is not unimportant; on the contrary, private celebration is prominent among the really not very many ways we have to let love be known. But you knew that, didn't you, young I? The knack to a successful lie lies in lying first to yourself and then in believing your lie. Don't worry, it is a skill that improves with experience and one day you too will be able to lie convincingly, like a grown-up. In 1954, however, you couldn't pull off a believable lie; your demurral sounded imitative, it lacked conviction. When you were turning fourteen, your parents announced early in the summer that celebrations of your birthday were over. Scavenger hunts, fish fries and story hours continued, along with other delirious summertime festivals for children in the neighbourhood, organised by your mother and led with a flair that was the only remaining expression of her innate theatrical vocation, sacrificed to propriety and an early marriage. But celebration simply of you and your arrival on earth was finished. No more being lured out of the house to help your father weed or prune in the garden and act as if you didn't know that your cake was being baked and decorations put in place, the feigned surprise, the songs and paper hats just for immediate family, never any friends or guests. Of course, you would have agreed that babyish stuff had become redundant, had anyone asked you. No sophisticated celebration replaced the old shindig as I recall, nor did you – later I – receive so much as a birthday card from your family during the decades of disapproval. But woman's memory can be a self-pitying bitch. And blame is a shabby substitute for understanding. I hope you understood then – you do now – that the decision no longer to celebrate your birthday was nothing more than a political affectation: birthdays, like graves, were supposed to go unmarked in the households of those who fancied themselves progressive intellectuals and lefties.

When I was very young, Mother told me proudly that she and my father met for the first time in the early 1930s at a young Communists' summer seminar in Indiana. This story was not repeated later, however; the terrifying strictures of the McCarthy era did for it, as I sometimes suspect they also did for the indisputable love my mother and father once had for each other. Birthdays, shmirthdays! I never knew the dates of my parents' birthdays and only learned them when I was old enough to find out for myself; I don't recall celebrating my brother's birthday in April either, not after he passed the cut-off for individualistic bourgeois pretensions. He had to be barmitzvahed, of course. Neither of my parents was attached enough to enlightened atheist principles to risk battle with my paternal grandparents who would have been wounded to the quick and for ever had their first grandson not had his barmitzvah. Besides, when a faith collapses, it always leaves behind sentimental and superstitious residue. Non-practising Jews fast on Yom Kippur; old hippies march against globalisation and then go home to play the market on-line; and there are plenty of Christians who break nine commandments regularly and will kill for a tenth.

I like my birth month, September, I like its industry and its crispness; I like its position on the calendar, leading in months of more than one or two syllables. Nevertheless, my birthday has always been preceded by days of malaise as if I must be sickening for something. And of course, September is a month when the Western world has classically sickened for war. Crops are coming in, meat is being smoked and salted, hibernating animals are getting too sleepy for the chase, local females are as usual pregnant, lactating, past it, or mere babies. Hell, let's go out and make trouble for someone before someone makes trouble for us! All four versions of trouble – one's own, trouble in the family, trouble for others, and trouble for mankind – occurred in September of my travelling year. Birthday blues were well in place when Mother in the United States took a fall that put her in hospital with a fractured pelvis. Thus, instead of heading for Heidelberg to pick up the spoor of my old trail, I found myself installed in Mother's house near Princeton in the community she calls 'geriatric gulch' making daily visits to the nearby nursing home where she was recuperating.

It was a three-mile walk to the nursing home. By the seventh day I had done more than forty miles back and forth, all on foot except once when the spinster sisters next door gave me a lift on their way to church. Mother's neighbours leave their gated community to shop, to pray, to fly to Miami for the winter, to keep doctors' appointments, go into hospital and be buried. They have a golf course in the precinct, but no cemetery. I once spent a sepulchral winter alone at work on a book there while Mother was paying her annual visit to California where my brother lives: a journey she was not going to be able to make again after her fall. At Mother's ninety-odd not much is left to do but breathe and remember. Ageing is a process of small bereavements: one desire, one pleasure, one function after another gone inexorably, though their losses can appear wilful to the young who think they will never allow it to happen to them. In truth, the sole recommendation for old age is its alternative. One day that winter, after the thaw, I'd had enough scribbling and I was on my way to catch the bus for Princeton, forty minutes down the road, the nearest feasible place and not so gruelling as Manhattan that lies fifty minutes in the opposite direction. As I was hurrying to the gate, a small, stooped, ancient figure suddenly appeared and stood foursquare in my path. I recognised the curtain-twitcher who lived six houses down; she had been espying my comings and goings from behind her window during the snowbound months. 'Who ARE you?' she demanded, stamping her little arthritic foot peevishly.

Before I could answer she drew nearer, squinting, then nodded her head. 'I know, I know,' she said triumphantly. 'You're a daughter!'

One of the grim sights in any retirement community is of grey-haired daughters pushing wheelchairs or slowing their pace on daily strolls next to mothers of ninety and ninety-five with whom they live in bitter captivity. There are several such in Mother's community; I shudder to see them. There is one live-in caretaker son whom I used to pass on my way to the nursing home; a shabby bachelor in his early seventies, he shuffled along alone in the bright September mornings, smoking the cigarette he was not allowed at home. Particularly in America much in life and life itself depend on money, never more than at the end. Fortunately, Mother husbanded the inheritance my father left her and nursed it cleverly into a tidy sum. Private agencies exist in America for offspring who cannot or do not choose to cope with the care of an aged parent: one of them is bluntly and honestly called 'Rent-a-Daughter'. Guiltlessly, I set arrangements in motion for Mother's care when she left the nursing home to recuperate, probably for the rest of her life: we would hire her a daughter, a model of the type – bought and paid for, unmarried and childless too – who would care for her, like her, admire her, adore her even, never dispute a point, and do as she was bloody well told because Mama knew best. For over a week I visited Mother daily in the ward of the nursing home and meanwhile also prepared her house for my surrogate, which entailed once again burrowing through the detritus of the past and adding a few more to my small collection of cards posted to my parents from the Study Abroad tour in 1954, now returned to sender. One showed a picture of Koblenz: 'Writing this on a boat on the Rhine. Lovely though confusing Germany! Guilt, sympathy, antipathy, pity and appreciation all mixed up in me. We are passing a castle, home of a medieval lord, and where Hitler met Chamberlain. Oh, life!'

Oh life! Just as Mother seemed organised and on the mend, and I was seeing my way clear to returning to London and the road, trouble happened – big trouble – this time to others and to us all.

On Tuesday, September the eleventh I started out for the nursing home not long after sunrise, intending to catch an early bus for the fifty-minute journey into The City, as Manhattan is known in those suburbs: The City – the only one on earth. Once out of Mother's community, pavements and sidewalks give way to a rural landscape familiar from my childhood and rapidly being blighted by industrial estates and dormitory communities for commuters to Manhattan. I timed my morning walks to avoid the worst of thundering traffic that bisects cornfields bronzing in early frost and has demolished forest trails where towering trees, bent when they were saplings by local Indians, used to point the way. A narrow place on the four-lane road forced me in towards the verge where I nearly stumbled over the carcass of a racoon, the biggest I had ever seen, nearly the size of an Alsatian dog. Its head lay against the bank, eyes open and still watchful behind the bandit's mask. The car or truck that knocked the life out of the magnificent animal and threw it aside had caused no visible wounds. My immediate impulse was to bury it: to hide the decomposing of its beauty as a villain might hide his tracks or a geisha her unseemly laugh behind a fan. But I was squeamish and besides I had no tools. For the rest of my time in America, on my daily walks between the retirement community and the nursing home where aged lives were eking out, I was going to pass the racoon twice a day; it lay noble and entire, never a sign or whiff of decay attached to its imperishable beauty, perfectly preserved in a time of dreadful endings: a pharaoh of the animal kingdom.

One of the nurses needed to talk to me about Mother's blood count and bowel movements and similar geriatric priorities, so I let the early bus pass. There is always another bus to The City. Thus I was sitting next to Mother's bed when hell broke loose. Nurses were shouting out loud, from the highway car horns blared; only the incessant racket of longevity suddenly ceased: the aged stopped moaning and raging – they slumped in their wheelchairs or lay abed in eerie silence. A male nurse ran past Mother's door: 'Turn on your television!'

'It must be a trailer for a Schwartzenegger film,' said Mother.

Had I caught the early bus it should have been just at the point where the Manhattan skyline can be seen raising itself grinning out of the Jersey marshland. Damn! If only I had caught the early bus, I would have witnessed with my own eyes one of the seminal, terminal moments of American history.

'I guess there won't be a bus into The City today,' I muttered stupidly.

161

Just then, on the television screen suspended over the foot of the bed, a man hurled himself from one of the crumbling towers; for an instant it seemed the miracle he and we were praying for had happened: the great law of gravity had been suspended – a splayed human figure was actually going to fly. But the body fell according to nature and plummeted to earth. After seeing that terrible suicide there could be no room in any heart for anything but dumb horror.

A week or so later, on the empty plane to London, I riffled through back issues of the *New York Post*. On an inside page, away from continued reportage of the local disaster, was a little story that completed heartbreak.

'Camels killed in car wreck,' it read. 'Two runaway camels from a travelling circus were killed when a car smashed into them on a road near a small German town on the Rhine . . .'

Ten

'1954: Early start and a hard travelling day. I am writing this on the bumpy bus, on the road to Switzerland. Soon we will see the Alps. And then on to Italy: dear old Italy, at last. Spent a night in Frankfurt. Yech!'

Half a century later, on the second lap of the journey in your gentle wake, after the usual mundane anxieties of departure, silence lay behind me. No farewells or popping corks. Nobody required the journey of me, nobody was waiting for me, nobody on the road ahead knew me or needed me; such is the bliss and melancholy of solitary travel. Charing Cross Station is my favourite departure point from London; the incoming morning horde is more raffish than the suits who pour into Liverpool Street and it is a short walk from my flat. To start a long journey on foot returns me to a childhood daydream of running away from home, not in anger: to explore the world, to find other places, another place, and another way to be myself, to become the source of my own pride. London was tender and grey and moist as a newborn moth in the mid-October dawn.

My compartment in the early train to Dover was practically empty except for a few dozing couples and, sitting alone in my line of vision, an older version of my Dutch friend, Annette, with the same handsome, mouthy face, pale-brown hair and slightly distracted eyes, a similar eagerness too, I sensed, to laugh at even the most feeble joke. The strange woman turned up later aboard the boat to Ostende where I overheard her speaking Flemish to a younger woman. There it was again: that inward busyness of Rembrandt's women who seem even in their finery to be mulling over kitchen problems and household accounts. A life-saving ability has evolved in us human females to change our allure and our very shapes according to prevailing taste; the characteristic abstractedness of lowland women, their restraint and air of preoccupation with issues more urgent than those in hand, must reflect what Rembrandt and lowland men desire.

In years of travelling, I have twice slept through discrete areas of the globe: Arkansas by Greyhound in the mid-Nineties was one, and a few years earlier on my way to Greece with my son, also by bus, I slept all the way through Belgium. Belgium was not on the Study Abroad itinerary and it has never been one of my ports of call. Indeed, the most enchanting thing I knew about the place I had just come across in a shipboard give-away publication. 'French fries' it informed readers should rightly be called 'Belgian fries'; they were invented there during a fishing crisis of the last century when locals tried to trick their hunger for seafood by cutting potatoes into sprat-like shapes before frying them. The boat arrives straight into the train depot, so with barely a glance at Ostende I made straight for the first of several connections to Heidelberg before going on into Switzerland and the Alps. It was a surprise to be told on the platform that a rail strike was in progress.

'In Belgium?'

'And why not?' the attendant said.

For an hour or so I cooled my heels in the extravagantly vast forecourt until a train finally set out pretty much in the direction I wanted to go; by the time it left, something subtle and ruthless had made itself felt behind the narrow, hooded buildings of the Belgian front.

The skinny young man at the table diagonally across from mine was a student of art ostensibly, ostentatiously even. As soon as the train was in motion he took a sketchbook from his backpack and a huge bouquet of coloured pencils done up in an elastic band. Then carefully and reverentially he brought out an autumn leaf the size of a dessert plate. It was touched by shades of advancing decay, richer and darker to my eye than the insipid orange pencil he selected. I turned away to the window to see what was specifically Belgian about the view before I left the country again, possibly for ever. Hunger for light was evident in the way houses were situated in open space or on top of rises, and there was a curious control and solemnity about the gardens and the pace of traffic, visible too on the pale faces of people waiting at crossings. Otherwise, an alien with nothing to go on but the view from a train window would have trouble distinguishing what he saw from Holland or northern Germany. Meanwhile, as we chugged alongside empty tracks, it had been dawning on me – dusking? – there was no way I was going to make Heidelberg by nightfall as I had intended.

As it turned out, I was lucky to get as far as Cologne – Cologne again – by midnight. And unlucky that a seasonal infestation of trade fairs and conventions had preceded me. Taxi drivers outside the train station, men of experience and prophecy, assured me there were no rooms available, not one, not anywhere in Cologne.

'Not for money, not for love,' a handsome Neapolitan cabby assured me with a lascivious wink that reminded me I was on the road to 'dear old Italy'.

And his wicked smile reminded me too that I was old, too old to anticipate with equanimity spending the night in a train station. It has not always been so, of course. Until age corrupted me I didn't mind discomfort and even danger on the road; on the contrary. Earning a destination established its value; being there was the reward for having got there. And getting there has incidental rewards too, for young attractive women.

One night a long, long time ago a general strike stranded me in a bustling railway station somewhere in France. I forget where I was going, probably returning to Paris from the south. Too broke as usual to rent a hotel room, I settled for a space on the floor behind a row of seats and curled up, shivering, to doze between announcements of delays and cancellations. At some point in the restless morning hours I found myself being gently covered and tucked into what felt like a rough blanket still warm from someone else's body. My heavy eyes opened to see a tall, suntanned French soldier no doubt on his way home from Algeria, in ferment at that time. I slept soundly under his greatcoat for several hours; when I woke, it and he were gone. But I could not forget the look on that young man's face while he covered me with his coat. There must be women accustomed to being looked at that way: protectively and cherishingly and uncritically. But not I, certainly not by a man, not by anyone who wanted nothing in return, not respect, not gratitude, not fuel for his vanity, not that I should change my ways or my mind; never by someone who wanted only my comfort and happiness. It would be good to keep that brief recollection shiny and pure. But the wry old busybody who edits my memory forces me to remember that a few days later a patch of infectious ringworm developed on my cheek where it had rested against his coat.

Planes are a purely pragmatic way to reach a destination, increasingly cheap and ever more uncomfortable. Since the propeller was outmoded, there is not any attempt by airlines to add the slightest glamour to a journey. Airline staffs are bossy and peremptory, and in economy class they are all but equipped with cattle prods; it is only surprising that weary, intimidated air travellers do not more often succumb to rage on board. Whenever there is time in hand I do not choose to fly. As for trains, they are becoming today's buses; they exist increasingly for people too poor or scared to fly, too poor or ill or old or just too ornery to drive a car. Vestiges of romantic expectations still attach to continental rail travel, however, even though outside commuting hours, train stations nowadays attract lunatics, beggars, junkies and low-life. The hopeful pretensions of many European terminals' façades make them all the more sad and sinister out of hours. Thus, when I learned there was no connection to Heidelberg until the next morning, instead of hanging around the station, I caught a late train and ended up just as I had in 1954, spending a night in Frankfurt. Yech!

'Frankfurt, yech!' I said it aloud recently, I don't remember why, in a crowded London pub. Whereupon an Englishman along the bar who turned out to be the husband of a German, resident for fifteen years in Frankfurt, took me to task and extolled its virtues: terrific shopping, clean streets, good transport.

'A great place to raise children. The weather's no worse than here. And if you want some fun, we have a lively student quarter,' he said.

Expats can be fierce warriors in defence of our adoptive countries, for in defending them we are defending our lifetime choices: we are defending our marriages. Of course, we are just as often the opposite: full of scorn and anger against our union, our destiny, ourselves. As a faithful expat to London, I hold that anyone wedded to a place because of its climate, or its student quarter, or because it is a good place to raise children, suffers arrested development. Consistently warm temperatures are good for the bones and bad for the brains: they melt wit. People over forty who hang around student quarters are a menace or a joke unless they teach, often then too. And wherever is known as a good place to raise children turns out to be safe, antiseptic, segregated and stultifying for adults.

It was convention season all over Germany, apparently. After an exhausted sleep in a hotel room constructed around the dimensions of a travelling salesman, I descended into a lobby packed with groups of people wearing name tags and consulting earnestly in French, German and English. Frankfurt's train station itself was gripped by a trade fair of sorts. Stalls manned by dark exotics filled the huge central space, purveying bright cottons, spices, sweets, and ornamental elephants carved in wood and fake ivory. I must have suffered a periodic crisis, the sequela of communication deprivation, because in the midst of the hullabaloo I found myself deep in conversation about coffee with a plump American conventioneer. She was still wearing an illegible name tag while waiting for a train to the airport and her plane home. We agreed that Italian coffee was the best in Europe; diplomatically, I granted the USA greater variety. The Turkish polyglot who ran the refreshment stall where she and I had bumped into each other put in a word for his own national brew. On the vexing question of whether coffee is bad for us, did we not agree that man does not live simply in order to go on living? An uncomfortable image crossed my mind of the inmates at the nursing home where I had last seen Mother. 'Only when we're toothless, blind and bedridden does staying alive become the sole pleasure and purpose of being alive,' I said.

'Well, I don't smoke any more and I never drink alcohol,' the American replied. 'But I sure do like my coffee. Coffee is my only vice since I found Jesus . . .'

The Turk and I exchanged a nervous look. Gosh! Was that the time?

I took my assigned seat by the window on a tram-like train with hardly any space for luggage. Across the table was a fat, powdered woman dressed for a garden party; it was bemusing – it always is – to realise the old biddy was probably my own age, possibly a year or two younger. Next to her a bespectacled, youngish man read a thick book without a dust cover. As a short delay in departure edged towards fifteen minutes, then twenty, with no public announcement or explanation, she fidgeted and twisted her fingers, which were linked to her like big white sausages. Finally, she tugged the young man's sleeve and whispered in his ear. She must have asked him to find out what was wrong because he bowed his head and carefully put a bookmark in place, before he left the compartment.

'There has been an engine failure, Madam,' he said on his return a few minutes later, speaking first to her in German and then to me in excellent English. 'They are waiting for the arrival of a part.'

'So British trains are not the only ones . . .' I said and he laughed.

Inspired by the big book and by a button dangling forlornly from the cuff of his suit, I asked was he a professor?

Yes, he was, of linguistics at the ancient and esteemed University of Heidelberg. 'And may I ask what you're reading?' He nodded towards my paperback.

It was a translation of *The Rings of Saturn* by W. G. Sebald. A British resident since the 1970s until his untimely accidental death, Sebald wrote in his native German, but the professor did not know his work. I handed the book over to him.

He skimmed several pages with the speed of light. 'Erudite man . . .' he said.

I said 'He doesn't wear erudition lightly. Proudly, a medal of honour. Whether you like his style or not, it is a style, a real style, original, layered, peripatetic . . .'

Suddenly the old woman, who had been watching us through narrowed eyes, began to speak in a querulous tone, unburdening herself from what I could make out of a detailed description of the heavy traffic she'd encountered on her way to the station. The professor offered automatic, distracted sympathy as a successful son or nephew might on a visit to

171

the family he has left behind. Our minutes of waiting were now drawing towards an hour. I offered the professor my mobile phone so he could call colleagues awaiting him at the university. The horrid gimcrack had been a dead encumbrance in my bag until then, though it was necessary, I guess. Mother had recently moved back home with her daughter replacement; she and only she had the number of the nasty new noise-maker. While the professor was warning his colleagues he might miss his first lecture, the old lady glared at me steadily; as soon as he was finished she started to pontificate on what to my ear sounded like the prohibitive price of good beef and the dangers of, with a glance at me, mad cow disease. Dexterously, he talked her down. Our train was finally in motion. Through him, I asked if she wanted to use my telephone to call friends awaiting her at a stop outside Heidelberg. Thanking him, not me, she accepted. While she was busy, he delivered me a pithy dissertation on the kinship of German *geist* and English 'ghost'. 'It makes me sick to ride backwards on the train,' the old lady interrupted shrilly, or so I heard her words; there was no mistaking the homicidal squint my way even though it was I, not she, who was riding backwards. Then she launched what I would swear was a geriatric tirade against the loss of all good things in life: good beef, good bread, plush and punctual trains, good manners, demure women and the respect of children.

I turned away to the window and a view reminiscent of autumn in upstate New York, there was the same genre of foliage and a similar lie to the land; it all looked lightly stamped upon, however, German hills flatter and German leaves much less bright. The old lady had paused to give her professor the opportunity to sympathise about the lack of flavour in soft fruit these days.

'Had I not missed the early bus,' I heard myself saying, 'I would have been in Manhattan on September the eleventh.'

A hit! A palpable hit! I felt almost sorry for the cow. The field was mine. What could she do beyond flashing me a look of perfect detestation when she finally left us at the stop before Heidelberg?

'August 1954: Midge and Evelyn are suffering from a crush on Tony, too. Ev has it bad, much more seriously than I do. Last night I overheard Tony say to his friend Jeremy, "She'll make good old bones." I was watching them in a mirror and they were talking about me. Funny thing to say! What does it mean? Is it a compliment? Maybe he means my young bones aren't so hot. Jeremy left us today. He is darker and fatter than Tony and stand-offish. Ev spends hours in the bathroom and she is forever asking Midge if she looks OK. Before breakfast today she asked me and I said, "You look very 'kempt' and very 'hevelled'." Oh dear. Doesn't it ruin a joke to have to explain it? I don't want to be a snob, but . . .'

Hang on a minute, young lady. About those old bones? I understand your confusion – compliments are for immediate

173

consumption; they don't keep in cold storage. For all I know, Tony and I have passed each other without a second look several times in the years I've lived in England and his antique compliment is of not the slightest use to me now. If I were you – and I was you – I would forget what he said, and I shall. As for being a snob, of course you wanted to be a snob; others wanted you to be one, too. Snobbery is judgement based on credentials inherited or acquired, genuine or faked, just as long as they are persuasive enough to lift you to a level where there is small threat of being humiliated or – and this is utterly unthinkable, my dear – of being humbled. The creation of snobs is part of what higher education is about; why else call it 'higher'? Nowadays all education is mainly about money, of course, and so is most modern snobbery. Back in 1954, however, a cultural swan through Yurp still added the kind of lustre to an American girl's finish that a nose job does now. Joining Study Abroad was all your own idea and you paid for it with your own savings. Nevertheless, the trip had parental approval; it raised a girl half a notch in the market and was a lot less of an undertaking than, say, piano lessons. I was about ten when my parents arranged for me to go to Miss Barnaby's house once a week for piano lessons. We had no piano at home and I had to practise alone after hours at school, which I managed only once or twice a week as it entailed dragooning a resentful student-teacher to stay and supervise me.

'You have no interest in music. You will never play,' Miss

Barnaby said, turning away from me in disgust after my fifth or sixth bungled lesson.

Through quick hot tears, I looked down at my fingers on the unexplored miles of keyboard and, young as I was, I knew the anguish and helplessness of being sentenced for a crime I had not committed.

Of course, your family never dreamed, nor did you yet, that a summer's tour in Europe was going to uproot all desires and make you unavailable to an intended destiny or, for that matter, to an intended. Otherwise they might have bought a piano and kept you at home making music. Oh yes, unpractised child, while we're at it, from where we sit now I recall perfectly well that you used the 'kempt' and 'hevelled' routine a few times back at Columbia until someone – I hope it was your own good sense – persuaded you to shelve it.

When our train finally arrived in Heidelberg, the gentleman professor had missed his first lecture and with time in hand before the next one, he offered to take me on a quick tour of the city. He led me from the station straight on to a bus and into the old quarter where the university is based with a breakneck haste that revealed clearer than words how deep is the divide in Heidelberg between town and gown. Unfortunately, I'd bought a suitcase in London that combined an expansive soft top with a hard base to protect bottles and breakables, and of course, it had wheels too, not ordinary wheels to make the going easy; these wheels had been designed unquestionably by an Italian, perhaps the very he who designed motor scooters, and mainly they made the going incredibly noisy. Rolling to Charing Cross early the previous morning, the clatter that accompanied me alarmed residents of Central London in advance of bedside clocks and it later put the wind up placid Belgians trying to bask in unseasonable sun. But the racket that had gone before was a muted timpani compared to the sound of those infernal wheels at speed over the cobblestones of old Heidelberg. Like the tumbrel of revolutionary Paris, our approach startled and terrified citizens within a wide radius. And who among men is more maddened to be made unable to hear himself think than a university professor? The poor man couldn't wait to abandon his Cook's tour of Heidelberg and leave me on an ancient corner to fend for myself.

'August 1954: Heidelberg is like walking into a fairy tale or an operetta with its old castle high on a mountain. There was some sort of celebration going on. Everywhere everyone was tipsy and singing, and it didn't take us long to join them! After fifteen hours here I still do not know where people live, only where they drink. Perhaps they don't live at all. Perhaps they just leave the stage and disappear? This place is full of history and thought, so different from Germany north of here, it could be another country. Almost.'

Tipsy, were you? And not for the first time. Or would you prefer to forget the previous December when you stayed with a patrician classmate, Judy R, in her granny's Park Avenue apartment? Wangling the permit that was required back then for Barnard girls to spend a night out of the dorm required you to neglect mentioning that Judy's aged grandparent was not actually resident to chaperone you; she was in Palm Springs. Who would have dreamed buildings could weave and wobble the way New York's skyscrapers did after half a bottle of granny's cognac? It has taken decades to break bad habits you were starting then, susceptible child. Did you have to spend twenty years of your life as a hard smoker, for instance? When you were fourteen and confessed to your mother that the gang was planning a secret smoking party down by the lake she, an occasional smoker, insisted you take along her cigarette lighter and holder. Of course, what impressed your friends was not your Zippo and slinky cigarette holder; they envied you your swell mom. You were also the only kid in the fifth grade whose mother made caviar and cream cheese sandwiches for you to take on a school picnic. Why, oh why, did you have to acquire a weakness for the cigarettes and not the caviar?

Nobody was carousing in Heidelberg this time. Perhaps they don't carouse there any longer. You sure don't, sugar. However, I must agree about the prevailing ambience of operetta which apparently goes back a long way: a kitschy tableau in the municipal museum purporting to represent locals of prehistory shows them as fine-boned and blond, the females smartly dressed in furs. Even my hotel advertised itself with a self-conscious simper as the hostelry that once turned Goethe away. Can anyone blame them? I started across the bridge towards the Philosopher's Walk that winds through parkland of the opposite bank, but any practising cynic had to turn back halfway there discouraged not only by strong winds, also by the merry young hedonists on their way to the same place and clearly burning to exercise their tenets to a logical conclusion. Instead, I tackled the formidable hill to the castle and at its summit had the pleasure of sweeping views over the picturesque town and surrounding landscape. In a small side room that contained only a suit of armour and a few easy chairs with attached headsets, I gorged on Schumann's *Papillons* until a lengthening queue of doddering romantics waiting for their turn put me to flight.

I was taking a late lunch in the cool open air of the crowded main square, the Marktplatz, when with barely a sketchy by-your-leave a stout ageing couple platzed themselves down at my table. They told me right away that they were Viennese tourists, a case, in adorable Heidelberg it seemed to me, of bringing Newcastle to the coals. The man, whose English was superior to his wife's, wanted to talk. Uncharacteristically, I did not. But it is a pedlar's inheritance, this compulsion to show my wares even when I would prefer to read or daydream.

'Are you travelling alone?' the man asked.

When the woman heard me say yes, I was alone, she shook a power fist of sisterhood that caused her diamonds to sparkle. Nevertheless, in her belying eyes was contempt: where were

178

my diamonds? Where was my substantial husband? While he told a tedious story about the frequent business trips he used to make to Houston, Texas, before his retirement, her suspicion of me was freezing into dislike, a phenomenon every bit as common between strangers as attraction. Before I could catch the eye of a waitress and make my escape, the husband leapt into position to take a photograph of me. How naïve and amusing worldly travellers find natives in far places when they hide from our cameras lest they steal pieces of their souls. But as the cursed lens was winking in my face, I shuddered. Even now I shudder to think of an over-furnished Viennese dining room where the overstuffed couple are show-ing holiday snaps to their overfed friends. 'And this is an interesting American woman Helga and I met in Heidelberg,' says the husband, passing my image over reeking plates.

'Ach, Helmut, you think all American women are interest-ing,' says his wife.

Guests shuffle their feet and there is an uncomfortable pause while everyone remembers hearing about Helmut's clumsy infidelities in Houston, Texas.

'Travelling alone,' says their host at last. 'German name but couldn't speak a word of German.'

'Don't be such an old fool,' says Helga, licking cream off her fingers and grabbing my photograph out of her husband's hand. 'Can't you see? She's a Yid.'

Attracting the hatred of every second woman over fifty in Germany was getting me down. Consolation came next

179

morning when I found myself across from two young Australian women on the train to Switzerland and Lucerne. They were curious, friendly and nearly as predisposed to go out looking for revelation and self-discovery as my generation of Americans used to be long ago, before America became arbiter of everything worth having, by jingo, and its own only myth.

'Are you travelling alone?' the redhead asked me and when I said I was, she asked if I wasn't afraid.

'Of what?'

'What if you get sick?'

At her age such a thought would not have entered my mind. Only now it does sometimes: what if I fall ill? What if the fatal disorder probably already gathering in this old body strikes me on the road? What if it does? So what? Then I'll die in German or French or Italian, and be no less dead for that. I hope when the Aussies got to Zurich they found the miracle neither of them had ever yet seen: snow. When I waved them goodbye from the window of the train, I was wondering whether it would be the brunette or the redhead who upon her return to Melbourne found it too far, too young, too small to hold her. My money was on the brunette. Naturally.

'July 1954: Bound for Lucerne and at last a glimpse of the Alps. Fortunately, it is a grey day or I would not, could not, believe my eyes. No metaphors here, no similes. Beauty solid and aloof: the mountains forested at the bottom, then tundra and finally crags and snow. The bus went around curves "like in the movies". Lucerne is a clean and shining city on a lake; everything looked silvery. Oh yes, we changed drivers at the border. "Off widdershanks, Fritz!" I said, or something that sounded like it. Our new driver is Italian! A real Italian! From Italy! His name is Giorgio. He's funny and a flirt. And he is about one hundred years old.'

You were privileged to climb into Switzerland by breath-taking twists and turns. I envy you. Trains tunnel in, each dark passage opening into an achieved landscape where hills are sharper, peaks no longer rolling but higher and higher and cresting. Although announcements on board are in Ger-man and English, the exuberant graffiti outside Basle station hint at a ramshackle Italianate influence that also peeps out of gardens with too many pots and unruly plants. Roofs slope steeply to shed snow, and local sheep in apparent obedience to Darwin seem to have evolved with legs shorter on one side to help them graze dizzy inclines. I had phoned ahead to a hotel in Lucerne gleaned from a guidebook I had browsed, standing up in a London bookstore. I shouldn't have bothered, Lucerne is well stocked with hotels and bed and breakfasts, and I could have trusted to luck and instinct as I generally do. The woman who took my reservation was called Irma too, so we immediately achieved an uncommon intimacy denied Marys or Catherines who meet on the road.

181

My urban heart sank, however, when the taxi she advised me to take from the station zipped through the gleaming city centre, then right past substantial suburbs where the very air reeked of money, and finally far, far into sloping fields, bright and green in October sun. Below our road, I watched to my dismay as Lucerne first stretched then grew small in the distance. What is a big-city girl supposed to do with herself in the country? And in a foreign country, too.

'Take a walk?' suggested my short, blonde, buxom name-sake.

'Is there anything to watch out for? Any local hazards?'

She gazed thoughtfully through the big window beside us; there was nothing to see but unadulterated, rolling landscape. 'Man-eating crocodiles?' she suggested, an Irma after my own heart.

'1954: Not to get too carried away by the big scene; little Alpine flowers are in their way as beautiful as mountains. Heidi didn't have it so bad!'

The breeze was clean and crisp and electrified; it trilled on my skin. Halfway along the road a signpost pointed down to a vast field, I turned left and up, up towards the forest. On either side of the narrow way was a building, one a farmhouse, the other an inn shut up tight. Beyond them were meadows where sheep grazed, the clang of their bells muffled in wool. Sauntering towards me down the middle of the road appeared a handsome young ram, his bell clanged too, briskly, in time to his pace; I stood aside in deference to his majesty, and his horns. Then, suddenly, the forest drew me in and closed around me. There is no sound as telling of earth's benign indifference to the individual as the creak and rustle overhead of wild trees. Beside the wide trail a stream of bright water licked my shoe and scampered free in a channel of its own design. How like a cathedral it was, I thought, looking up at the ribbed vault far above. No. No, the forest came first. A cathedral is its urban representation: soaring pillars, cold hard floor, shrines and shady side chapels for intimate communion. What luck! To have a chance to see again how nature does it with no help from us.

The air was growing cool and the sun was dropping. It has been very long since I have seen starlight pure and undimmed by a red urban sky. Reluctantly, I turned to retrace my steps and return to shelter before nightfall. Were I much younger – as young as you, child – or not a lot older, were I not still in the years of mortgage and responsibility, I could not have resisted the temptation to walk on and on, to vagabond and lose myself.

Eleven

While travelling around western Canada, Swiss Irma and her husband had stumbled upon a town called Irma. 'Isn't that a surprising coincidence?' she said.

It was surprising to me that an alpine couple would choose the Canadian Rockies for their second honeymoon; strictly speaking, however, Irma finding Irma – even this Irma finding that Irma who had found Irma – does not qualify as a fully fledged coincidence: not in my book – not enough incident. Coincidence comes close to the tidy conceits of fiction and in real life plots thin a lot more often than they thicken. Coincidence is like love at first sight, a perfect accident, a collision requiring at least one and, at its most stunning, two moving bodies; thus, to travel attracts coincidence. Unlike every other thrill, coincidence alone happens increasingly with age as one acquires more to be coincident with.

There was the portly American tourist in a baseball cap, for example, whom I encountered at Dover port several years ago. He was travelling with a group of 'senior citizens'. All

crossings had been delayed for an hour and we found ourselves neighbours in the queue for coffee.

'Where do you come from?' I asked.

'California.'

'Oh really. My brother lives there. Where in California?'

'You wouldn't know it. A little place called Carlsbad.'

'Of course I know it. Believe it or not, that's the very place
my brother lives.'

'No joke. What's your brother's name?'

'Kurtz, Michael.'

'Not Doctor Michael Kurtz?'

'Yes!'

'Oh my God!' he cried out and again, 'Oh my God!', for
coincidence is a glimpse of the miraculous and can inspire
or restore faith. 'Oh my God! Your brother . . .' he began,
shook his head hard, and then this stranger from the land of
all that is literal said, 'Your brother saved my life.'

And there was the time I was stuck out of season in the
bus station at Tijuana in Mexico. The shuttle I awaited was
probably going to turn up eventually and possibly go on to
the airport, perhaps in time to catch my flight south. Who
knows? Maybe. There was only one other hopeful passenger,
a young man in his twenties on his way to Mexico City, he
told me. We sat in the sun, chatting; I had heard him earlier
speaking Spanish at the ticket window and his fine English
had a slight musical accent. When our bus materialised,
although it was empty, we chose to sit side by side.

'I love this Baja landscape,' I told him. 'I have a friend who used to live in the Balearics. She moved here about ten years ago. She lives in a geodesic dome at the very bottom of the peninsula . . .'

'My God!' he cried. 'Roberta . . .'

Not only had his mother, it turned out, been my friend Roberta's neighbour in the remote village where they both lived on the island of Majorca; it also turned out that on one of my visits there, when he was four, I had taught him how to play tic-tac-toe.

And four or five years earlier, a young Greek sitting next to me, the only other foreigner on another Mexican bus, this one overflowing with locals bound for Oaxaca, told me after a little conversation that he was the assistant and interpreter for a professional astrologer, an Englishman, who had retired to Rhodes.

'Oh my God!' I cried, for his employer was a former drinking chum and colleague whose column two decades earlier used to run next to my own in a glossy London magazine.

When a pixie-faced Swiss opposite me on the train out of Lucerne wanted to talk about the war, I actually had to think for a moment about which one he meant. I had been spared newspapers and television for forty-eight hours or so and wars move fast these days; blink and another one has started, blink again and we're in a commercial break. It was impossible to take the elaborate conspiracy theories the guy was spouting very seriously; he was reading du Maurier's *Rebecca*, for crying out loud. I was not sorry to see the back of him when we changed trains in Olten. On German trains the smoking sections are full; in Switzerland, however, they are the carriages in which to be alone, and I chose one en route to Milan. Through the first tunnel and high above us at last was the glint of snow. The next tunnel opened into a landscape of tarnished silver and streams that streaked like mercury around strands of firs before commingling into waterfalls. The compartment was empty except for a young couple in the seat behind me. The boy talked incessantly, nervously, droning on and on in Swiss German to his silent girlfriend. Every time we entered a tunnel he stopped talking and whistled tonelessly, thumping his feet against the back of my seat so it beat the rhythm of a giant heart. His mother must have had an easy birth; the kid couldn't wait to get out of the dark.

'July 1954: Italy! Italy! We're on the road to Italy! Evelyn is really excited because she has family there. I feel as if I have family there, too. Maybe everyone has family in Italy. Giorgio is singing, and Tony said he was giving up being our leader for the day and went to sit with the boys at the back of the bus. We can't go fast enough to get us to Italy!'

Long ago when I lived in Spain, later in France, and always in my imagination, crossing the border into Italy has been

187

like flying on earth or turning table wine magically into champagne; there is an immediate lift and what is flat becomes buoyant. You, my young I, would have been over that border quicker than you can say 'Ciao, bella!' So what made me decide this time to spend one more night in Switzerland? Gazing out at the sunlit alpine villages, I admired their chic invention, even the wood stacked against winter looked designer-arranged, and when the announcement of our next stop came, I liked the sound of it in all three languages, I thought, 'What the hell?' Could there be a better place to test freedom or a more paradoxical place to break out of the constraints of your compelling itinerary, my young predecessor, than in a town called Brig? 'Why, perhaps', I heard myself telling you, in apology for my delinquency, 'I'll meet a few brigands in Brig. You'd like that, wouldn't you?'

Humanity nestles in Switzerland and crouches over nest eggs in the hollows of mountains higher than hope or ambition. Ever since an ignominious mudslide, not quite an avalanche, tried to wipe the pretty town of Brig off the face of the earth not long ago it nestles, yes, and cowers too, in the shadow of the encircling giants. Despite the clear weather, from the moment I left the station, mountains always at the corners of my eye gave the impression of impending storms. Although it was early, I found myself hurrying in quest of a roof and protection. Night, when it arrived in a few hours, was going to fill the jagged blue cup overhead and wall us up in solid black. From several all very similar hotels near the station, I chose one capriciously because I liked the bright abstract painting behind the desk. Nobody appeared until I rang a brass bell on the desk and started an immediate commotion in a glass-fronted office on the small mezzanine overhanging the lobby.

'Have you a room for one for tonight?' I called out.

'But I know that voice,' came the reply.

A woman appeared at the top of the short flight of stairs.

'Oh my God! It's you . . .'

We did not believe it. Who would? Who could? When Diana and I had last seen each other in the late 1960s she was engaged to marry an English friend of mine. She and I used to meet in London during their liaison, not often, always with pleasure. It must have been 1970 when Diana and my friend broke up. Soon afterwards he told me that she returned to Switzerland and married someone else; he returned to disport himself manfully on the field of play where he has more or less remained a player to this day. Even after their split, he mentioned her often and I had a sneaking suspicion they used to meet from time to time. Years ago, he told me that Diana was divorced; I had no idea, however, that she lived in Zurich, nor that she was originally from Brig where her son owned and managed a hotel. He had asked his mother to cover for him while he took a few days' holiday.

'If he hadn't asked . . .'

'If I hadn't changed my plans . . .'

If my old friend in London had not taken a skiing holiday

189

in Switzerland back in the 1960s to the resort where he and Diana met; if she had not been a petite blonde; if instead of breaking up they had settled down in Clapham; if I had not broken my journey impulsively in Brig; if he had given her as a gift one of his gloomy paintings and not the cheerful abstract that caught my eye: a coincidence is the resolution of all but infinite 'ifs'. What is each of us before he is born, if not a coincidence waiting to happen? Fancy meeting me here!

'There is no elegant way in English to say "*bon appétit*",' said Diana, over our dinner together in Brig that night.

'Nor to say "*au revoir*", my friend,' I replied.

'July 1954: Over the last stretch of the Alps. To Italy!!!!! Twisting tunnels were a squeeze for us. We are only a few miles out of Switzerland and the country has taken on a jolly sloppy look. Clothes lines are outside every house. I haven't noticed clothes lines anywhere else. Where do the other Europeans hang their clothes? The English in the cellar; the Swiss in the night; the Germans probably have a complicated machine that dries their clothes secretly and the Dutch wear them wet, I guess. Only the Italians hang them in the sun.'

Have you begun to train for a future in popular journalism? You show a precocious gift for sweeping generalisations. Guard it well and cultivate it. Except for sedentary boffins who are cut out to specialise – train spotters, plane spotters, puzzle setters, mathematicians and similar harmless compulsives, most of them men – life is too short for an eager mind to do anything but leap to conclusions. So generalise to your heart's content, my old, old girl, and save us both a lifetime creeping among endless maybes. Only try to remain observant and flexible; love the exceptional; never expect anyone to act according to your expectations and never think anyone *should*. Oh yes, and try not to imagine that the things you like are perforce likeable, and things you hate must to all be hateful. By the way, what did you want to be when you grew up? Beyond a vast and amorphous, growing and consuming lust to see the world, I recollect no specific ambition after you stopped thinking you were an actress.

'What do you want to be when you grow up?'

In fact, it was a question nobody asked a girl-child in the 1950s. It hardly mattered what she thought she wanted to be, because eventually every good girl must marry and be supported. Around their fourteenth birthdays young Americans used to be subjected to aptitude tests, perhaps they still are, a series of puzzles and multiple choices intended to show what we were cut out to be with no reference to our dreams or desires. I found the psychologist's summation of my aptitude test crumpled in the bottom of one of Mother's cardboard boxes: 'A girl of indisputable gifts, she should of course use them some day to make a beautiful home and raise a family in elegant surroundings . . .'

Of course. In his expert opinion the way for me to make

191

use of my various skills while I killed time until the most important day of my life would be 'to edit a music magazine'.

'And what do you want to be when you grow up, little girl?'

'I want to edit a music magazine, please, Sir.'

'Don't ever, ever, *ever* get married, Irma!'

That was your mother's forceful injunction every other Thursday evening when she and her friend Marie used to meet to discuss a chosen book they had read in the preceding fortnight. It astonishes me to reckon that both grown-ups were about thirty years younger than I am now when they invited me from about my tenth year to join them, admire their perceptions and cautiously to chip in my two cents' worth on Aldous Huxley's *Brave New World*, for example, and Philip Wylie's *Generation of Vipers*. Mother's seminars took place under the beady scrutiny of a swarming fish tank in the 'reception room', as we called the waiting room of my father's dental surgery. My father was relegated to another part of our ugly sprawling flat on these occasions, probably wearing his thundercloud face and his mouth downturned like a capsized lifeboat.

'Do not ever, ever get married,' Mother used to tell me again and again, impassioned and vibrant and histrionic, while Marie nodded agreement and sometimes chimed in: 'Do not ever, ever get married!'

Marie was a large, sad woman. Memory may be confusing her with another of my mother's acquaintances when it gives her a withered left arm. But I know she had an unhappy marriage. They all did. Nevertheless, telling a girl of that era never to marry was as good as telling her never to have children, never to have sex, never to have a life in which her body participated. Having made her point, Mother came up with no attractive alternative. She imagined me living alone in a bijou flat somewhere in Manhattan, I dare say, possibly teaching, probably holding down a job in the social services as she had for a while before I was born. Mother had published a few short stories, too, in small literary magazines. Classic tales based on my father's lower East Side childhood, they were highly narrative and seemed made to read aloud. But I doubt she saw the slightest hope of my going down that road, not judging from the way she blue-pencilled my school essays and sometimes wrote them outright. Mother was not abusing her power, not even exercising it; down deep she believed herself powerless: it was all make-believe and showing off. Did she long to have restored the childhood torn away by her father's early death? I will never know. Her tales were of my father's childhood in lower Manhattan, not her own in the sticks, and her memories now when we talk are mostly edited versions of my own.

So what did you want to be when you grew up? Until you crossed the ocean in 1954, you had no idea and probably thought you had no choice. You were always open to impulse, never much of a planner until age and responsibility required it. From your very first sunrise at sea, and your journey across the mighty Alps into the Italian sunshine, a conviction was growing within you that was going to replace all conventional ambition: you were a sailor in your soul, a traveller and an observer, and born to work your passage.

'1954: And so to Italy. About time, too! At the Italian frontier I had a grand time flirting with a grey-eyed officer. Land of marvels! Their uniforms were trimmed in sunny yellow; they looked handsome and happy. Happy! Only the hotel in Milan was vile, sterile, white and called "The American"! Is that what they think of us?'

Our train burrowed through the great Simplon tunnel under the spell of geology and time itself to emerge at last in Italy. No flirtatious border guards this time, not much of a border at all. But the train was suddenly crowded as trains always are in Italy. And under cover of the tunnel Swiss German had changed into something more comfortable, so the prevalent language when we emerged was Italian. Outside were red roofs, a forest of TV aerials and yes, just as you noted all those years ago, laden clothes lines were hanging in every garden and swinging from every balcony despite the cloudy weather. In the midst of merry disorder, only the cemeteries were laid out neatly with a fresh bouquet on every tended rectangle. It was lunchtime in a nation that has good reason to be devoted to its food: the stations we passed through were empty, towns and roads empty, and empty fields levelled into a desolate foggy plain. Across the table from me sat another solitary woman traveller. Apparently she made this journey often; when she glanced through the window it was with impatience and boredom, almost disgust. She was of an age to be visiting a geriatric parent in a mountain rest home. But the way she covered her eyes from time to time with a trembling, manicured hand suggested grief more acute and unexpected than attaches to an ageing daughter's terminal duty. I patted the mobile phone in my bag, pipeline to Mother and her carers in America, and prayed it would stay quiet. No question the woman was Milanese. Her scarf was going to remain just so all day long in understated harmony with the unstructured jacket, her simple gold wedding ring and her scent of fresh mimosa. Englishwomen are too easily seduced by idiosyncrasy to pull off such consummate *comme il faut*. Rich Latin-American and Spanish women cannot control their taste for big jewellery and heavy perfume. As for spendthrift North Americans, they wear their expensive clothes psychically inside out, label first. On this planet, when a silk scarf is tucked into the neck of a cashmere pullover as hers was, the woman wearing it is going to be Parisian or Milanese, and of a certain age. Only Japanese women accustomed to Western dress ever sometimes achieve similar seamless perfection. Even when she slept, I thought, it would be in a cocoon of perfect chic that has gone quite out of fashion and will be buried with her generation of well-bred women from Paris and Milan.

Milan, when it gathers itself together out of the mist and
flatland, is not the sun-drenched picture of an Italian city
stored in your heart, my fond young traveller. Only the clamour around the train station is hectic and altogether Latin.
Because it was Italy, I was neither astonished nor suspicious
when the young woman outside the station of whom I asked
directions offered to show me the way to a hotel, one of
a featureless chain usually found near the train station that
I often choose to save time in big cities. Her name was
Giuliana. She was seventeen. She was a student. She lived
with her family in a suburb of Milan. She had relatives in
Boston whom she hoped to visit some day. She had a boyfriend but it wasn't serious: he wasn't serious. She had
recently had her appendix out. She did not like to see women
smoking in the street. And her favourite colour was blue.
'It's good for me,' she said, waving away my thanks in the
hotel lobby. 'I need to practise my English.'

Milan's industrialised grime and grimness make little
surprises all the more enchanting: gardens that overhang
balconies and roofs like shaggy green wigs, for instance; a
bookstore so cluttered and cosy I longed to be able to read
Italian fluently enough to browse with intent; an entomol-
ogist's shop window full of bright wings belying death. In a
street market of paintings and small-scale sculpture, the
artists, amateurs and professionals, men and women of every
age, preferred kibitzing to making sales. Women shopped for
food in enticing grottoes where each purchase was handled,

196

sniffed and discussed with the butcher, the greengrocer, the fishmonger; only the corner supermarket where I stopped to buy a bottle of water was sad, not very clean and full of skinny foreigners speaking Eastern European languages. Two handsome armed policemen stood in the shadow of the Duomo smoking cigarettes and loosely holding the reins while their white horses champed at the bits. And there was the fantastic sugary heap of the Duomo itself. Italophiles are generally dismissive about industrialised Milan; nevertheless, in very few continental cities can so much charm still be found in the space of six or seven city blocks.

'1954: The opera! *Tosca*! It made me cry. The Italian man next to me was singing along softly in places; I didn't mind. It's his opera, after all. Italy is opera.'

Lucky girl! Word that I was in town must have leaked out to the mischievous travel gremlins; they raced ahead and installed ballet at La Scala, knowing that I see the dance as scaffolding on music. While a sudden shower passed overhead I mooched around the opera house museum and coveted Verdi's last desk, his pen, his inkwell. On such a day sensible people head indoors, but the cafés in the great square around the Duomo were packed. Bags decorated with logos of world renown were carried by women and many of the men, too, as they patrolled the piazza. A local couple were seated next to my table. As soon as a timid sun emerged from rain clouds, the woman riffled through the anonymous plastic carrier bag that had kept her things dry and took from it another carrier bag, this one made of thick paper and fashionably emblazoned 'Luisa Spagnoli'. She transferred the plastic bag and its contents before she and her escort strolled off with the better bag swinging from her arm. A quick stab of affection overtook me, almost homesickness for Manhattan where slightly too fashionably dressed women are often to be seen leaning against skyscrapers while they change from sneakers into designer shoes out of Prada bags before going up to their meetings. Milan is the only other city I have seen where schlepping à la mode is endorsed as shamelessly as in New York.

'July 1954: Milan, and how they flirt! Midge complained (not very seriously!) that every time she turned around, some man was ogling her. But the truth is we have been ogling them, too. It's hard to take flirting seriously here, it's just a reflex, like winking when there's something in your eye. Even Giorgio goes in for it and does not let the fact that we are all probably half his age restrain him from whispering "*bella, bellissima*" to the girls every time we climb back on board the bus. I suppose things like a major age difference don't matter here.'

Italians are not the only men to flirt with women half their age, honey; you had better know that every man this side of the grave does that in the normal course of things. On the other hand, you will also discover that in Italy, and everywhere, any man who flirts with a woman twice his age or near it will turn out to be depraved, deluded or a conman. As I loitered in the café like an old trout in the shallows, I watched the men. Near me was one of the local faces: green eyes, lots of nose and a pointed intensity, an animal single-mindedness that relies for its beauty on being young and slim. With him sat a girl whose back was to me. Every time she lowered her head to her plate, he sent a long, blazing look over to a table of young women nearby. They seemed oblivious. But they weren't. They stretched and plumped. He was jiggling his knees unceasingly, too, in a way that indicates sexual excitement in a male, or so Midge had whispered to me in practically that very spot fifty years ago, and she was majoring in biology, after all. I polished off lunch, merely a sandwich yet a delicious reminder that food can feed more than the belly. Then I started across the big square and soon found myself captivated by the man in front of me. He was unaware of me, unaware of everyone, of anyone, aware only of womankind en masse: his adoring audience. An expensive raincoat worn open swung around him like a cape; his head was high, his hair swayed in gleaming ringlets to his shoulders. He walked briskly, confidently, hips and cock slightly in advance of the rest of him. Could I have been transported suddenly to such a height that all the figures in that square became dots under me, I would have known that dot as male; it had to be. From a height of one thousand feet or more not only would I have identified such a swash-buckling dot as male, I would have known it as an Italian male dot, too.

Nowadays I find 'vile, sterile' hotels not such bad places to come back to after a day of gadding about. To be made anonymous by the anonymity of my hosts, made comfortable in every ordinary way then left alone, can be restful for a compulsively gregarious loner like me. I sat contentedly in the assembly-line bar over a glass of red wine finishing Luigi Barzini's pugnacious book, *The Italians*. Only filial love tinged with self-contempt can produce anger and sorrow to equal his about his countrymen.

Thunder rumbled all night and lightning split the sky like an overripe black plum. In the morning a small cyclone of starlings lazily spun across the grey sky in front of my window, watched by a solitary magpie perched on a TV aerial. The previous night I had taken dinner in the dining room of my hotel. And an extraordinary dinner it was, too: fresh fish marinated cleverly and grilled to pink perfection, crisp vegetables, and – most rare treat for the abstemious traveller – a drinkable wine by the glass.

At the table nearest mine a big local family was celebrating grandfather's birthday. While they waited for their special menu to arrive a little boy of about four began to grizzle impatiently. Mom and granny and two other female relatives whisked him away to one side out of earshot while his sister, a year or two older than he, womanly and poised, watched from her place at table. Was this then the making of an Italian man? This stroking and cajolery by his women, their fussy attention that looked like pride in his noisy outburst; is this what will send him out one day swaggering across the piazza with the hilt of an imagined sword thumping his groin? I looked away quickly before the womenfolk noticed my interest. Since the advent of middle age, flirting with babies has not only become one of my pleasures on the road, it is also a ploy for getting to know their moms and through them a little more about the place. In Italy, however, native mothers turn their prams, or their backs, and shield offspring from the eye and attention of an unknown grey head.

Milan station defines turmoil. When I asked the girl at the information window about train times for Venice, she wrote the schedule out cheerfully and laboriously by hand, no Teutonic electronic printouts here. I was lucky to find a seat on the morning train. It was on the aisle next to an old man who had a small carrying cage on his knees from which emerged unholy noise. A continental traveller soon becomes accustomed to seeing dogs on leads aboard urban and inter-urban public transport; a woman with a parakeet in a cage had boarded my bus in Amsterdam, but this old Italian was transporting a cat and they do not travel well. Its tawny nose was pressed to the grille and even though it was on its way to Venice – fat cat city – it was not a happy moggy. Only its owner was impervious to his pet's demonic yowls and slept soundly. Each time yet another shattering complaint

201

rose from the cage, passengers exchanged shrugs and looks of amusement; there was not a trace of northern outrage, not on our own behalf, not on the cat's.

'July 1954: I preface this day with a solemn vow: I vow to come back to Venice. There is no place on earth like Venice and I do not need to see them all to know that. The volatile gondoliers and fragile gondolas, the sewer stink and floodlit palaces, handsome men and dangerous fruit, rats and glory! Italy is a magnificent, free, sunny, dirty country and Venice the most divine, freest, dirtiest place in the world. I never knew a city could be like this.'

'Dear Ones,' I wrote on a postcard showing the Grand Canal at sunset, 'Venice is everything it is supposed to be. Italy is a continuous and ongoing Renaissance. I hope you see it too, some day . . .'

How fortunate you were to see Venice when you did, while it still belonged to its history, to its art, to itself; and while you still belonged to fairy tales. Venice lives best as first seen, in memory; it is one of the most rewarding cities on the Continent to visit with a virgin traveller. Twenty years ago, when I took my son to see Venice, it had already begun to appear overproduced for tourism to my old eye; not to my boy, however, who was seeing it for the first time.

'This is wonderful. You didn't exaggerate, Mum,' he said, as we cruised the Grand Canal. 'For once . . .'

'Your city is incomparably beautiful,' I said to the hand-some old man behind the hotel desk.

He glanced to the open street door behind me where a pair of Swedish tourists entreated passers-by for directions, hopelessly; everyone passing was foreign and lost, too. 'Beautiful, yes,' he said. 'But not ours.'

Some parts of the globe present themselves as backdrops for frustrated travelling players. They take one look and are persuaded that this desert, this jungle, this city is the place for them at last to give the performance of their lives. Venice has ever been of those cities in Europe – Paris was another, Barcelona will be the next – where a few tourists every season look up at overhanging balconies and are seized by a desire to do more than admire; they want to move in and act out the roles they believe they were born to play: grande dame and her seigneur, artist, writer, playboy, thinker, saint, lecher, whore – roles they cannot play at home for fear of being laughed off stage, or imprisoned, or because they cannot afford local real estate. Never mind that the new arrivals have barely a word of the language and slight knowledge of complex local history; arrogance is part of the mix for expats and, as a rule of thumb, it is in proportion to the warmth of their adoptive climate. Usually the buyer into paradise is American or British, increasingly in Italy, these days, he is German. Many ads in the windows of estate agents in Venice specifically request foreign buyers. Who else can raise prop-erty values beyond the purse of locals? Of course, there is

203

resentment, I heard it in the voice of the man behind the hotel desk, sensed it in the flowing streets, saw it on the faces of waiters and the gondoliers waiting to be hired as living stage props.

'July 1954: Here I sit, scribbling incoherent postcards. How can I describe this place? Dear veined Venice. My God, but how she smiles at me. We have spent three perfect days here, and this is my last day for loving Venice. From here on, I must love a memory. How am I going to do it? I have never felt this way before. Spent the day on the lovely Lido beach, got into a private part of the beach with the help of some convenient Belgians. Got a new view of Europe: the playful rich. I like it. Then to St Marks and music and the wonderful clock, if only it would not make time pass! What it must be like to fall in love here! It is set for a great love. I don't want to go. Goodbye, Venice. Dear Venice. With a little praying and lots of work I will come back. I had to get silly to keep from crying. I don't want to stop writing now, to put the final period. No, I will end with a dash –'

Yes, yes, yes, I guess I agree, young one of me. Rest assured that Venice remains beautiful beyond belief and the Venetian light, ever sheer and spectacular, continues to discover colours not to be seen anywhere else. The clouds of a sunset I watched from the Rialto were edged in gold, not the chrome of a mundane palette, not even gold that is weighed in carats;

an utterly new and sensational hue. For a moment, in that celestial glow, I understood willingness to die just to have lived for a while over the Grand Canal, up high with a balcony and plants to tend. But what a lonely place is Venice in which to be alone. Swedes, Germans, British and American couples are everywhere kissing, lovers drift two by two in gondolas under laden clothes lines like maternal chidings overhead, flapping and ignored. I cannot recollect you will ever conduct a love affair in Venice, only come close once thirty-odd years ago with a Chilean poet. We picked each other up on the beach at the Lido. Between us we hadn't enough money for a hotel room so we strolled the canals and in dark places where only rats can copulate we drove each other half mad with what could have been love. When dawn finally came triumphantly, as it does in Venice, we sat silently in the train station, drinking coffee, worried, and parting finally without an exchange of addresses or surnames. He was heading south-east to Athens an hour after my train left north-west to Paris; we had both come too far alone to change direction and we had not gone far enough together to kid ourselves there was a hope in hell. By the by, that wonderful clock in St Mark's? The travel gremlins will hide it under their ugliest scaffolding fifty years later when you visit Venice again for probably the last time in this life.

The ghost waiting for me was not one I had expected to find. Strictly speaking, it was not a ghost I knew. Thirsty for astringency and hoping to outdistance the hordes of tourists

who were conscientiously ganging up on Renaissance culture,
I made for Peggy Guggenheim's collection of twentieth-
century art, housed in her former palazzo on the Grand
Canal. It is a collection that betrays the collector: the collection of a man's woman – it reveals her lack of inner confi-
dence, her superficial vanity and her acquisitive nature. Like
the clothes of some rich celebrities, taste is in evidence, yes
indeed, but subsumed under tragic and unappeasable hunger,
so the jumble of mainly fine pieces ends up being altogether
disconnected and scattery. It was as I stood where Peggy
Guggenheim's ashes were scattered by a memorial stone
against a wall of her garden that a phantom memory tapped
me on my shoulder. I saw a white-haired woman with her
back to me. Slowly she turned her knobbly potato face and
eyes that were empty of curiosity or logic, the mad, avid
eyes of a collector, slid over me in search of someone or
something interesting. Peggy Guggenheim had never met
me. But a long time ago, not in Venice, probably in Paris, I
suddenly remembered that I had once in the home of a
mutual acquaintance almost met her. Next to her memorial
stone is another engraved with the eight names of 'My
beloved babies'.

'Gosh, were they all her babies?' a young American behind
me asked the friend she was travelling with. I had seen them
earlier taking it in turn to photograph each other with their
heads stuck through a hole in a Henry Moore.

Cappuccino, Baby, Sable, Pegeen, and the others were

Peggy's dogs. Her daughter, a probable suicide, was called Pegeen too. Had the dog been named after the child? Or before her? Peggy's son was called Sindbad. There was no dog of that name. Later, I dreamed about Peggy Guggenheim. On waking, the dream was forgotten; it left but a chill and the lingering question that apparitions always put into the minds of those who feel their presence: why me? Only four people attended the rich American's funeral and my guess was that nobody who had known her in life had ever bothered to visit her memorial stone. Why was I chosen for her chilly visitation? What power summoned her ghost? It must have been the power of disappointment, posthumous disappointment, disappointment lofty and eternal ruining her peace in death as it had in life. Yes, a mourner had arrived at last to sigh over her ashes, and about time too, but it was a nonentity, a nobody: only me.

The waterbus to the station is always crowded with tourists on their way home. On the open deck I found myself pushed next to a couple of stout American women, mother and daughter they told me, from Indiana.

'Why,' I said, 'so is my mother.'

Indiana seemed pretty gosh darned small and far away there, on the Grand Canal.

'Mother went to Indiana University,' I said.

'Isn't that something,' said the older woman with the flat Hoosier intonation my grandmother used. 'That's where I work. Now that's what I call a coincidence.'

In the end, what defines a coincidence, I was thinking as we passed between the glories of Venetian architecture, is also what defines love: the number of times it does not happen.

Twelve

Across the aisle on the train to Florence sat an English family, mother and father and two daughters in their late teens, possibly twins, it was hard to tell; one had bright bottled yellow hair and the other bottled red. Both girls were dressed in artful rags and studded here and there around brow and mouth; the one closer to me sat in the lotus position reading a paperback copy of *Trainspotting*, her ears were plugged into a headset connected to a portable CD player in her pocket. Her sister sat eyes closed and tapped on the table in time to something hissing into her ear through her own portable CD player. Mum was turned to the window though there was nothing to see but fog. Dad read an English paper: devoured it, rather, gathered it into himself letter by letter, with the twitchy absorption of an aardvark at an anthill. Not one word was exchanged among the little family. Only when the parents went silently in search of coffee did the sisters put their heads together and whisper quickly. The moment mum and dad reappeared making their way back down the swaying coach the girls separated and wired themselves up again.

'August 1954: As our bus passes along narrow cobblestoned streets the people turn and stare, arrested in the processes of a daily life so different from ours and closer to the past. Was ours like this once upon a time? Here sits a woman shelling peas, there a child playing with a puppy. There is no difference between street and sidewalk; people sit on the street, sometimes we drive along on the sidewalk and peek into little shops – blacksmiths and carpenters – dark and cluttered, enticing, so different from our cities. The traffic is made up of bikes and motorcycles. Poverty is in evidence. The paint chips and signs are pasted over signs. Kids are barefoot. A lot of them ask us for chewing gum and cigarettes. Dopey Earl says we shouldn't give them anything because "it encourages them". To chew? To smoke? No. He means encourages them to beg. I wonder what he would do if his family was as poor as some of the people we see here? There are rows and rows of identical signs plastered on every building, making their points over and over and over again, for gelati, for Communists. Wherever we stop there is a church and in every church is something wonderful. The hills are cultivated and fall into rich folds. Evelyn says she is very proud of being Italian. I don't blame her. But it is funny, isn't it? Nobody remembers we were at war with Italy, too. Nobody on the bus has the same bad feeling a lot of us had in Germany.'

*   *   *

Good point, bright eyes. The Italians invented fascism; their flair for it remains evident now in the high-handed tactics of police and petty officials, and granted, they do get a kick out of uniforms. However, evil itself when it appears to be scatterbrained must seem more charming than infernal. Even after Mussolini accepted the edicts of Nuremberg, while Germany marched into its Third Reich with characteristic messianic fervour, Italy seemed to tag along, uncommitted and distracted, looking around for a hedge against the opportunism and self-regard that to this day make chaos of its traffic and politics. Italy can be a tricksy nation, annoying, and sometimes deadly: Italy simply cannot, however, be unlovable. The old boot, heel and all, has a soft spot in every civilised heart. To say one dislikes Italy or finds it dull is to say one dislikes music and is bored by the greatest flowering of sensual art in Western culture. You will observe in your travels, young I, that nations too are ruled by dominant traits of inherited beliefs and behaviour: nations have personalities. There are inconsistencies, of course, and internal contradictions, nevertheless, numerous and quite profound national differences continue to exist on the continent of Europe, and they remain distinct enough on the whole to submit to a high degree of generalisation. There will come a time, when you can sit on a continental train as I did – as I – on the one bound for Florence, and with near-perfect accuracy know which country each of the other passengers comes from by the way he or she dresses, sits, communicates and reacts to strangers.

Destination, destination, destination: that is what travel is all about these days, especially on the continent of Europe. Your journey by road in the 1950s meandered through fields and forests and down the main streets of villages where life unrolled outside the windows of your bus. You young Americans were as rich a source of astonishment and enlightenment to the people you passed as they to you. Nowadays, even had I chosen to travel by road instead of rail it would be on dedicated torrents of haste and waste and commerce you could not have imagined. The transformation of the European continent into a theme park had barely begun in your day; now in every season tourists queue for the main attractions, and tons of them are American. I envy you your impromptu pit stops in Italy, the uncharted churches; I envy you the children waving and cadging cigarettes or chewing gum, the passing faces looking up in surprise; I envy you the last granny on a straight-backed chair outside her front door, shelling peas. On our wide roaring highways there is nothing of human interest to see and even less of the landscape from a car than from the window of a train.

At least on the train fellow passengers offer entertainment and enlightenment. The neatly dressed young man, for example, seated alone and with absent-minded affection stroking his genitalia as he read a local morning paper; the businessman across from me who wore a beautifully cut suit in disturbing contrast to the wiry black hairs springing from the knuckles of his fingers. As we left Venice he was on his mobile phone saying, in Italian, 'I am on the train . . .' Outside, farmhouses of yellow and umber with terracotta roofs designed for sunshine looked as lonely and stranded in mist-filled valleys as big seashells on a chilly beach. Then, for the length of every tunnel we found again our own reflections hovering in darkened windows.

'Look! We are beside ourselves,' I said to myself: to you.

A long tunnel and beyond it the mist was gone, the clouds were broken. Both girls now stared blankly at the railway embankment on their viewless side of the train. Mum had nodded off and dad, having at last digested every dot of his English paper, kept looking hard at me whenever he thought I wouldn't notice. Please, let him not be one of those harmless nutcases! One of the unimaginative spotters! One of the arch loonies who never forget a face no matter how briefly it has flitted by on their TV screens, no matter how small and out-of-date the picture above the byline. I turned my head and watched the businessman pull a brochure out of his sharp handmade briefcase, its title in English I read with surprise, 'Seminars in Vascular Surgery'. Not a businessman, after all. The thought of those simian fingers daintily repairing a human body was faintly repellent.

Swept along in a flood of Japanese tourists disgorged by the train in Florence, I found myself wondering if there was an affinity between Japan and Italy. There are ostensible similarities: Japanese and Italians both reverence craftsmanship – the density of handmade paper, the perfect gilding of

213

a frame, the silkiness of fine fabrics – both hold the family as a cornerstone of society and sons as their highest blessings; Japan and Italy have each produced an idiosyncratic cuisine: both nations love noodles. Both Japan and Italy are passionately devoted to display. True enough, at first sight their natures could hardly appear more different. Japan is austere and self-sacrificing in a way that makes dangerous soldiers; Italy is flamboyant and life-loving to the point of physical cowardice. Affinity, however, is often at the core of apparent differences: pairs who appear to be utterly unalike – cops and robbers, say, drunks and teetotallers, men and women, saints and sinners – are as two ends of a circle stretched in opposite directions to the same point. The Japanese manage their unusually highly strung feelings by imposing rules of conduct, ritual and etiquette as matters of honour. But the Italians for all their emotional pyrotechnics are not so very artless, either; histrionics too are a way of disabling emotions and making them cool enough to handle and use.

My thoughts were circling east because I was going to spend a night at the home of my dear friend, Kimiko, 'La Japonesa' as she is known in her neighbourhood. For a long time Kimiko, first as a separated wife and recently as a widow, has been living in the hills overlooking Florence; her two children practically grew up there. My friend is a rare expatriate to Tuscany; she has not only learned language and patois, she also maintains complex and textured relationships with her Italian neighbours, a dwindling community of farmers whose rural ways Kimiko sometimes romanticises, never patronises or overrides. Florence is a city best seen from above and there is no vantage ground I prefer to the porch of Kimi's pretty house. Glass of good white wine in hand, I watched the Arno catch and hold the last of the light that was lingering too on the domes and turrets of Florence; they could have been made by men expressly to give the sun its due. While inky Rorschach shapes rose up from the flaring horizon, swelled and shifted and gradually filled the sky, I began to think that a woman could do worse than to grow ancient as a reader of Italian clouds.

'July 1954: We went to a restaurant in the hills outside Florence for dinner. The sun set in an improbable splash of colour and then the sky darkened into star-sprinkled black and the lights came on below us. It was being completely isolated and surrounded by night and stars. I walked off on my own. I couldn't tell where lights began and stars ended or sky stopped and earth started. I walked further than I realised in the dark. But Tony missed me and was worried, and scolded me when I got back. I will never be afraid of being alone. Why fear being alone? Anyway, nobody ever travels alone as long as someone you leave behind is thinking about you.'

But it all depends, dear, upon what they are thinking about you. I, for example, have left you behind and do you think about me? According to you, I should have died fifteen or so years ago; your age group always believes deep down that women should drop dead when they stop being objects of desire. And there is your family, too; yes, they thought of you while you were away. But what were they thinking?

'Our shining hope is just another Mediterranean beach bum,' Mother was going to write to you in the early 1960s at the start of your expatriation.

At the time, I am proud to recall, you were flat broke, in love, and living with a mixed bag of Anglophone old beatniks and ur-hippies on an undiscovered island called Ibiza. It was late afternoon, fishing boats were hurrying home and liver-splotched hounds were barking in the town below. You were all alone, weeping, on a salty, wet rock with the letter in your hand. After a while you began to wonder what in the world your mother thought she knew about Mediterranean beach bums? She was the second generation on her maternal side to be born smack-dab in the middle of America; had she ever been to Europe? Had she ever, even once, travelled all by herself to an unknown destination? Or walked alone by the sea except as a two-week tourist? You looked again at the words 'our shining hope'. You could not recollect then, you do not now, that anyone had ever hinted you were a 'shining hope'. Education in the 1950s was designed as an obstacle course to put girls like us in our place.

'I will not continue speaking', said a celebrated professor of Greek Literature as I crept into one of his lectures at our brother college, Columbia, 'until the woman leaves this hall.'

I looked around. He had to mean me. I was the only woman there.

'Shining hope?' Not so you knew about it, dear girl! Praise was sparse at home to discourage the dreaded affliction of a swelled head, and instruction was pretty much restricted to criticism of all you were not doing right, or doing well enough. Was it the same for your little brother? When we compare notes on our childhood now, he seems to have grown up in a more relaxed and approving family than yours. Even your five uncles got in on the act, warning your father in your hearing that you would never find a husband if you did not fix your nails, your hair, your stuck-up intellectual pretensions. Perhaps you were lucky, after all: familial hopes are like aptitude tests, connected to conventional expectations and resident disappointments; had you known that you were your parents' 'shining hope' you might have felt compelled to settle for an obedient imitation of a life to satisfy them. Instead, there you were, a black sheep on a warm, alien shore, struggling to discover your own hope and to find a way to say, to show, to live to its fair limit all you felt welling up like libido and youth and the surrounding sea in a great swell that snapped the last lines to obedience and conformity, unfurled my sails and set me adrift. It was then, in the moments of a Spanish sunset when time shifts gears and friction is suspended, in those silken moments, you became I, child: I began.

*   *   *

217

'July 1954: Everyone shopping like crazy in Florence. Evelyn and Midge skipped sightseeing today to shop some more: to hell with Botticelli for a bargain and you know what you can do with Da Vinci for a silk scarf and a pair of new shoes! I escaped again and walked by myself down by the banks of the Arno. The banks of the Arno! I had a sort of vision: we are not born to a place but to the whole globe. If I just kept walking, could I see it all? I wish I could see it all! It is so beautiful and full of wonderful things. Michelangelo's figure of twilight is the most beautiful sculpture ever! Golden gates glitter on the church. It is hard to explain. The more I see, the more I want to see. Looking at so many wonderful paintings and sculpture and architecture, I wish I could make something beautiful too. But I can't paint. Maybe there is an art form not yet discovered? That's the one for me! Or maybe we can make a work of art of our own lives?'

You shopped, too, snooty child; you always will. When you are too broke to shop you will acquire pebbles, seashells, broken bits of tile and once, in India, the shed skin of a cobra. There were no emblazoned T-shirts yet in the 1950s, or china mugs, pens, underpants, handbags, mouse pads, stamped boldly with the name of the city to shout on your behalf back home: 'Look everybody, look where I have been! Have you?' Our souvenirs were examples of handicraft in everyday local use. If mementoes carried the names of the cities in which we had bought them, it was on small hidden labels; nevertheless, connoisseurs back home recognized a leather belt so perfectly tooled it had to be Florentine, that glass was Venetian, the plate must come from Delft, of course, and where did you find that amazing perfume? Where but in Grasse, lucky girl! On your first trip to Florence you bought yourself a passport case of pale calfskin. Retired now from active use, it holds in state eight defunct passports. A list of gifts you bought there and their prices are scrawled down the side of a page in your journal: a silk tie for Dad ($5), a comb for Mother ($3), she still wore her long hair in a crown of braids, high and pointed like a Russian head-dress, a wallet for my brother Mook ($4). The scarf ($2) you bought as a gift for Grandma Annie more than half a century ago was black silk stitched with emerald green. I remember that scarf; I see it even now drifting across my mind's eye because it became attached for ever in your mind – more lately mine – to the word gossamer.

And that lovely thing was for a woman you hated. An emotion reciprocated, by the by. When the unhappy old biddy was dying, my brother was at her bedside, and he told me years later that one of the last things she said was 'I never liked your sister'. During summer holidays in the country you used to sit under the catalpa tree outside the kitchen and listen to her whining on and on to your mother, complaining in her flat Midwestern tones about your father: 'that man'. Did she sound off about you, too, when you could not hear? And call you 'that child'? You wondered then, you have to wonder now, if your mother agreed with the old cow about you as she did about your father – that you neglected household chores, that you put on airs, that you were too smart for your own good. So you see, what they think of us, the ones we leave behind, does not always brighten solitude; what they think of us can make our way dense and harsh. As for you, child, whom I have left behind, when I think of you now I wish I could go back and whisper faith and encouragement into your ear. For you, sweetheart, you really were my one and only shining hope; until my son was born, you were my only child.

Once in Florence, no longer hovering over it, the city remains lovely to look at but I find it hard to like. Perhaps I should have queued with the tourists in the morning for a ticket to allow me to queue with the tourists in the afternoon for entrance to the Uffizi Gallery. The Pitti Palace turned out to be a peaceful alternative during an unpredictable lull in its tourist intake. Out of the higgledy-piggledy collection, a puffy and depraved Caravaggio, *Sleeping Cupid*, made my day. I let the lunch hour lapse over a beer in the square of the Uffizi where masses of fully clothed people from all over the world were chastely ogling the most famous naked man since creation. Later, I walked the backstreets and noticed how many of the ancient brass bell pulls are engraved with brand-new German names. Here and there were wisps of the sounds and smells of my first trip to Florence when artisans now dead or very, very old worked in shadowy, cluttered shops carving and painting and restoring objects of classical purity and innate beauty: objects, indeed, of virtue. I bought something for myself this time too, of course, a waistcoat of Florentine silk strands cleverly knotted in a traditional local manner.

'People do not want these things any more,' said the ageing proprietress of the cubbyhole shop as she gazed sorrowfully out of the window at the passing horde in tracksuits and trainers made in China.

As men of Milan swagger, so men of Florence scoot. Armed with an imaginary fly swatter, I muttered 'Splat you!' every time another devilish *motorino* shattered any struggling affection for the city. Happily, unlike many Latin cities Florence has not only public squares, but also a vast and leafy park, the Boboli Gardens, where it is possible to escape the most alarming street noise known in time of peace. Absorbent leaves let fall a memory of when I passed through Florence with my son seventeen years earlier, two months before his thirteenth birthday. We were returning by rail and bus from a ramble through Greece and Italy. And it was in this very park he and I had our first monumental quarrel. He broke away from me and ran into the crowd around the big fountain where we had been sitting peacefully on a bench until a moment before. He disappeared from sight. He spoke no Italian. He had no money. I ran after him through endless green corridors and terraces. Strangers turned when I called his name. I looked down, surprised to see that I was wringing

my hands. What had we quarrelled about? Nothing. Everything. We quarrelled because a few days earlier he had started
to become a man.

We had spent the previous weekend on a beach in Sorrento
before heading north to Florence.

'I want to do that,' my son said, pointing to a paraglider
so high above the beach he could have been a distant gull.

The driver of the speedboat towing the parachute was
flirting with a girl in the seat next to him and absolutely
inattentive to the figure high above.

'I want to do that,' said my son.

Men in my family did not trust their lives to such contrap-
tions; their women did not permit it. I came from cautious
stock.

'OK,' I was horrified to hear myself saying. Where had it
come from? What rogue gene sent that 'OK'?

'You'll let me?' my son said, amazed.

We both watched the paraglider dropping like a spider on
a strand of silk towards the unfriendly ocean where the best
he could hope to be was bait.

'Do you really want to? Are you sure?'

'Yes,' said my boy. He swallowed hard. 'Yes.'

The congenitally flirtatious driver received only monosyl-
lables for his pains. Two lives – not just my son's, my own
life too – were suspended over his oily macho head as we
zoomed back and forth out at sea. Every string of my beating
heart was attached to that faraway billow of silk from which

dangled the little doll that was my baby. On shore and earth at last, breathing normally again and in one piece, my son's eyes were radiant with achievement and joy, and with something else, too. A girl's coming of age is up to Mother Nature who marks it clearly on the sheet. A boy, however, whether by tradition or something much, much older, has to pass through fire and fear and be received by his fellows, in my son's case the Italian beach merchants and lifeguards who were even now laughing and ruffling his hair as they undid the harness to the parachute. When he turned from them and looked at me, there was a difference in us both: he had become a young man, and I, his mother? I was one of the women.

I have tried from the day Marc was born, the most beautiful day in October, to allow him to become and to be. Probably, I have tried too hard not to criticise or interfere. He is my respected son; he is not my creature, not a projection of my will or my judgements or my fantasy; he is not my hope, though I hope with my very soul that he loves his life as much as I love him. Nevertheless, the quarrel in the Boboli, whatever it seemed to be about, was because for one aching, weak moment I had wanted my little boy back again. But he was gone for keeps. Instead, I found the young man waiting for me on the very bench by the fountain where we had parted in anger. I sat next to him, put my arm round his shoulders and refrained from kissing him. We stayed like that quietly for a while, then strolled off; he was tall enough, already almost my own height, so we could walk arm in arm to a café for two bowls of strawberries with cream.

'3 August 1954: We were scheduled to stop in Siena but we got a flat. While the men changed the tyre I wandered through fields. We went straight through Siena, squeezing through the narrow streets. I really am sorry. From what we saw, it looked lovely. Tony said we missed something special, but it would give us all a reason to come back some day. I do not need a reason. I will come back.'

And so you did. The train out of Florence was a mere six minutes late, a snip on the Italian timetable, not worthy of announcement such as the one broadcast in several languages for the train to Rome: 'The local train, second class only, due to leave at 10.45 for Rome on track number five instead of six is forty-five minutes late instead of thirty and will leave on track number seven instead of six.' Our approach to Siena was through golden fields tilled and cultivated for generations into a landscape fit for battle and ambuscade. Cypress trees added their distinction to the countryside, and clumps of green bamboo bubbled beside the tracks. The schoolboy across from me reached into his backpack for a digital camera that fitted into the palm of his hand, and a mini-disc player the size of a cigarette pack. These perfect little works of man were in sharp contrast to the dilapidated buildings outside our windows; were it not for the ubiquitous laden clothes line, most of them would have been taken for derelict. An unusual number of young women were on board, travelling two by two to work or shop. They were animated and vivacious, hair and eyebrows here and there unruly, noses unpretentious; the girls possessed a variety of body shapes, of skin tones and hair colour, and large expressive eyes. Italian women by and large are mavericks, distinctive thanks to their variety; they are the great beauties of continental Europe and have somehow escaped globalised prettiness that would have all women as one young, fleshless woman standing between two mirrors.

Siena's small train station was buzzing in several languages with rumours of an imminent rail strike. Those tourists who spoke Italian, a smaller proportion it seemed to me than speak French or English or even German as a second language, relayed to the others information gleaned from the laconic old fellow behind the information desk before he suddenly and arbitrarily pulled the 'Closed' sign down in front of his window and disappeared.

'So, what is the upshot?' cried an irritable German in English.

'What's going on?' a young Australian backpacker asked a French couple with a baby.

'Do you know what's happening?' the Frenchwoman asked me.

'What did he say?' I asked a bearded young Englishman closest to the window. 'Is there going to be a strike tomorrow?'

'If I understood the old man correctly,' replied the English-man, 'the answer is: "Maybe".'

In Florence young men of fashion that season were dying their hair yellow; in Milan they swaggered; in Siena I noticed through the window of the bus from the station the men about town tend to a slouching pose, hands in pockets of jeans, keeping tabs on their crotches. From the same window I spotted a small, nondescript hotel that looked right for me. Was I just lucky in my glancing encounters with the women of Siena? Everywhere, the Sienese women were bright and friendly, and I often heard the cunning laughter attached to the wit of the harem. When I asked the girl behind the desk if she knew about a rail strike scheduled for the following day, she immediately telephoned a friend who worked at the station.

'My friend says not to worry,' I was told, after a long animated telephone discussion.

'Oh, thank goodness. No strike, then.'

'She didn't say about a strike. She just said why worry?'

The glass wall between the sexes in Siena, the philosophical humour of the women, a purported lack of street crime and a quality of self-containment, of permanence almost: the very spirit and tempo of Siena derive from an annual sporting event, a horse race known as the Palio, that is led in by days of celebration and marching bands and gorgeous page-antry in the main square. The Palio takes place twice a year in the summer, purportedly to honour the Virgin and commemorate her miracles, and it involves the entire populace as well as innumerable camera-laden tourists from all over Italy and the rest of the world; it is broadcast too, these days, on national television. Everyone I asked was coy about the Palio's origins; I suspect it is not quite as old as the medieval costumes that attend it or the sublime Gothic architecture of its surroundings. Nevertheless, the Palio has a hold on the hearts of Sienese men as strong and enduring as an ancient religion; when they are not actually presenting the event, they are constantly rehearsing its music, its formations, and all its rituals.

'Siena has the atmosphere of a university town,' I commented to a young woman from whom I was buying yet another roll of film.

'We have a university,' she said. 'But foreign students complain they cannot study because of the noise of the drums all night long, rehearsing for the Palio.'

Although the Palio is a competition among the seventeen districts of the city – the Noble Eagle District, for example, the Snail District, and my favourite, the Noble Caterpillar District – the women I spoke to in the town assured me that little unscripted violence accompanies the annual event, almost every iota of testosterone being reserved for the explosion of pomp and procession and intramural competition. Were a sociologically inclined researcher to collate the dates of local conceptions my guess is an inordinate number of Sienese would be found to begin their miraculous trek into

227

life late in the night of 2 July or 16 August of any given year.

I am sorry you missed Siena first time round, dear heart, you would have loved it. It is a fine place, light on motor traffic in the old section and full of accessible delights; among them one of my favourite works of art in Italy showing the lonely triumphant passage of General Guidoriccio da Fogliano by Simone Martini. I always smile to see again even on a glove box or a fridge magnet that chinless profile and the huge galumphing horse every bit as magnificently caparisoned as its master, and infinitely more handsome. It took some time to find the gallery where the General is kept, thanks to Latin courtesy that would rather misdirect a confused tourist than disappoint her. My enjoyable quest took me as far as the municipal cemetery outside the city gates, on the edge of enticing countryside. Even though it was not Sunday or a holy day, old women in black swarmed silently among the graves, distributing flowers. As soon as they saw me noticing the way they tended their dead, they turned their backs protectively just as younger Italian women do when I flirt with their children.

I headed off early in the morning for the first train to Rome. Very early. Too early. Nobody told me clocks had been set back one hour at midnight. Not everyone knew. The girl at the hotel desk, for example, bade me a cheerful farewell though it was, in fact, a few minutes past five, not six as the clock on the wall was telling us spitefully, and she was not due on duty for almost an hour. At the train station, however, time became relative to motion: there was plenty of the first, practically none of the second. Platforms were desolate; silent rails dwindled in both directions. Oh yes, a strike was under way.

'But why do you want a window seat?' asked the girl at the emergency office set up at the train station to sell bus tickets. 'There is nothing to see, only autostrada.'

With hours in hand, I went to absorb a few coffees and whatever conversation was going at the counter of the station café. The waitress was a French Moroccan whose bounding energy would have made her too big for the narrow space behind the counter even had she not been wide in the hips. Obviously a favourite with the male counterman, he smiled at her and made unnecessary trips to the kitchen for an excuse to rub against her while the middle-aged woman behind the till watched them grumpily.

'I have two boyfriends, one of them is Italian,' the girl told me. 'I liked him a lot. But he just said to me last night we cannot ever get serious. He dumped me, in other words,' she said with a delighted laugh, as if being dumped were the next best thing to being tickled pink. 'Because he said that he cannot introduce me to his family.'

'Is he a racist?'

'No. No. It is not racism here. Italians are not racists, not like the French. In Italy,' she said, 'it is not racism; it is a matter of pride.'

Girlfriend as accessory is what I understood her to be telling me, a labelled bag to be carried on the arm: in matriarchal families given to display, boys would be boys, but as soon as it came to taking a wife, a girl from beyond the pale lacked the credence of an old in-house brand.

'1954: The morning was spent on the road to Rome. I could travel this road for ever! The countryside is lovely. If I had this to look at every day, I too would be a saint.'

It was good to be on a bus again. I felt closer to you, the old young me. A bus is a more intimate capsule than a train; it has a visible chauffeur and there is no constant passage of strangers in the central aisle. It was good to be free of the suitcase, too, know it was safe in the hold and not going anyplace without me. Across the aisle a woman pulled closed her curtains. Someone always does. At least we were not being overlooked by a big, blind mechanical eye like the one on a bus I took last year to Vera Cruz. As soon as we'd pulled away from the brouhaha of Mexico City every curtain on board was immediately drawn, the man behind me leaned over and drew mine too, as if in terror of the sere and ancient Mexican landscape that sings straight to the heart as no other I have seen. As soon as all the windows on board were darkened, everyone could watch a Latin-American soap opera that sprang into life on the television set suspended behind the driver.

230

'My heart is breaking! He loves me no longer!' cried the heroine, while on the other side of the curtains a volcano as old as the hills was puffing lazy rings into the sky.

Once out of Siena, the land was striated with dark-red bands of old corn; the bare fields were of precisely the same rich umber as the farmhouses. I wondered if the stands of cypresses at their back doors served, or ever had, the cloacal purpose of cacti around the peasant houses of Mexico. About an hour beyond the city the countryside becomes wilder, more overgrown. Hill towns appear here and there suspended over rivers running green and fringed with hollyhocks of the feral pink that butterflies prefer. The nature of local traffic begins to switch into the Roman style, which means that even in relatively open spaces every vehicle seeks another ahead to tailgate. When a mobile telephone at the back of the bus rang a mad tune, and a woman's voice said '*Pronto*', I recollected wandering into an extraordinary exhibition of illustrated manuscripts at the Libreria Piccolomini the previous afternoon in Siena where I overheard two middle-aged Parisian women complain bitterly to each other that the Italians no longer speak French. 'English, all English! Twenty years ago all Italians spoke French.'

Not so the woman on the telephone; her '*Pronto*' had transmogrified into rapid Russian.

We passed a company selling swimming pools. Farmhouses began to look less shaggy, more like trim fortresses, second homes for the people of the city. Great Caesar's ghost!

231

Was that actually an ostrich farm? The poor exotic captives walked in a line, their pinheads turned towards the capital while chicks as big as Christmas turkeys scampered away from the noise of our engine.

'August 1954: As we approach Rome ancient ruins spring up more prominently. Rome! I am actually going to Rome! *Arma virumque cano* . . . All roads . . .'

Yes, dear, we know: they all lead to Rome. But do you really think it is proper or right for a virgin on that road to sing of arms and the man?

Thirteen

'August 1954: Rome! Too much! Far too much to condense here! Another opera! This time it was *Rigoletto*! In the ruins of the ancient amphitheatre. The voices were rich and mellow! And the atmosphere was . . . my goodness! Fun! Not as pompous and overdressed as the Met. Afterwards, we were caught up in the crowd. A bunch of boys surrounded Midge and Evelyn and me and serenaded us. What fun! Nobody could be lonely or sad in this fascinating city. We spent the next day wandering through the Colosseum. I will not forget it. Being face to face, heel to toe, shoulder to shoulder with antiquity is an infinite thing. I was so glad that I had studied Latin. Thank you, Mrs Kryzak, for keeping us kids at it! Tony said Rome shows the futility of power and the folly of all things we cherish. But I don't think so. I think Rome shows that things endure and carry forward something of the men who made them. They were here! They were really here. You can feel them. You can touch stones they touched. In the Forum we saw where coins had melted into the ground by fires, our guide said, when the barbarians finally overran the city. You can hear them: "Bar-bar-bar . . ." We partied with Tony and his friend last night. Just Midge and Evelyn and I, and white wine. Midge said she was surprised Evelyn did not speak better Italian. That was a bad thing to say in front of Tony. Evelyn got very annoyed: "I'm as American as you!" Tony had to calm them down. Midge sat next to me on the bus today and asked if I would share her room at our next stop. She says Ev is getting on her nerves. The trouble is, Ev asked the same thing. She says she's tired of Midge knowing it all. Damn. Damn. Some day I will come back to this city. Alone. Or with someone I love. I would like to live here when I am old. Feelings are beautiful. In Rome you feel more and think less.'

I am glad too that you studied Latin and made stabs at the *Aeneid*. Fifty years later hardly enough of the language remains in the net between your ears to translate the chiselled graffiti of ancient Rome; however, parsing its sentences and struggling with its masters gave enduring insights into the logic and structure, into the very philosophy of language. You, dear enthusiast, you will never be old enough for Rome. And Italy is no country for the young. Immature music and fashions, juvenile demands and puerile lusts do not even now flood Italian high streets quite as they do all others and control its markets. Youth's so-called culture is less palpable in Italy than elsewhere in the Western world, except perhaps in Salt Lake City and similarly fundamentalist American backwaters. Especially Rome remains in many ways Europe's leaky old bastion of commandments and faith. By the way, girl who used to be I, do not fall into the trap that was avant-garde in your time – old hat now – of placing 'feminine' feelings higher than 'masculine' thoughts. Feelings are corruptible too and more corrupting than thought. Only think how many crimes, crude and subtle, are committed every day in the name of love. Friendships too, intense and powerful as they can be between women, deliver gratuitous pain. The squabbles of Ev and Midge are nothing compared with the rough judgements and true grief that will be visited upon you in years to come when sisterly attachments turn sour. Like most expatriates, you made a family of your friends and some of your women friends, sooner or later, were bound to display the acrid, envious sisterly vices. Only now you are old do friendships with your own sex run smoothly, now you are hors de combat, as it were. Do not grin at the pun. Unintended?

Can you believe that when you are I and we are old we will find ourselves disenchanted with Rome? The ancient stones had lost the power you felt humming off them, hedged in and fenced off as they are these days to protect them from modern vandals and the river of tourists flowing and breaking around them. Within moments at the sidewalk restaurant where I took my first meal the city showed itself to be brusque and bad-mannered. Italian restaurants are in general male

235

provinces. Contrary to waiters in other continental countries, increasingly even in France, who are almost always new immigrants, the men – for it remains mostly men – who wait on table in Italy are locals and they form a fraternity, closed and reactionary, similar to the brotherhood of taxi drivers in London or cops in New York, and every bit as venal. In Italy a woman with the temerity to enter a restaurant on her own can expect to be hidden with contempt at a table near the toilets. Partly, yes, she is scorned because a solitary female in man's country is obviously undesirable or past it, pathetic, a failure of her sex. But there is also a lot less to it than that. I have waited on table in my time, and I know that a waiter of experience can see the minute I walk in the place that I'm a real small spender, one dish maximum and one, maybe two, glasses of wine. Furthermore, I am bound to occupy a two-seater table and thus halve the expected tip for that station. Fortunately for me, waiters all over Italy undertake stints in the restaurants of Soho in London to perfect their English and when I managed to make it known – twice in Venice, once in Milan – not only that I live in London, but specifically in Soho, I benefited from their gratitude to the Bar Italia, a block from my home, where a wall-sized TV screen broadcasts the Italian football matches day and night.

In Rome, however, I had no luck. The waiter greeted me with a snarl, cared nothing about my provenance and snatched the menu out of my hand when an American couple turned up for an early dinner. After that, the sunset I had been looking forward to seemed heavy on rude orange tones before it sank finally into pretentious imperial purple. Admittedly, the bad mood I found myself in was partly my own fault; my taste for contrasting literature had gone too far: to take Dostoevsky along as a reading companion to Italy was like taking a brain surgeon to a seance. The Russian genius is all wrong for that place: too morbid, too analytical and at odds with Italy's sloppy allure.

I looked up from my overpriced pasta and my page in *The Double*. Another woman had entered the café alone; she sat with her back to me. She put a pack of Marlboros on the table and I heard her order a pint of beer in English. The contempt of the waiter meant less than nothing to her; her own greater contempt neutralised his. She took an English newspaper out of her big handbag and started to read with ostentatious concentration and the occasional head-tossing of one already in the know: one who knew the score. She knew it all. I wanted her to turn round so I could see her face; at the same time I dreaded that she would. I knew something, too. I knew her. Oh yes, I knew her. The stiff back, the reddish hair, now dyed, worn shoulder-length to hide a thick neck, the conflicting messages her posture sent out – 'look, look how fascinating I am!' and 'peasant, how dare you look at me!' – belonged unmistakably to a friend of my early years in London, a good companion and amusing colleague who in one ugly convulsion of her soul became an enemy. Oh yes, I know her. She is vain, self-dramatising and vindictive. I thought I had been catching glimpses of her all day: at the Forum, at the Colosseum, at the Trevi Fountain where neither of us threw in a coin. To have an enemy is to have no rest or freedom as long as you both shall live. Why had fate sent the bitch to Rome now, and to this very restaurant?

I can take no pride in her hatred of me either, because her hatred is rank and common. Sooner or later she hates everyone. I have not seen her in ten years; others tell me the arrogance and scorn that once animated her beauty has begun to rot and shrivel it. She turns to signal the waiter and I see her face, frowning and imperious. But it is not my enemy's face; it is not a face I know; it is the face of someone else's enemy. I scribble a note instructing myself never, never again to read Dostoevsky on the road.

Returning in the sudden dusk to the little family-run hotel recommended by a well-travelled friend of Kimiko, I turned a sharp corner and collided with a young man coming the other way. He was casually dressed and carrying a large McDonald's container of Coca-Cola. Tall, broad-shouldered and muscular, his dark eyes were of the canine variety many girls raised on black-and-white movies grew up to consider sexy; they met mine with a little explosion of interest, and slid down to where small things were surprised to be remembered. Once more those lapdoggy eyes looked straight into my own; all this happened, of course, in a split second. While holding my gaze seductively, he slowly and deliberately tipped ice and Coca-Cola down the front of my pullover. When I jumped back, he sang out '*Scuuuuusi, signora! Scuuuuusi . . .*' in a way that would have thrilled Midge and Evelyn and me in the old days when we went out scoring vowel sounds from the young men of Rome: '*preeeeego*', '*beeellaaaa*', '*scuuusi*'.

Only later at the hotel, while I was peeling off my sodden clothes, did I realise I had been the victim of an attempted street robbery. The old man behind the hotel desk, the boss himself, had warned me that very morning to watch my bag. Thanks to him and the anecdotal evidence of innumerable travellers to Rome I had shortened its straps so it was tucked tight under my arm thus, the accomplice of the Coke fiend, who had certainly been in place behind me, was unable to dip it while I was distracted. So much for the weird sexual ploy my overheated imagination suspected at the time. Damn. To this day I would rather be used even unwittingly for ill-gotten pleasure than ill-gotten gain.

'August 1954: Racing along the Appian Way. Bumpy, eh? The Appian Way! The handsome Italian policemen in dazzling white suits must have trained with Nijinsky to learn such balletic movements. Fountains sing everywhere. A group of nuns sitting at the side of one fountain were singing, too. I bought a rosary as a gift for Anne Burke and stood in a crowd of pilgrims. How Chaucerian! And I held up the rosary so it could be blessed by the Pope. He stood on a balcony high above the crowd. He was all in white, a little china figure. His voice was warm and gentle. Perhaps the voice of a saint?'

Anne was my age, the oldest of the four Burke children, three of them girls, and playmates of childhood summers at our house on the lake. On our paternal sides at least, the Burke kids were as close to the sod of Ireland as my brother and I to the shtetls of Eastern Europe. Anne and I sometimes engaged in babyish theological conversations and she often innocently admitted her astonishment to find herself friendly with someone descended from the killers of Christ.

'Anne, Christ was also a Jew!' I cried the first time this happened, but won no argument, only a sweet, pitying smile, marginally less wounding than the snowballs hurled at 'dirty Jews' when there was no harder target on the street where we lived in Jersey City. As I raised Anne's rosary to the distant figure of Pius XII, I was not praying, not even hoping; I was, however, daring an epiphany, coaxing it, challenging even just a wee little surprise to leap out at the crowd of pilgrims and make itself known. Not long after I gave Anne the blessed rosary, she became a nun. But there was not the least surprise in that. One of the Burkes was bound to take holy orders and Anne had always been the most pious and docile.

I have been through Rome a few times in the past few decades; never before had it appeared so clearly to be a single-industry town. Garbed clerics, many of them African and

Asian, were everywhere in groups more numerous on the approach to the Vatican, base of their corporate religion and head office of a highly successful globalised faith. They walked slowly, made no eye contact with the rest of us in the street and appeared almost to be floating a foot above the ground. The Pope was not in evidence at St Peter's; there was, however, a serious armed police presence, trained for bullets in these days of new terror, dear child, and not for ballets. Tourists and pilgrims filled the precinct, inching, milling, forming and reforming queues. I nearly stumbled over the small, dark American woman in front of me when she suddenly fell to her knees for prayer, crossed herself, then rose and took three flash photos of the effigy of Jean Paul XXIII. In one of the gift shops I bought a small dispensation for ironical tendencies: a fridge magnet of the current Pope. The sales clerk was a nun of about my own age; as I paid her there passed between us a quick, fierce, silent exchange of curiosity and distaste.

More or less dragooned into a queue, I shuffled along between a couple of German youngsters who were necking erratically and a noisy bunch of Swedish teenagers, one of them flicking cigarette ashes on the marble floor. By the time I realised we were waiting to see the cupola, not the Sistine Chapel, it was too late to turn back. Eschewing the lift for the infirm and aged meant walking up, up, up the staircase heavenward that at one point narrowed under a ceiling so cruelly sloped it forced us practically to hands and knees.

Finally, I burst through into sunlight, well ahead of the Swedes, and the Germans too who had folded up in each other's arms about halfway through the ascent. There at the crown of St Peter behind the gigantic statues of the apostles, I found a Roman memory. You left it for me, young I – I that I used to be who used to be I. In the shadow of those towering backs barely sculpted, dazzling white and monolithic against the scurry of clouds and facing out over the remains of earth's greatest city, I remembered being you in just that place fifty years before; I felt your delight, your pure untested strength. And for a moment I felt the wonder and thrill of beginning.

'August 1954: Midge and Ev are friends again, kind of. It's a little edgy. After the Vatican, the three of us sneaked away for a glass of white wine and sitting there in a café on a side street a funny thing happened: all of a sudden I really caught Rome's tempo. I began to love the place even more than I had before. Yes, I could live here when I am old.'

And so will history repeat itself in Rome. For on the way from St Peter's to the Forum, a funny thing happened. I started to catch the tempo, and dangerous it is, too. Walking around Rome is a death-defying sport. Stoplights count for nothing, pedestrian crossings are as doodles in the sand, and he who would cross the mad streets with impunity must conduct himself as a torero pitted against onrushing fury. At one hairy junction, in a spasm of terror I grabbed the arm of the stranger next to me, a local woman who hurled us across the boulevard with incomparable bravado. On the opposite bank she freed herself from my grip and left without a word. I needed a glass of white wine. I chose the terrace of a café on a side street near a fountain of no particular fame. At the table next to mine was a big middle-aged American woman, handsome as a horse, wearing a few pieces of expensive, self-consciously arty jewellery and a voluminous hand-printed caftan; she was obviously at home in Rome. A much younger Italian woman shared her table and listened with overdone, flattering attention to her companion's flood of Bostonian English. '. . . and it's all so vulgar. Nobody wants short stories any more,' I overheard the American complain, and immediately there opened before me a glimpse into one of the expatriate types of Rome: self-deluded or exiled writers and pseuds, old and rancorous, and with money.

At a large table nearby were four women, gossiping. The only man among them tried and failed several times to get a word past the machine-gun rapidity of his companions' exchange. The single sound he finally added to the uproarious fusillade was '*Ciao*' when he and his wife rose to leave. Thus spins the macho coin and falls regularly, too, on the side stamped with the head of the mother.

Around and around the fountain strolled a number of heavily made-up women in tight skirts. A lone man, not young, shabbily dressed and graceless, canvassed the square and stopped to talk confidentially to the lounging men and to each male newcomer, while gesticulating towards the circling women. Sex, of course: just about the only thing humans do out of uniform between birth and death. And it was at that moment, over my glass of Orvieto white wine, I started really to like the place, almost to love it as much as you had in 1954.

'It took me eleven years,' said my young waiter. He had the keen, dark face of a revolutionary or a Romantic poet. He had been raised in France and was brought by his parents as an adolescent to Rome. 'At first Rome is . . .'

'Curt,' we agreed was the word.

'It waits', he said, 'to make the . . .'

'Touch?'

He nodded. 'And the day comes one finds one has begun to like Rome. Or . . .', he added thoughtfully, 'I guess you could also hate it beyond measure.'

My long ramble took me into a tunnel with a narrow pavement for pedestrians. A taxi passed, threading through traffic at full throttle; the driver was leaning on his horn and holding a white handkerchief out of his open window so it streamed as a visible siren. At the other end of the stinking tube was a different city, more old than antique, juicier and seedier than the high tourist areas; there were street markets, neighbourhood cafés, sex shops and useful boutiques. My eyes were streaming from the tunnel's fumes, and I entered a small church at random to rest. Behind the simple grey façade was a scene of ebullient reverence; cherubs of tarnished gold tumbled everywhere under a painted ceiling that had cost as much sweat proportionate to the artist's gifts as the one in the Sistine Chapel. The only other person in the cool, spiced space was a well-dressed man in his fifties who knelt beside an effigy, probably of the patron saint, laid out in a coffin. Seeing him at prayer, I remembered how I used to envy the Burke kids their kneeling and crossing and confessing and medals and rosaries that seemed not only to add glamour to ordinary life, but also to relieve it of immense burdens, though just what those burdens were I could not then have said. I watched the man press his lips to the waxen mouth of the simulacrum. The burden of solitude was one, I thought, and the burden of death, and the burden of incessant choices.

'. . . I was happy as never before in my life. As though I had suddenly found myself in Italy – so strong was the impact of nature upon me . . .' Dostoevsky's words from *White Nights* drifted into my mind at four o'clock on my final Roman morning when I was awakened by snores from a neighbouring room, and again at five by a rogue mosquito, and finally at six by someone else's alarm call. Bleary from the pre-dawn impacts of Italian nature, I trailed downstairs for breakfast. The aged proprietor was on the telephone under a handwritten note that told us guests the swipe machine for credit cards was out of order and only cash could be accepted

245

in settlement of bills. The sign had been there since my arrival and I had asked several times in the preceding days whether repair was under way, for I did not relish the idea of walking even two blocks in Rome carrying a bundle of cash. Each time I'd asked, he shrugged: 'Who knows?' and said with perverse pride, 'This is Italy.'

Two elderly English couples were already installed in the breakfast room. We exchanged 'Mornings' and settled into our separate English silences. I had just buttered a fragrant roll when the air was ripped by a scream of rage from the desk. We could not see the old man, but we heard him. We, who spoke a language that expresses anger mainly in spitting consonants, were astounded by the enraged vowels that flowed around us like lava in a searing wave, then dropped into a rumble, and rose again and again and again into a swelling torrent of every possible variant of 'e' and 'a', breaking here and there on a short sharp 'uuooo' like the yip of a bad dog. For a full ten minutes we listened, jaws dropped, coffee cooling. And when the old man finally appeared, flushed and triumphant, at the door we rose as one to applaud his performance.

The second lap of my journey, and yours, was ending. It was time to return to London or to London's synonym in my inner vocabulary for more than thirty years: to real life. Work, bills, esteemed and beloved son, tea not made with tea bags, weekly transatlantic calls to Mother, dentist's appointment, theatre tickets, encounters in the street with first-name acquaintances: real life. Only a few hours left, enough for a visit to the Capitoline Museum before I caught the overnight train to Zurich, then to the French coast and finally on to England: home. As I was passing the desk I paused to ask the old man, 'The credit card swiping machine? It will be fixed today, I hope?'

He looked puzzled and it dawned on me his earlier histrionics had not, after all, been undertaken to chivvy the repairmen, as I assumed at the time. The next moment his silky smile as good as told me that the swipe machine was not really out of order; it never had been. I slapped my metaphorical forehead: of course! The euro was due very soon to replace lire at who knew what loss to tradesmen? And besides, cash warms hands and pockets, and can escape the taxman too, as plastic never will.

'I understand,' I said. 'I will stop at a hole in the wall and bring you cash for my bill.'

His smile now was beatific; I had caught on at last. 'There will be a small discount,' he said, 'there always is, for cash.'

Uproar in the Rome train station defied sanity. But I had begun to take with equanimity queues that queued for other queues that ended nowhere. With two hours in hand before the train, I went outside to watch a final Roman sunset. The sky was alive with starlings; they flew together making funnels and cones and perfect formations for which there are no names on earth; then they rested for a moment like a hundred

247

thousand musical notes on a clef before soaring off again into another display of evanescent geometry. Commuters and panhandlers had stopped in their tracks to watch and wonder too, perhaps, with me if the ancestors of these Roman birds performed for the Caesars and for Cleopatra when she paid her fatal visit to their city.

'Red or white?' impatiently demanded the girl behind the station bar when I asked if they served wine by the glass.

'Blue,' I said.

She hesitated and then we shared my last Roman laugh.

Fourteen

Strange beauty, a romantic tradition, unforeseen encounters: travelling overnight on a continental train continues to have the ingredients glamour requires, even a whiff of brimstone. And admittedly, whiffs a hell of a lot more earthy too assault the traveller in crowded compartments of couchettes. I used couchettes all the time in my salad days; I would rather not, now I am old and grand – a certain amount of grandeur commonly accrues to age – not unless wagons-lits are fully booked, as they were pretty much throughout Europe after September the eleventh. Fear of flying is probably roughly proportionate to self-importance of the kind that I guess must chronically affect bankers and the sort of Roman business-people in a hurry to get to Zurich; they left not one wagon-lit berth free on my train out of Rome. Fortunately, the elderly attendant had a solid Italian sense of propriety; he hurried me into a compartment of six couchettes with but one other occupant, a pretty woman in her early twenties for whom a duenna was wanted.

'Lock the door,' he said and hurried off to stow away – far, far away from her youthful pulchritude – all lecherous male passengers in smelly socks.

My companion's name was Ayalla, she was from Brazil, and of Italian ancestry. Half a lifetime ago I was given a free ticket to her homeland so I could write about it. The Brazilian airline that invited me went belly up the day before I was due to leave London. Disappointing, yet preferable to being stranded flat broke (as usual) had they declared bankruptcy the day after I'd arrived in Rio. Or perhaps not. Perhaps I would have made a Brazilian life of bliss and achievement. Who knows? Who ever knows? I am too old for Brazil now. And Ayalla was too young for Italy. She had been travelling there for several weeks, and she said that in her opinion the young Italians she'd met were swinging back to the family and traditional values. But the Italian social pendulum is ponderous, I think, and she had not yet seen any other country in Europe.

'That's not a swing, Ayalla, it's a twitch. And it is not towards tradition but away from it. Italian youth is just putting itself in line with the rest of the swinging West, only forty years later and much, much more cautiously.'

While Ayalla slept soundly, I woke from time to time to the ghosts of a daytime world outside our window. Near Florence I opened my eyes to see a magnificent chandelier; unlit so late, it glittered in moonlight where it hung suspended over the living room of a run-down flat near the tracks. Close to the Swiss border a cross and steeple were silhouetted against the stars and hardly taller than an old pine, yet what unimaginable devotion it had required to build a church stone by stone atop a needle peak. Devotion, too, from parishioners in the town below who aspired to its services. Soon another fat pink dawn arose, sucking its thumb behind the mountains. Lights in waking houses were Swiss silver instead of Italian gold, and the motion of the train had shifted in the night, so a body's liquids sloshed heel to toe, no longer side to side. Drifts of pristine snow reminded me of childhood and multiplied the thrill of being homeward bound, as if I were heading for every place I had ever called home: our house on the lake, Manhattan, Paris, the sloop *Stormsvalla*, and at last, London.

In London the next day were waiting messages to tell me one dear friend had suffered a serious heart attack, another had not beaten his cancer after all. The washing machine had broken down. Expected cheques had not arrived. It was the tail end of another year. And nobody had missed me. But there was a box of clean white paper on my desk. The window boxes had survived an early frost. My son was keen, smart, balanced and happy with a stunning new girlfriend. Hopes grow fewer and desires contract with age; what remained of mine, however, were still and for a little longer bright as new-minted coins.

'Dear ones, this trip is the most wonderful thing that I have ever done,' I found on a card sent to my family from

IRMA KURTZ

Rome, 1954. 'I want it to go on and on and on! I want it never to end! I want something new to see every day, and every day something more beautiful. Only I am feeling anxious about all of you, having heard nothing in so long. Is Jersey City still there? I love you. If it weren't for you, I wouldn't give a damn. I love you. I really do love you.'

Do I not detect a note of protestation, young lady? 'I love you' needs to be said only once in a letter or conversation, you know, only the first time; said more it means less about itself and begins to intend apology. And 'I love you' said a thousand times too late cannot make up for an early failure to say it once. I am not suggesting you did not love your parents and little brother, child, or for that matter did not care about your homeland. However, looking back at you – and me – I see that a new love was growing in your young heart and I think you were starting to feel its incompatibility with the old.

'1954: When Tony called us all on to the bus today so we could hit the road, eventually to Genoa, I had a sudden urge to run away and take to the sunny road all by myself. Eat berries and fruit off the trees, sleep in barns, maybe rent a room in Rome or Venice and . . . what? Teach English, I guess. English is all I have to sell.'

The sunny road is no longer the one I prefer, certainly not for travel in continental Europe where warm weather brings out swarms of schoolchildren and the timorous old tourists, too, who move in a solid bellowing herd from site to sight. I leave summer to you, nubile child; winter is my season now. I chose to start out on the last lap of my journey – our journey – one frosty dawn a few days into another new year. The paunchy elderly man behind me on the train to Dover talked interminably in clinical detail about the breakdown of his car while his wife, who was wearing a little too much make-up and Dame Edna spectacles, complained that carless, they would not now be able to bring back the anticipated amount of cigarettes and alcohol from their outing. Such day trippers are known in the cross-Channel trade as 'French flyers'.

'Sorry, Sir,' I overheard an attendant on board the ferry tell him when I happened to find myself sitting near him and his wife later. 'I'm afraid you'll have to get off at Calais even if you are a French flyer . . .'

Poor chap. Instead of plundering the ship's shop *aller–retour* for cheap fags and booze, and returning straight home to put his feet up, he was going actually to have to disembark in Frogland along with all the other boomerangs from Kent. What if he were compelled to eat some of that French muck! What do they call it? 'Queasy-een'?

'I don't wanna get off the ferry,' he said to his wife.

'You hafta . . .'

'Don't wanna . . .'

'Maybe we'll have time to go to the shops before the next sailing . . .'

253

'Yeah,' he said, sounding a little mollified. 'Get in some more fags . . .'

The ferry to Ostende was out of service. After more than an hour of hanging around the glorified shopping mall that serves as a port in Dover, we passengers bound for Belgium had finally been shipped out to Calais where a bus was laid on to carry us to Belgium across a landscape devoted to factories and industry. Piped music played on board. The passengers, day trippers except for me, permuted dirty jokes about driving on the wrong side of the road; a girl behind me kept shrilling, 'Fuck! I'm gonna wet myself!' I let myself drift away into memories. There was a day on the Channel about forty years ago aboard the single-mast beauty, *Stormsvalla*. We had been moored in Cowes for some time, outfitting the craft for a foolhardy and dangerous assault on the Bay of Biscay and straight on to Gibraltar. All of us were inexperienced hands except for the first mate, Douglas, and the skipper, Michael, who used to say the only thing wrong with *Stormy* was that once aboard her, he could no longer watch how she flew and capered under sail. Brief practice runs out of port had been part of the drill, but this was our first open-ended voyage all the way to France. I remember the cliffs of Dover rising sugar-white behind us, and how the hiss of our wake made the very same sound skis make on crisp snow; deep water was a rolling power under my landlubber's feet; salt spray cleared the air of terrestrial pollution and threw little rainbows here and there. While the day trippers on the bus to Ostende were shouting profanities overhead, I was recalling how fortunate in geography Britain appeared from *Stormy*'s teak deck, and how privileged by nature to have such a noble body of water as her moat and border.

'You don't wanna get married,' an old man's voice said from the seat behind me. 'You're too young.'

'Yeah,' replied the girl who had threatened to wet herself. 'But I'm pregnant.'

On the road to Ostende, I was impressed again by Belgian solemnity. Every shop, the very ornaments on windowsills, looked muted and grave, pedestrians passed at a head-down, get-on-with-the-job pace that keeps small caged animals on a treadmill, and in humankind inspires renegades, comics and serial killers. My fellow passengers were all heavy smokers and after an hour on a no-smoking bus their throats were dry with craving, so they had gone relatively quiet.

'Let's come over here sometime and go clubbing,' piped the voice of a young girl at the back of the bus. Something must have charmed her in the stretch of low-income housing, corner bars and cheap furniture shops we were passing through.

'Why not?' replied her friend.

'I wonder what they wear? I guess they're quite conservative.'

'Yeah, it'd be a challenge . . .'

Thus endures a spirit of daring and enterprise in descendants of Channel pirates.

255

On the train at last between Ostende and Brussels, grass beside the tracks was frozen stiff and water birds walked on the ice. Across from me a boy studied a loose-leaf notebook with deep concentration, eyes fixed on the page. It is rare these days to see a student unplugged to any device and studying notes in longhand.

When I asked in Brussels about a wagon-lit for the overnight journey to Milan and Genoa, the young ticket clerk said sorry, they had to be booked in advance. 'But have a word with your attendant on your train. And . . .' He made a gesture as if rolling a cigarette. 'A *pourboire* . . . know what I mean?'

Money has never been our favourite abstraction, has it, child? For your father every dollar saved represented an iota of brute security – food and shelter – against unknown vicissitudes that could lie ahead as sharp as those of his childhood; extreme poverty is never left behind, it becomes part of the very fingerprint and leaves a film of itself on everything for a lifetime. For your mother, money was and remains power and control in a world where her strengths were never appreciated or used to great effect. Your brother enjoys money: he plays with it, and collects old coins, and puts it aside too, probably less than he thinks he should – there are few rainy days in southern California where he lives. For you money will always be a by-product: waste material that gets nastier the longer it hangs around. Every time you pull yourself yet again out of debt in the years ahead, my girl, and have a few coins in hand, it will only be quickly to acquire debtors. Bribing and bargaining, like gambling, remain as foreign to me as dancing a minuet, and I make a mess of them when I try. The moment I saw how the middle-aged Italian porter lounged against the side of the train like a lazy cowboy, I braced myself for trouble.

'There are no wagon-lits remaining,' he said and added the word 'truthfully . . .' with serene emphasis, like a blessing, to let me be warned that we were now through with truth: from here on in, it was business. 'I can fix it for you to have a couchette in a compartment on your own.'

I sighed. 'How much?'

Such amateurish bluntness made him smile, but only for a moment; his rugged face clouded. How much, indeed? Money as he and his forefathers had known it for centuries – sweet fruit of minor graft, ripe and fat and soft from passing through the caressing hands of fellow citizens – the great, nourishing lire in all their millions, they had overnight become no more. Silently, we eyed each other, both doing clumsy sums in our heads. I opened my wallet and showed him a crisp euro note, four days old: the equivalent of about twenty pounds.

He looked at it, his lips moved, his gaze switched to the middle distance; he shook his head to clear it and began again. 'OK, OK!' he cried angrily and snatched the immature note out of my hand, a man watching bread being torn from his children's mouths, a player deprived of his game.

257

He showed me into an empty compartment of couchettes and put a finger to his lips: I must not tell a soul. As if I would! But the moment he left me alone I was surprised by a spasm of criminal psychosis, the paranoia of Capone and Bugsy Siegel in a world where only dead men can be trusted and terror is the ace in the hole. What if the bastard cheated me? What if the train filled up in, say, Strasbourg? What guarantee had I he would not renege on our deal? How could I be sure the double-crossing son of a bitch wouldn't usher strangers into the compartment I had bought and paid for against the rules? And if he did, what the fuck could I do about it? Corrupt and self-serving greasers of palms, rich American broads who want to be alone, can hardly make an appeal to authority. Furthermore, the heater in the compartment was jammed on high; the window would not open without a key. And when I went to look, there was no attendant in the corridor or anywhere on the train as far as I could tell. The dirty rat had made a break for it with my money in his pocket. I would have to suffer in my overheated cell. I lost my rights when I did wrong.

The world outside my oven was a vast, snow-covered wedding cake decorated with neon signs in primary colours that flashed no language known by day: RiRi, AILATE, MMMMMM. Factories were going into morning shift. Behind a plate-glass window a young man struggled into a protective suit, a butterfly in reverse. I could see he was singing aloud. To whom had he made love last night? Towering constructions of industry were as beautiful in their functional design against the brightening sky as any Expressionist sculptures; street lamps in the towns could have been modelled on a flower of my childhood; it is a dainty blossom, parti-coloured in pastels, convoluted and reminiscent of the iris only smaller, with a hanging head, and not as splendid. When my unfortunate and slow-witted grandmother lived with us at our summerhouse near the lake, she used to cultivate it in her perennial garden and yell at us kids when we threatened it with our badminton and ball games. What is it called? That pretty flower is a tiny black hole in my memory: I have never been able to hold on to its name. I forget it now.

Disembarking in Milan to change trains, I felt for the first time in decades a full blast of the lift and joy of being in Italy. The train to Genoa was already in the station with time to spare for a strong coffee before boarding. We even pulled out, uncommonly for Italy, on time. I had been caught in the past when the city I was bound for had more than one major station for disembarkation as Genoa does, so I chose a motherly figure across the aisle to ask in my childish Italian if the first of two scheduled stops there was the 'Central Station'. When she replied in English that yes, it was, we began to talk in earnest. I moved to the empty seat next to her and in no time we were exchanging histories candidly, with animation, as only solitary women can when they meet on the road. Her name was Paula, which suggested to my self-referential analytical mind, albeit not as strongly as

Edwina or Josephine, that her parents would have preferred a son. A maintained blonde in her early sixties, the bones of her face were fine under abundant flesh; she had fair skin and blue eyes, and it was no surprise when she told me her mother was German. Paula had been raised in northern Italy where she lived until she married a banker and moved to his home town south of Naples. Italy was many states and two distinct nations, she told me, north and south, with separate customs and practically different languages. After her husband's death, she remained an outsider in the southern community that had never accepted her, not even when her son was born there, not after thirty years had gone by. Her greatest pleasure was to visit northern friends, such as the one she was going to see in Genoa. I happened to look down and notice that her fingernails on both hands were bitten beyond the quick; the skin around them was raw and bleeding in places.

'I have bitten them ever since I had teeth,' she said, seeing me see. 'My mother was a cold woman. She never hugged me, or kissed me goodnight, or said she loved me.' Paula glanced at my nails, worn and shabby but unbitten. 'And your mother?'

My mother? A fatherless girl, a lonely little show-off looking for the audience she never found. My mother? An actress stuck in a long-running soap opera: comfortable but not exercised. My mother?

I said, 'Fun-loving.'

Only a few minutes later when Paula suggested exchanging addresses so that some day we could travel together to Sardinia, my alarm bell sounded. Friendships on the road are about nothing but themselves. Like one-night stands of passion they can endure past the deed only rarely. What is an aged woman afraid of when she travels alone? Among other things, she is afraid of not remaining alone. It was as well Paula and I were not getting off at the same station in Genoa.

'August 1954: What a brawling town Genoa is! Almost ugly compared with Florence and Venice. Genoa is certainly a lapse from the opulent beauty that Italy has shown us so far.'

Now just you listen to me, honey bunny, Genoa is an untidy, nervy, handsome city, and from the moment I stepped out of the station into the shadow of the statue of Christopher Columbus, I loved it this time. In pace and tempo Genoa struck me immediately as similar to Manhattan when I was young: when I was you. It seethes as only a port can, breaking down the constant influx of new ingredients into a digestible stew. Streets bustle with South Americans, Africans and immigrants from every colourful corner of the globe. Unlike your Venice and Florence, much of Rome and most of Manhattan these days, Genoa has not sold its soul to tourists. It does not belong to the buyers and sellers of souvenirs; nor does it belong to the Genovese. Like New York in the 1950s

261

and right back to the beginning of the twentieth century when my father was growing up there, Genoa belongs to the alert and musical newcomers who live in wary proximity, a simmering miscegenation that sharpens wits and keeps the police force on its toes too, I'm sure. The knot of ancient narrow streets near the port was long ago abandoned by locals and the properties divided into rooms and flats to be let at exorbitant rents to the new immigrants. Or so I was told by the Peruvian brothers who ran the hotel I found near the station.

'Genoa is a mess,' said the elder brother. He looked out at light reflected from water never far and the street of oriental bargain bazaars and sex shops tucked into architecture of far, far better intentions; someone was playing loud, strange drums. In a tone I have only ever heard from old New Yorkers, rueful and passionate and true, he said, 'I love this city.'

'August 1954: Today was a miracle! Midge and I spent the day with Evelyn and her relatives who live in a big stone house in hills outside the city. Amazing! Fifty or more happy, noisy people and all of them related! Lunch at a big table in the sun under trees! Kids drinking red wine! Everyone was very kind and didn't seem to mind my lack of their language. Someone played an accordion. The old men danced with us and the young ones flirted. If I had grown up here, I'd be married to the boy next door by this time. But what a great place to visit is this Italian family life! One of the happiest

days of the trip! Why is it so much harder to describe happiness than unhappiness?'

Why? Because unhappiness attaches itself to sharp and specific causes – loss, failure, insult – all too easy to describe.
Happiness, on the other hand – real, singing happiness –
requires not only fortuity but also suspension of judgement,
and what is description, if not according to one's own judgement? Also, face it, child, happiness goes in a flash; unhappiness hangs around long enough to get a grip on it. In Genoa
I was delighted to follow your lead, to smile where you had
smiled, and find myself alone this time, but happy again.
When the stallholder in a vibrant street market sold me five
mandarin oranges and asked for 'one euro and sixty-seven
. . . atomic particles!' he and I laughed together, then settled
into a serious if linguistically mangled conversation about the
lack of an existing word in Italian for 'cents' or 'centimes'.
When I left, he and his co-workers were in explosive debate
about whether the euro was a wonderful thing. Or a German
plot, said the seller of sausages. Or a piece of seductive French
subterfuge was the opinion of the baker and his wife.

Humming, I explored the bright, open port area. On a
lucky impulse I bought a ticket for the aquarium and walked
into wonderland. I used to keep fish. I like to be around
them. Fish excuse simile – the lookdowns, nose to tail like
silver dinner plates on a shelf, the red scorpion fish, gussied
up like Miami Beach matrons and wouldn't you know they're

263

poisonous? – yet fish are impervious to sentimentality; they resist anthropomorphism and we can't make slaves of them: fish won't play. In corridors arranged with extraordinary submarine empathy, I wandered for an hour or so all by myself, an invisible swimmer in a wondrous world. Afterwards, luck held in choice of restaurant for an early dinner: seafood, it happens – I really do like fish. The only male member of staff in evidence was a cheerful and creaking grandfather who showed me to a table with courtly ease. Unusual in Italy, everyone else, even the cooks, were women and a cordial, funny lot they were, too. I walked back to my hotel on the dark streets past groups of lounging men who observed me idly, out of habit the way New Yorkers do, to see what I had worth having. They didn't scare me. Familiar threats can be comforting in an unknown city. The trick is to keep a steady pace and glance back at them precisely their own way, calculating and scornful, but never long enough to hold a gaze.

'August 1954: The food Evelyn's aunt cooked was amazing! I cannot believe pesto sauce and I have been around and not met before! I want it on cornflakes! I want it in my coffee, on my ice cream! I want pesto sauce on everything! Evelyn's great-aunt wrote the recipe out for me. I didn't say I could not read one word of it. She has big, rough, warm hands.'

I found the recipe tucked into your journal. It is written in fading pencil on crinkly paper that used to be known as onion skin and has gone the way, I think, of carbon paper and typewriter ribbons. The writing is utterly illegible now as then and redolent still, I swear, of sweet basil. And, oh yes, the flower that memory refuses to present on request? The one that droops its head like an Italian street lamp? I remember now. Columbine. It is columbine. Columbine. Three cheers for columbine! What did that graceful stalwart of granny's garden ever do to you, my child, that you buried it alive in our memory?

Fifteen

'August 1954: We drove to Customs. Will I ever get over the thrill of crossing borders? We don't have borders where I come from, not real borders that are guarded by men in uniforms, borders that separate languages and customs and even the way people look. And a new stamp in my passport! When I'm old, I want to read my history in my passport. What a wonderful world! My first real look at the Mediterranean and there is no body of water so lovely. I hated to leave Italy. But I will go back some day. I must. And it is the only way to get to France. France! I am in France! And so is Paris! I am where Paris is! And I will be there soon. Flowers in profusion and the water a blue-blue that is amazing and stays blue even when one swims in it. In Monte Carlo you hear every language on earth being spoken. And guess what! I saw Lena Horne! She was walking into the casino with a man who must be her husband. What a thrill! I wonder why? She didn't see me. Monte Carlo has a kittenish look. Monaco feels solid. Nice is not so exciting but it has a beach and the ocean. Ev says she misses Italy. I do, too. I miss everywhere we have been. But I feel somehow more at home here, maybe because I have more of the language. Nice is nice.'

Yes, yes, yes. And Cannes is canny, and Toulouse is to keep, and Pareee is *sans pareil*, and London undone you; and please, please can you not stop doing that? Now! Before it's too late to stop me doing it, too. Punning is an old man's game. Celebrities, on the other hand, mainly impress the young. Ever since I saw Ernest Hemingway on Fifth Avenue when I was ten, I have been trying like you to understand the thrill of spotting a celebrity in the wild. Could it be surprise to find oneself in the right place at just the right time? Or does the meretricious brilliance of celebrity mimic for an instant the revelation souls are born hankering for? It was the wrong season for celebrity-spotting on the Riviera this time, darling. Palm trees were cringing in the cold bright morning and celebrities, being hothouse flowers, were a thousand miles to the south and west.

I had indulged myself in a first-class ticket from Genoa to Nice, a minor indulgence, as there is small difference in price and only a little more in comfort between the classes on most continental trains. Across from me a woman in her early forties with her much older husband read an Italian newspaper over his shoulder; the pages trembled in his hand, her own hands were strong, freckled, wedding-banded and clasped tightly over a snakeskin bag. The other passengers in our compartment were three pretty young women from Milan where the train originated; two of them dozed and chatted across from their companion who was absorbed in her Sidney Sheldon novel in Italian; she put it down only to retouch her eye make-up five times in an hour. She alone of the three was blue-eyed. On our port side a two-lane road ran between us and a chilly, choppy sea bristling with masts in harbour; to starboard, dark yellow houses reminiscent of city tenements or beehives rose in terraces to the summit of the encircling mountains.

A lone derelict cottage suddenly came into view; it was made of local stone and set in a small olive grove overlooking the sea. Before that delicious little house was out of sight I had furnished it with rough-hewn tables and brass lamps, and had just got around to setting a few logs alight in the fireplace when the announcement was made, in French at last, for our next stop. Frontiers of continental Europe may not be as formal as they were in your day, young one, the romantic rigmarole of crossing them is kaput, and the stamps in your brand-new passport that you used to look at again and again with the intensity of a scholar, or a lover, are no more. Borders do continue to exist, however, in hearts and habits. France was immediately French. It was tidier, greener and more purposeful than Italy. Especially the women among commuters on the platforms looked unselfconscious and comfortable in neat skirts or pressed fitted jeans and leather jackets, their faces regular, sharp and focused. Suddenly the pretty girls from Milan were wearing too much make-up, heels too high, outfits too fussy and matronly as they trooped off the train in Monte Carlo, for a naughty weekend was my guess.

Among the postcards I found from your Study Abroad trip is one that shows the bay of Nice in 1954; there are verdant hills in the background, not yet solidly built up as they are now, and the happy pedestrians thronging the broad esplanade were not bothered by today's lanes of solid motor traffic. 'Beautiful people and sunshine everywhere!' you wrote on the back. 'Everyone is happy here. And the blue, blue Mediterranean smiles!'

You must have been starting to know for sure that you would have to run away alone one day soon, break all their rules, destroy their 'shining hope' and give them reason to doubt your love, because you then once again stated it: 'I love you' – and restated it: 'I love you guys' – and overstated it: 'I really miss and love you guys!'

I found a small relatively cheap hotel next to the Negresco that looks down with disdain on the nouveaux riches in nouveau Nice. Along the Promenade des Anglais there promenaded mostly couples, not all Anglais by a long shot, a lot of them elderly and many with mobiles in hand should their children call from abroad; others looked down from the terraces of retirement flats at a steaming, streaming river of cars and buses between them and the sea. Your blue, blue Mediterranean, child of my heart, is now a vast warm bath for packaged tourists; even off-season it appeared none too clean at the edges. The neighbouring table on the waterfront terrace where I stopped for a beer was taken by a conservatively dressed couple, not young, pretty typical of the majority of folks out and about. The man was tanned, and scowling; his wife wore a fixed smile that showed teeth. They come from their home in Quebec to their holiday flat in Nice every two months, he told me within a moment of making eye contact. His wife smiled.

'Nice is full of thieves. Don't get me wrong. Ninety per cent of the immigrants are good people. But the others! As for the French,' he said in French. 'Shop-keepers! Penny pinchers!'

His wife smiled on.

'We usually stay only two weeks. We are staying longer this time,' he said in an angry voice. 'I have a health problem.' His eyes glinted red in the setting sun. His wife kept smiling. In a rage, clearing the word from his throat, he spat out 'Cancer'.

His wife winced and smiled.

I chose a big, cheap, cheerful brasserie on a side street for my first French dinner. While I was giving my order to the weary blonde who appeared to be the only waitress, three men in their late twenties and early thirties, and a younger woman took the table next to mine. Two of the men were North African; the other was bearded and fair. The woman was brunette, thin and glittering; she was smoking when she came in and lit one cigarette from another while the men quickly ordered wine, then settled down to study the menu.

The younger of the two dark men turned suddenly to me and asked aggressively, 'Where do you come from?'

'I'm American,' I said shortly, taken off guard.

'Only red Indians are American,' said his dark companion, possibly his brother; they had the same squinting eyes and a defiant glare that one was just younger enough to have picked up from the other.

'You speak pretty good French,' said the fair man, turning in his chair to eye me straight on. 'We speak it, too,' he said, gesturing towards his companions so the sleeve of his denim jacket fell back to show arms tattooed to the elbow. 'But it is a language imposed upon us. You understand? French is not a language of our making or our history.'

'We don't want to speak French,' the older dark man said; the younger one nodded. 'But we have had no choice.'

'No choice,' said the younger one.

'It is part of our enslavement,' said the fair man. 'We are enslaved by the pigs, the bastards.'

'Pigs,' said the younger dark man, 'bastards.'

While the men gave their orders to the waitress, who really did look too old for the job and very tired, the woman lit another cigarette and coughed slightly, her eyes fixed on the fair man, her primary lover; I had a hunch that she slept with all of them.

'And where do you come from?' I asked the fair man.

271

'I am a Berber,' he said, with a challenging edge in his tone.

One of his dark companions called the waitress back to the table and held up the bottle she had brought them earlier. 'This wine is corked,' he said.

She hurried away on heavily veined legs to fetch fresh wine.

'One day', the quiet dark man said and turned his burning eyes my way, 'it will all change. We the people will have our birthright returned to us. You others know nothing of what has been done to us, what has been stolen from us!'

The waitress returned, sighing, with my omelette and a new bottle for them.

'*Bon appétit, Madame*,' they said to me in chorus, before turning away to their food and wine.

'1954: At last I can use my French, abuse it too, with anyone who lets me.'

Your French? Yours, indeed! Unfortunately, upon entry to university you passed an exam to place out of French language courses. I wish I could go back and make you fail it as you deserved to do. But you were inspired by Judy B across the hall in the dormitory. She was a prodigious virgin who was dating a French sailor and she promised if you passed your French exemption exam, she would fix you up with one of his mates next time their ship was in port. You studied ferociously and sailed through the exam. Meanwhile, however, Judy's Frenchman got fed up and dumped her so you never did learn French properly, or improperly, when you were ripe for it. Even now, subtle tenses desert you the moment you are tired, or as soon as a native tells you that you speak his language well, or when your inner voice whispers, 'Listen to yourself!'

After decades of nipping in and out of France, its melodious, well-ordered language remains a distant second best to your English and not as fluent as it should be, my girl, and would be, too, had Judy's French sailor tested her virtue longer and harder before throwing in *l'éponge*.

'Shall I wrap it for you?' asked the young man in the Nice bookstore where I bought an emergency portable French dictionary. He looked at me, assessing: 'Or will you eat it here?'

The woman of whom I asked the quickest route to the station for a day trip to Monaco was going in that direction, so we walked together for a block or two and shared a gossip. She carried a paper carrier bag, well-used, and wore flat shoes run down at the heel; she was probably a hotel maid or a charlady. The Monégasque train station was an absolute marvel, she told me, a veritable Taj Mahal of railway termini; it had no equal in the whole of Europe. 'Suitable for millionaires,' she said, as if the very rich these days would dream of subjecting themselves to the vagaries of rail travel.

'Thank you,' I told her when we parted. 'You people of Nice are welcoming and helpful.'

'Oh, but I am not from here!' she cried. 'I came here from Poitiers twenty years ago. People of Nice are two-faced hypocrites. They say one thing and do another.'

In fact, among countless casual contacts of the promenade and streets, I met not one native-born resident of Nice. And I heard so many complaints like hers from long-time residents, it made me wonder if the entire population of Nice was composed of disillusioned settlers from other parts of France. Or if moaning about their adoptive city was a curmudgeonly mutation of contentment, a local perversity similar to the way Parisians will say 'It is not cold, today . . .' instead of 'Oh, what a beautiful morning!'.

'1954: There is a feeling of money in Monaco. Money feels sticky. But it never sticks to me! Odd how hard it is to tell if a man is rich unless you see him in his car, when you pass him just walking along, but women show it right away: they wear money. And some of them look silly, too. It was hot enough to swim today and did we not see a woman strolling along in a fur coat? Tony said it was sable! "How do you know?" I asked him. "Dear girl," he said . . . dear girl! "I hunt the noble beast, though only for food, of course. Sable for the table," he said, which for some reason sounded very funny, very English. To be rich must be like living inside an unbreakable bubble. I know I will never be rich. I don't see the point.'

*   *   *

And a good thing, too, that money never made part of your daydream. Penury is one price of parental disapproval where you come from and until you are old, until you no longer long for any pretty thing, you will earn every last penny you spend: no presents, no windfalls and no handouts. The Study Abroad summer itself was funded by part-time jobs, the most ghastly of them was washing test tubes in the college botany department. You won a few cash prizes, too, always second place, in debating competitions and poetry-reading contests fashionable for schoolchildren in the 1950s. Good on you, darling! Whatever cost endless work and worry may be to self-confidence, and probably to longevity, there is no way as sure as self-sufficiency to manoeuvre against defeat.

Rich and sticky Monaco was just down the road on a train continuing on into Italy. A redolent old drunk sat on the aisle nearby; he was chewing a baguette and mumbling to himself in French, 'I am going to Italy to eat well. I am going to eat well in Italy. I am going to Italy to eat . . .'

Indeed, Monaco has a magnificent station, full of long bright corridors on many levels, so many levels, and so few people around of whom to ask directions, it was practically twenty minutes before I found the exit I wanted out into fresh air. Once on the flat, however, and in the vicinity of astronomically expensive boutiques, the pavements sported a blue carpet, presumably to make window shopping easier on the soles of the well-heeled.

'Don't be fooled. They are not the rich-rich any more,'

said the young Italian waiter at a café I chose for a coffee break, next to the succulent food market. 'Here we have the false-rich and the tourists. Monaco is mainly a tax dodge. In the winter it is empty.' He was married to a local and, yes, he had learned his English waiting on table in Soho. 'I love the Brits,' he said, looking up at the nearby battlements, lowering symbols of decaying fortunes that put us in their shade. 'The Brits make me laugh. They know how to play around.'

I stayed only for a few hours; it was enough. Back in Nice, waiting for my late lunch on the front, I smeared yellow mustard on a piece of baguette and the sting on my tongue returned me immediately to hunger as I had known it in Paris when I lived there in a small hotel and could afford only one cheap bistro meal every other day, on good days. Back then before American tourism was in force and importing the gastronomic demands of a nursery, butter was not often seen on the table, and bread with mustard used to serve as my chief free appetiser while waiting for real food to arrive, as I was waiting in Nice. When will I learn that in any area ruled by tourism, local specialities should be ordered only in the very best eateries? Ordinary cafés and brasseries churn them out mechanically, the way factories plaster the Mona Lisa on umbrellas and mouse pads, ever further from the inspiration. When my 'Salade Niçoise' turned up at last it was a shamelessly inferior assembly-line product.

While I rummaged in it for the good bits, an immigrant

gypsy in long skirts carrying an armful of drooping roses pushed her way on to the café terrace. 'Please buy my flowers. Messieurs, Mesdames, I beg of you. Please, please, please . . .' she cried. After an increasingly tearful circuit of the crowded terrace without selling one blossom, she turned at the exit, shook her fist over our busy, bobbing heads and shouted, 'What a bunch of scumbags!'

I pushed my plate of overdressed finery to one side. I had to agree with her. Once in Boulogne sur Mer where until recently I owned a small hidey-hole in the old town, I was stopped on the crowded main street by a beggar I knew well – an upright old chap in ragged clothes with the sharp eye of a hawk, he used to see me coming from blocks away. As I was handing him his due, there was a sudden squealing of tyres beside us and a Renault saloon car pulled up. A bald, fat man in winking glasses leaned out of the driver's window, shaking his fist at me. 'Don't give him a penny! Don't be a fool! He has more money than you! He has more money than any of us! And he does nothing for it! Nothing!' he shouted, then rolled down his window before I could tell him what I think.

I think beggars are wayside shrines; I think when we pass them and they ask us to give something for nothing tangible in return, it is a refreshing change from the ordinary base commerce of the streets. I think that without beggars, richer men cannot rise higher than the pavement: coins and notes are nothing but stuff until a beggar implores us to search our conscience for metaphor. We can then enter the moment creatively with a few coins in hand to represent altruism and life-saving generosity. Or we can refuse and roar away in the family car, only after examining once more, however, our justification for withholding what we have more of than we strictly need from someone else who needs it more than we. I, for example, would have bought a rose on the terrace in Nice, I should have, except that I feared the opprobrium of strangers; that is where my cowardice lies, and my shame.

Banks, bars, brothels, theatres and beggars: what else are cities *for*? Thinking about beggars, I strolled beside heavy traffic to the far end of what was once Europe's most elegant thoroughfare into a cheerful complex of narrow streets and funky boutiques around the flower market. Two French-women in their middle fifties, laden with packages, walked in front of me.

Suddenly, a young man staggered out of a doorway and accosted them, not for money, merely to express himself. 'You are shit,' he said to them. 'Go back to the shit you come from.'

'And where do you come from?' asked the older one of the two amiably.

'Marseilles,' said the angry man.

'Well, go back there, go back to your kif-kif,' she replied.

'And you go back to your shit.'

'Kif-kif . . .' she said.

'Shit . . .'

'Kif-kif . . .'

The younger woman turned to me, shaking her head: 'My sister will talk to anyone.'

After people and the sea and the flower market, unlike most resort towns Nice has a few galleries and museums to look into. I chose to see the collection of Raoul Dufy paintings, because I relished the seaside walk to the modern art museum where they were being shown. It turned out that Dufy's stylishness, his colours and shimmering sunny line, could not anywhere look more important or appropriate than there in his old painting ground on the opposite coast of France from the chilly grey northern one where he was born. Afterwards I stopped at a café in a busy backstreet for a beer, as I would every afternoon should I retire to Nice, which I shall certainly never do, and I studied postcards of Dufy's work that I'd bought at the museum. He died in 1953, the year before my maiden voyage: just as I was planning to see the world, the artist was closing his eyes on it.

'Do you know Mori's Bar? M-O-R-I,' a handsome craggy man next to me was asking his much younger female companion. 'We had some fun there. Oh my. I will never forget Mori's Bar!'

'Fond mementoes of Mori's,' I whispered to you, young phantom punster at my side.

In front of me were four Australians, two of each sex, not much older than you were, baby face, the summer of Study Abroad. They too, I soon realised, were part of a group of students and on their first tour of the Continent.

279

'You should have gone to the Louvre with us. We saw the Mona Lisa,' one girl said to the boys.

'Quite small, wasn't it?' the other girl said.

'Paris was a real experience of life,' said the first girl.

'Yeah, like, we got seriously ripped off,' said one of the boys.

'Hey, did you see how our great white leader, Paul, was furious with Mary?'

'Well sure,' said one of the boys. 'Everyone had to wait while she was being sick.'

The girl shrugged. 'She's a slut.'

'1954: Midge and Evelyn and I had a triple room in Nice the size of a ballroom with a private bath and breakfast in bed too, my dears! Midge drank too much red wine last night and was sick in the bathroom. Ev whispered to me that she was disgusting. "I could tell you things about her . . ." she said, and she probably would have, too, except I got out of there in a hurry. Ah well. I will come back some day, alone. We all swam today. It was a pebble beach. But that doesn't matter, not as long as the pebbles are French pebbles! The food is so good, we are all getting fat.'

There is enlightening marginalia on this page: 'Breakfast: black coffee. Lunch: no pasta. No roll. Meat, greens, fruit. Dinner: soup, meat, greens. No potatoes, no roll, no dessert.' So you worried about your weight, did you, slim? A real worry, too, if it made you push away esoteric cheeses and desserts containing the very flavour and history of France. I had forgotten that even in the olden times of your youth girls and women fretted, though not so chronically as now, that they were fat and growing fatter. Compulsive calorie counting and self-denial are part of the struggle for control over elements of new confusion: over sex and work and freedom. But why don't women who feel in danger of losing control eat, eat, eat? Why do we try so hard to make ourselves lightweights? Why not make ourselves too big and fat to be swept away, too heavy to be dragged by our hair into the cave? Oh, but of course, we do that too, don't we? There is just no logic in the relationship to food of our food-producing sex. Or is there too much logic in it for our own good? The way women eat in the rich Western nations has become both the sin and its penance.

The hotel I had found was part of an apartment complex and required two keys for entry, one for the street door and the other to the reception itself at the far end of an enclosed communal courtyard. As usual, I had gone to bed early and was up well before six on my last morning in Nice, reading in bed the *Collected Stories* of Saul Bellow. Bellow is hopeful about intellect being sexy in men. Well, he would be, wouldn't he? But it is not a man's intellect that attracts the majority of women, it is the status intellect gives him in literary or scientific circles. Also, the particularly low opinion of females which is never far from high thought in men is

281

irresistibly attractive, particularly to unsure and daddy-scorned women. Men of extraordinary intelligence rarely court the company of intellectual women; admiration, not conversation, comfort not challenge, are what genius wants at home. Bellow was quite a rare catch for a woman of my years and temperament; handsome old intellectuals of his monumental vanity prefer to be seen and see themselves with younger, prettier women, particularly in bed, and I was enjoying myself with him when I was startled from the page by a key turning in my lock.

The door flew open and there stood a young, short North African man. Behind him I sensed the presence of another, taller man.

'What the hell are you doing here?'

'We have come to clean the room,' he said, his glance darting past me to clock my bag hanging from the arm of a chair, my camera on the little desk, my old coat with a fake fur collar on the foot of the bed.

There was not a thought in my head; I felt no fear, no rage, nothing stronger than irritation. 'At this hour! Who are you kidding? Get the hell out of here! Just you get out fast and close that door behind you. Close it!' I said coldly, pointing my finger his way as if it were a gun. 'And bugger off!' I said, not the least bit surprised when that was precisely what he did.

He had found, or stolen, or perhaps been given a set of keys to the outer doors, it turned out later when the manageress arrived and I told her what had happened. He let himself in at an hour when there was nobody attending the desk so he could help himself to the individual room keys.

'Can you describe him?' she asked me.

She herself was a tall, commanding woman in her fifties with the upright posture of an ex: ex-actress, ex-ballet dancer, or rich man's ex-wife.

'He was young and rather short,' I said, and then with reluctance that was practically self-revulsion, 'North African.'

'No doubt from Marseilles,' she said. 'Marseilles is a world apart.'

The only other guest in residence was a nonagenarian Frenchwoman on an annual visit from her home in California. She too had been reading in bed, the Bible, it so happens, and the moment our transgressor appeared at her door, she handed over her wristwatch and jewellery. Such good sense must account for her great age, though it became clear after a short conversation with her that she herself puts her longevity down to her chosen reading matter.

Only much later on I started to wonder, and still do, if there is a moment of the day or night when we do not go in ignorance of peril. Ladders, scaffolds, drunken drivers, ice on the pavement, window-panes falling from shoddy frames, armed lunatics on clock towers. Not just the streets and seas and jungles are full of danger; danger imminent and immanent is within us, too. Arteries explode, hearts give out without warning, single mad cells go on homicidal rampages, brains collapse into walnuts and blood overflows its little channels to make sudden whirlpools. We can even smoke ourselves to death. Smoke! Weightless by-product of fire, the quintessential human discovery! Smoke can knock a six-footer right into his grave. From start to finish, life is a near-death experience.

It was well I was thinking on these lines and steeling myself to fate, because danger of a different order was waiting down the road in Cannes.

Sixteen

'Only pertinent themes assure full recollections . . .' says Saul Bellow through the narrator of 'The Bellarosa Connection'.

Good words to read on the train to Cannes while I was preparing myself for a flood of recollection on pertinent themes of love, adventure, sex and the sea. Only later, after I had checked into the first feasible hotel I came across and had a look around, I began to wonder. Can anyone ever be sure, having forgotten, that what is forgotten has not as much pertinence as what is remembered? Why should it not sometimes have more? Tall, smart old Bellow's tall, smart old protagonist gives the reader negative evidence of what he means, he tells us that there are murderers who cannot remember their crimes and this, he says, is 'because they have no interest in the existence or non-existence of their victims': the victims have no pertinence. But surely it could equally be that the victim is forgotten precisely because his life at the moment of the taking of it is more pertinent to the murderer than his own. The lesser cannot encompass the greater; deed and victim must be lost to memory in case recollection stretch the faculty beyond its limit and destroy it altogether. What you don't know certainly can hurt you; it can demolish you. I wanted that tall, smart old author with me in Cannes for a while, if only to prevent me talking this way to you, myself.

Cannes had changed, of course, in the forty years since I lived there and the nearly fifty years since I first dropped in with Study Abroad. But what puzzled me from the moment I stepped off the train was that nothing about it was familiar. Absolutely nothing felt pertinent.

'1954: On the whole Cannes seems well moneyed, with a fair show of minks and diamonds, lots of playboys on La Croisette, and a few sallow children with governesses. It has the F. Scott Fitzgerald charm of rich people at play.'

No playboys this time round. I stumbled on a few noisy bars for playful boys, and plenty of bad boys on street corners, showing the alert shiftiness that attaches to the drug trade; and an awful lot of old boys, too, who passed rather slowly on rollerblades, hands clasped behind them like ice-skaters; as for old girls, they were everywhere airing salon dogs on leads. Boulevard La Croisette on a winter day appears now to serve as a promenade for pampered poodles and enlarged prostates rather than playboys. By the way, what made you imagine, unworldly Yankee child, had you bumped into a playboy you would have known him from a toy boy? Or a beach boy? Or a tallboy, come to that? One spry girl, mini-skirted and swinging her arms, skipped towards me out of the parade of dotards; when we were close I saw that her bob was lacquered black, and her taut, lifted face glumly set as she exercised frantically against time and gravity. Except during a few weeks of the film festival and the rubbish it leaves behind, Cannes out of season is a raddled version of Nice: not so nice as Nice, you would say, girl, yet somehow a little more shady and appealing.

But it was not Cannes I wanted, not Cannes I sought. Forgive me, young I, I must abandon you for a little while. For here in the Old Port were memories you have yet to make. Here, I am going to live for a year at the start of the Sixties aboard the good ship *Stormsvalla*. Here was played out the pivotal year of my life, I can call it now, a year of classic adventure unscheduled for a girl of my upbringing; a year that taught me the value of courage and that the only limits to possibility are the limits of one's own imagination. Here I stole a year from more ordinary life, a year that influenced every pertinent theme thereafter: my year before the mast. I had to leave you here, my own child, and abandon the itinerary of your journal to walk down to the Old Port of Cannes where the last days of my extreme youth were acted out. Perched there on a bollard at the edge of the coast, I looked for landmarks to the past. I found none, not one; nothing appeared even remotely familiar. Had Cannes and the world changed so completely? Had I? Was memory a liar, unredeemed, and the past not worth the paper I write on? Near panic, I felt myself to be invisible, crazy, a ghost lacking genesis and effect.

'Get a hold,' I ordered myself. 'Remember!'

We cruised from Cowes to Gibraltar, under sail every inch of the way partly for the challenge of canvas, largely because *Stormy*'s engine was old and as unreliable as memory, so we had to save it for emergencies. Sixteen days to landfall: sixteen days on a liquid planet that was constantly changing, always unlikely and in every way outlandish. Sixteen days aboard a flimsy toy on the surface of a hostile element that could terrify with its power and tempt with its beauty and its secrets. Sixteen days, a number easy to calculate because I wrote about it later in a lost memoir, never published, of which I recollect the title: 'Forty-eight Meals to Gibraltar'. The number must have included breakfast because for me, cook and chief galley slave, breakfast was the most difficult meal to dish up, coming as it did in the gloom to the bad-tempered, sometimes in weather that required bowls of hot porridge and mugs of coffee to be passed down a line of hands while we stood, feet braced, to hold ourselves upright. Fresh water was rationed, so to wash dishes I had first to throw a bucket on a line over the side from the cockpit. Four decades after the fact, the palms of my hands all by themselves re-membered and felt again the chafe of the rope when the bucket dashed away on its lead. Then the industrial smell of the liquid soap, the only one that made suds in salt water, came back, eye-stinging and sharp as kerosene, while I sat there in the new wintry sunshine of the Old Port.

Bless numbers. They put a handle on so much that is slippery. We were eight. That was too many for comfort, or what passes for comfort on a racing yacht built like a shark. Michael, our hired skipper, was the only professional sailor. Older than the rest of us, a bachelor, he was a bearded redhead, English or more likely a Scot; in those days, before I lived in England, I could barely tell the difference. Michael was one of those increasingly superfluous humans endowed by nature to live on water: a born old salt. His command had poignancy because he was heavily lame and thus incapable of doing himself most of what he knew had to be done, and ordered us to do. Probably he had been invalided out of the navy or merchant navy. But I cannot remember what I never knew and because I was still a thoughtless girl, I did not ask. Many times I brought him a mug of tea on his dogwatch, and sat next to him in the dark to watch dolphins cut phosphorescent streaks around us in midnight's ocean; I could have asked him then, should have. Instead we sat there side by side and silent as blinking fishes in a bowl. Years later someone, probably Henry, said when Michael had to retire from the sea he went into the business of building swimming pools in the south of France. Salt-water pools, I hope, and one day Neptune will summon all those drops of Michael's lifeblood into a tidal wave to chasten dry land that never

289

made the skipper happy or at home. Of course, Michael is a very, very old man by this time. Or he is not.

Henry W, or Hank as everyone called him, was the owner of the boat and my best friend on board I know now; I would not have called any man my best friend at the time. And so, I guess, can recollection pre-empt the pertinence of a theme. He had finally married Rhoda E, subsequently Rhoda W, his long-time girlfriend and my classmate from Barnard, who was on board too, of course. Owner's wife was a role she played with élan and hauteur, especially when we were moored in Cannes. Hank too lived according to an outstanding romantic affectation: poverty was believed by artists of the time to be the only fit and proper ambience for their endeavours, pretty much the opposite of how they think now. Hank enacted a semblance of poverty because in spite of being born rich, he wanted terribly to be a poet. Poor chap. Try as he might to lose his money or give it away when Rhoda wasn't watching, family investments prospered and he was lucky even in poker, which he played with spooky success. Genuine squalor eluded him until years later when, remarried and with a baby on the way, he moved to California. There, he succeeded in shooting most of a million dollars into his veins and freeing himself at last for the muse.

'I'd like to try it,' I said to Hank once in London when he and his second wife were staying with me and I came upon them fixing heroin in my living room. 'Just once. To know what it's about.'

His horror, the way he said 'No, no, no! Not you!' was the truest declaration of affection any man or any friend was ever going to make to me.

A few of the letters I received from Hank somehow escaped a cold sentence of destruction I declared one day a decade or so ago upon all old correspondence I could lay my hands on, published articles, unpublished manuscripts and diaries: a folly almost as vainglorious as saving and cataloguing the hard copy and paperwork that marks one's passage. One of Hank's letters is from California, dated November 1979: 'God knows when I last wrote you; God knows when I will again . . .' It includes a poem he wrote based on lines from Baudelaire: *Mais les vrais voyageurs sont ceux-là seuls qui partent/Pour partir . . .*

> *Over the faulty Californian crust [Hank wrote],*
> *I bend with the will of the fractious few . . .*
> *Oh pilgrims! Oh pioneers of death!*

Oh, dear! Oh, Henry! A pioneer inward bound and desperately seeking a place to settle at the far limits of his mind. Another letter I received from him later contained a poem called 'A Refusal to Visit the Bedside of My Dying Wife'. That was in 1981, the year Rhoda, his first wife and my old classmate, began her long, hard death by cancer in London. After that he wrote a few more times to tell me he had kicked his habit at last, even stopped smoking, and he had written

291

a book he wanted me to try to promote in London. After that there was silence unbroken and now unbreakable for ever, I know.

'1954: We hired a motor boat to take us from Cannes to an island off the coast. Not very far, but what a wonderful feeling to be at sea again! It must be how birds feel, like flying. Sea is the sky of another world. Ev and Midge are being friendly to each other again, thank goodness. We three crept off on our own and went for a swim on an empty beach. Tony says people live on this island but we didn't see anyone. For almost an hour I walked by myself through pretty dense underbrush and along a rocky coast where the mainland looked glorious, like a dream. By myself on French soil!'

Hello there. Piping up again, are you? And interrupting me at my post-1954 reminiscing? Reminiscence is not unlike prayer, you know, for us old folks who worship life and who look back, not ahead, to its full glory. There is also something you ought to know about that island off the coast, for you will visit it again one day, and again. These days ferry boats with bars and bored staff on board leave for regular expeditions to the outlying islands and the nearest of them, Ste Marguerite, is probably the one referred to in your journal. It is big enough to lose yourself on for a little while, quite densely overgrown, with stunning views of the mainland. I made the short journey this time because like you, I wanted to be on water again. As soon as our ferry had moored at the island pier, I found myself hurrying along the rocky coast to the right while the other passengers strolled towards a hamlet in the other direction. I had remembered something, something you, my chaste little alter I and other ego, knew less than nothing about.

A twelve-metre racing yacht offers no privacy whatsoever. In calm seas what cannot be seen on board can be overheard, and in rough weather, however swift and silent her passage appears to be from afar, a sailing vessel is as noisy as a jet liner and the crew is too busy staying alive to spare time or energy for hanky-panky. Enforced sexual deprivation did not seem to bother the skipper, maybe it came as a relief; nor did it have apparent effect on the young Mauritian hand we had signed on in Cowes. He was a serene, dignified boy and the only member of crew who did not disdain giving me a hand in the galley. How shameful of me to have forgotten his name. He was hardy and adorable; I'll call him Columbine. In port, only Hank could afford occasional nights ashore. I dare say he and Rhoda stayed in a good hotel, too, as she was making no secret of how tough she found living on board and how disappointing the role of owner's wife. Every woman in Rhoda's family including her mother was dead by that time of cancer, taken in their thirties and forties. Knowing in her very fibre that she was born for a short life made Rhoda querulous and envious and sexually voracious.

As for me, I had only quite recently cottoned on to sex

with a handsome, uninhibited partner, Douglas, my Argentine lover. Covert couplings in the sea off the side of the boat and on the chain locker in the dank fo'c'sle were better than nothing, and if sex were a valve to open when pressure climbed into the red perhaps these illicit collisions would have sufficed. But I wanted more; I wanted it slower, longer, noisier. I wanted much more; I wanted too much. I was in love. Every few days my lover, who was also an experienced yachtsman, persuaded the skipper to set sail for Ste Marguerite, in those days practically desolate. On the island Douglas and I found a thicket so secluded we could leave a bottle of wine under the vines and find it cool and waiting on our next visit. The sheltered place became our boudoir for the kind of roofless lovemaking impossible on board the mother ship. When I hurried along to the right I was looking for our old bower, and I found it, too, carpeted in thick ferns and grass, shaded by towering trees now, and masses of hanging vines; it had been very well fertilised.

Nowadays, there are so many yachts in Cannes harbour nothing much is visible over miles of docks and aerials and masts; many of them decorative and attached to motor launches. When we were moored there long ago, the few times we managed to inveigle an intrepid paying charter and set out for a day or two of hectic sailing, once as far as Corsica, other crews used to turn out to watch our return and admire the pure beauty of our approach under sail. Hank sold *Stormsvalla* in Cannes not long after I left for Paris to live there with Douglas. Sweet, sexy, fey Douglas, we called him the 'silver fox' because his hair was prematurely white. Three years ago and three decades after he and I parted in Paris, a granddaughter from one of his marriages sought me out in London to tell me he had died not long before in South Africa after a long and tormenting decline of mind and body.

Suddenly, a thought rose to my mind as sharp as a splash of sea water; it had been biding its time ever since Genoa, ever since London. The rich man who bought *Stormsvalla* from Hank had no intention of cruising or racing, he wanted her as a bath toy permanently moored with mainsail up in stops. Yes, yes, all that was long, long ago. And yes, only look how Cannes had grown; how it had changed. But the new owner was a lazy rich man, and they live to be very, very old, don't they? Besides, moving *Stormsvalla* any distance required a crew and is not as easy to do as modern Mediterranean yachtsmen prefer. *Stormy* could still be there. Of course. Why not? She could at that very moment be somewhere in the vast bobbing parking lot, waiting to be found by one who had loved her.

The first person I asked for information was an Englishman in his late sixties, one of a handful of yachtsmen to be seen out and about that cool day. Clearly, he lived full time on board his boat, and had for some time. It was an old motor launch registered in London; tea towels and shorts were drying on a line stretched outside the main cabin, and there were crates of empty beer bottles stacked in a tower on the deck.

'A Dutch-built sloop, am I right?' he said. 'A beauty. Wooden hull. Yes. *Stormbird*. I haven't seen her in some time. But . . .' He looked out at the countless boats in the harbour and shook his head. 'You need an address to find an old friend in this floating city.' I had interrupted him while he was coiling stray lines very properly on deck. There were worse ways to live, I was thinking, and to die, than occupied with nautical minutiae and swilling beer while moored securely to the south of France. He suggested I ask one of the established chartering agents on the front and then, if I had no joy, try the harbour master after the office opened again at three. When I left him I felt cheerful and heroic, and certain, absolutely certain, there was no question in my mind that I was going to find *Stormy* and was destined to stand on her deck one more time in this life.

The boat chartering agency had a shopfront with windows on the harbour. The agent himself reminded me on sight of our most unlikely crewmate on *Stormy*, Martin W-T. Hyphenated Englishmen were a type I barely knew back then. Hyphens are like school ties, they can be falsely claimed and always hint slightly at disreputable potential. To be worn with style the hyphen requires a degree of irony, in Martin's case by inference and tone rather than quotable wit. Because hyphens often unite with mama, they carry traces of sexual ambiguity, not quite belied in Martin by his German girl-friend, a likeable pudding called Helga. Hyphenated or not,

Martin was a brave shipmate and staunch in crises. We missed Martin and Helga too when they left for London soon after our landing in Cannes, and it was to be almost a decade before I saw him again. Instead of selling real estate, or chartering yachts, he was selling art. At our final meeting he nearly bankrupted me for a small painting I could not resist by Liz Frink who was practically unknown then. Not long afterwards Rhoda, also resident in London, broke a long, sulky silence to ring and let me know Martin had died suddenly of a massive heart attack. Disorderly old death, to take Martin W-T so capriciously and out of sequence.

The yachting agent, though he was generally a hyphenated type, had none of Martin's foxy charm. He was ratty. He sized me up quickly: no furs, no gemstones, no husband – no sale. His effort to look awfully important and ever so busy was undermined by his being all alone in the big office, nobody attending the other desks, no pretty girl to sort me out at reception. 'Yes, yes. I remember hearing about *Stormsvalla*. A twelve-metre, right? Class A racing boat. Wet. Old. Uncomfortable.'

While he spoke, he was scooping papers from his desk into a fake crocodile briefcase. He stood, straightened his maroon tie and reached for a Burberry rip-off hanging behind him. 'Before my time,' he said.

'Do you know where she is?'

He shrugged and pushed past me to the door, then stood waiting for me to leave first.

297

'Can you look her up for me? Please. I'll come back later.'

'*Ça sert à quoi?*' he asked, locking the door behind us. 'What's the point?'

We were outside now on the pavement.

'Oh yes, of course, I remember now,' he called as he scuttled away. He stopped, turned and looked straight at me with his little pink eyes. 'I remember your *Stormsvalla*. It comes back to me now. She was destroyed.'

The world turned around me for a moment; the world turned around without me. There is more than one way to remember: to remember factually and sequentially; to remember sensually; and to remember with the soul. Under my feet the deck complained and stretched, a living thing born to fly; the big boom idled, waiting for a breeze. It was the night of our thirteenth day without sight of land; we were utterly becalmed and Michael trusted me at the helm. My mates, my company, my lover, my friends – my dear, dead friends, the other fools – were playing cards on the foredeck; a lantern cast their shadows monstrously big against the patient mainsail.

'*Détruit . . .*' the rat had said, '. . . destroyed.' Borne on that word, memory returned absolutely and gripped me entire for a single, searing instant of pertinence and loss.

'I don't know why he told you that.' The young man in the harbour master's office spoke soothingly like a doctor to a doomed old patient. 'It's true that we don't have *Stormsvalla* on our books. But that doesn't mean she was destroyed. She could have been moved. She could be . . .' we both turned to the window beside us and looked out at the spreading sea, '. . . anywhere,' he said. 'You could track her down. It would not be easy. But it is possible. It would take time. Have you time?'

'No.'

No. I had never felt more tired: tired in a new way – depleted. Earth was too big after all, too many ports and too many oceans.

'No,' I said. My voice caught. 'I have a train to catch.'

Walking back to my hotel near the train station, I stayed for as long as possible close to the water so I could hear the whimper of lines straining from land. Sand underfoot sparkled with bits of glass, silver foil, brass nails and small glittering fragments of once beautiful things, destroyed.

Seventeen

'1954: This must be the loveliest country in the world. Here where Van Gogh and Cézanne chose to paint and I would choose to live. A strange, tortured landscape: grey mountains, gnarled olive trees. I am making it sound dark and grotesque and it is in a way, but also inexpressibly beautiful. Red earth makes purple grapes. Oh dear! I open my big mouth and nothing happens. How can I describe the earth-coloured cottages covered in purple wisteria? Or the ruins of a castle destroyed by Richelieu yet holding on still at the summit of a windy hill. They must have been proud people who lived there. Unlike most impressive views it has a personal feeling: "This", one thinks, "is all mine!" Thirty of us stood there feeling the same way. We came back to Nîmes. And that night we went to see Katherine Dunham dance in the amphitheatre. Improbable! Sitting where Augustus Caesar sat and watching dance that has its roots in Africa! An unforgettable experience! But I will no doubt manage to forget it!'

*   *   *

Yes, dear, you will forget the Dunham recital. You went to a major league baseball game once with your father and you can't remember that either except for the hot dog that became a paradigm for the blessed junk food of youth. The French landscape remained familiar however and even in winter from the window of a train kept reminding me of your words: 'red earth makes purple grapes'. We passed red roofs, red fields, dark-red rocks tumbling down to the sea that rippled rosy in the late winter dawn. Inland was a hibernating landscape; misty chiffon lay over pruned vines in the fields, shuttered houses and drowsy olive trees. The old man dozing next to me on the train smelled of root vegetables and tobacco. Across from us, flirting with a handsome companion, was a fierce beauty: vocal and mobile, a superstar, a scene stealer, a real performer, laughing and brushing back gleaming long blonde hair with hands as broad as salad plates – a fantast who interpreted femininity too dramatically, certainly for an early morning train, too confidently and gorgeously ever to be real, an artist in a way: not a believable female. The only wholly convincing female impersonators – Marlene Dietrich, for instance, Marilyn Monroe, Mae West, Margaret Thatcher – always turn out to be women.

In Toulon I was supposed to change trains for Nîmes. That is what I meant to do: what I expected to do. But I was overtaken by the old need to stretch the strings and test freedom, to change a plan en route. Without a thought in our little head, young ancestress, on the prod of perfect impulse, to hell with Nîmes, I stayed on the train to Marseilles as you would have done too, my curious, curious young self. You, the traveller of your small family, the child who leaves for no reason except to leave, a sailor born to homesteaders who will watch your peregrinations with worry and with contempt, too: 'There she goes again, your sister/ daughter/granddaughter. You know how she is. She didn't get it from me!'

True enough, you did not get it from them. The least detour on the road to our house in the country threw our father into a sweaty panic. Where he was raised, on New York's lower East Side at the turn of the century, he soon learned the hard way that when a little Kike strayed into a neighbouring ghetto of Wops or Micks he came out of it hurt and bloodied, and minus anything of the least value he had happened to have on him. Your brother grew up in relative safety yet nevertheless shows milder symptoms of similar paranoia. And in spite of spinning wonderful tales from her anarchic imagination, your mother has always proceeded very, very cautiously in real life, scared to lose control of her vicinity which must be strictly ordered according to her opinions of how things ought to be. In old age she set alarms to ring when it was time to work on accounts, to stop, to take a blue pill, to take a red one. But her wardrobe is stuffed with clothes that have not been worn in forty years, detritus strains at every cupboard door and chaos has ever threatened at the corner of her eye. Why hang on for dear life to judgements, grudges and outmoded systems unless it is for dear life?

'1954: I asked Tony if we were going to Marseilles. I have always liked the sound of it. It sounds mysterious and exotic, a seaport out of Conrad. Tony winked and said, "You're too young for Marseilles." '

'Marseilles', my landlady in Nice had said with a disapproving shake of her head, 'is a world unto itself.'

Not so. Cannes, Monaco and Nice to this day remain the worlds apart, enclaves for those too rich to be real and for the aged who are retiring from the world's business, only not retiring too far, if you please: cemeteries are tucked out of the way and there must be quite a brisk trade in shipping empty old bodies home from the Riviera. But nobody retires to Marseilles: people live there, they die there – the city is entered through a graveyard and presumably it is left that way, too. I had passed through Marseilles only once before years ago with Douglas on our way back to Paris after an impulsive journey to Morocco. The city held no lurking memories beyond the revelation of my first true bouillabaisse. Descending the steps of the ornate railway station into a city – a real city – a French city of street wit and threat and savvy, spotting a kosher butcher down a small side street, mixing with the shills and office workers out for lunch, strolling in the smoke and traffic of Marseilles, a big-city traveller has to feel at home.

'Is Marseilles very dangerous?' I asked the old man from whom I bought a slab of gooey pizza for a street lunch.

'Marseilles is a pussy cat,' he said, watching with interest a woman of his own age pass, wrapped in a black lace mantilla. 'Of course, you won't go out alone at night. But that's only common sense, right?'

A gentle two-hour stroll gives constant small delights: exquisite green art deco tiles frame the portal of the Armenian Community Centre; bleached whores of every skin tone with flinty eyes and glossy red mouths lounge purposefully in doorways; the too familiar logo of a low-fashion international chain is squeezed between a pair of buxom caryatids left over from a more voluptuous age; a handwritten sign taped to the door of a legal aid office announces 'no consultations this week: the solicitors are on strike'! And then, with a fanfare of Mediterranean light, there is the big, wide, open port at the bottom of a busy street. Of course Marseilles is dangerous; you bet it is. It is a seaport with dens and bars and brothels and a vigorous underworld, guns are as easily accessible as everywhere else in France, neighbourhoods are inimical and the city shelters every sort of villainy, but Marseilles is not boring and it is not crass. Being off the American tourist trail now, as it was in the 1950s for us youngsters of Study Abroad, it has escaped the creeping Disneyfication, the sterilising and freezing and packaging and marketing that increasingly overtakes Europe's beautiful and ancient cities. Many of the places you visited in 1954, my junior version, as far as the twenty-first-century visitor knows or can tell, are ceasing to be living cities of complex texture and idiosyncratic nature and political clout; they are becoming showcases for T-shirts and novelty pens, selling, selling, selling all the city is famous for: a museum or a bridge; a horse race and Gothic architecture; china, silk, leather or glass; a celebrated restaurant squeezed between universal fast-food outlets; and for goodness sake, you cannot go home without a picture of yourself standing in front of that wonky tower! And how much are you supposed to tip the guide? And aren't you afraid to travel on your own?

Yes, yes, I know it is the way of old folks to exaggerate the shabbiness of things now that live fresh in our memories. But did you exaggerate then, too, young I, the soul-stirring delights of your first trip to Europe? No, you did not. And would you find what you saw equally moving now? Except perhaps in glimpses as if through a door in one of the Dutch paintings you admired so much, and admire to this day even as you shuffle before them half-drowned in an endless river of tourists flowing as fast as it can to the shop and the postcards.

'1954: Oh, what a delicious something is in Europe and foreign in my homeland. The theatre in London! The noise and spirit in Rome! What is it? There is a depth and

305

humanity. An elegance of history: I don't know what I mean, but it is all I can think of to call it . . .'

Elegance: the word in your lifetime will lose its gloss. But I know what you mean, young I: you mean old human ingenuity, its opulence and style, its silence in repose. You mean a depth of history, some of it cruel, and deep thoughts, some of them evil, which were thought in Europe for the first time long ago. You mean humanity that grew up in the locale and continued to pray there, to play, to stroll with their families, to work and eat in those places where now the hordes from Kansas and Kent leave no room for them. The fact is the Grand Tour has slipped downmarket. If you were young now, jetting over to continental Europe for the first time, of course you would enjoy yourself, and find here and there the enchantment you found almost everywhere in the 1950s. However, for the growing awe and sense of discovery you had with Study Abroad, for the mystery and captivation of an old, old world, a youngster needs nowadays to travel to the top of Peru, or the far Far East, and your great-grandchildren, I guess, will have to go to Mars as soon as they are able, before McDonald's exports terrestrial swill and Taiwan makes shirts and shoes to fit the little green men.

The only other English visitors I bumped into in Marseilles were a couple of travelling salesmen there to sell machine parts, not to plunder museum gift shops and cute boutiques; the only thing I had to queue for was a pizza. It would have been no misfortune to spend more time in Marseilles. It is elegant. Should I ever again get up and go for no reason except the impulse to be gone, it will be in that direction.

'1954: We are moving fast. Quickly, too quickly, through Avignon, one of the loveliest places I have ever seen. The mistral was in a gentle mood. A fairy tale castle was perched on a hill. A bridge, though half destroyed, sits quietly and daintily. The usual subtle French meal, a sort of soufflé in pastry with truffles, meat roasted very rare in wine with mushroom sauce. There are long waits between courses and food is family style, so we can serve ourselves. There is wine at every meal. I have seen Frenchmen having wine with their breakfast! Midge and Ev and I agreed to ban all pastry until we get to Paris, when it is too late to develop the habit. You don't know the creativity of humankind until you see the inside of a French patisserie! The hotel put on a little performance of folk songs and dances for us. Silly! I don't believe local people jump around that way when they're not paid to do it. Midge and I planned to mutiny. When we got to Carcassonne, we were going to remain there, hike or bike for a few days to escape the sheltering bus, and catch up with everyone in Paris. Paris! Paris! Ev was invited but she said we were crazy. She has been acting funny again, very critical, like an old lady. I don't understand. Nothing hurts like other people! As it turned out we did not stay in Carcassonne because of the expense and, to be honest, the oppressiveness

307

of the town. Broke the door. Soap in my suitcase! A day to forget!'

Anything to oblige you, sweetheart: consider the day forgotten. What door? What soap? It's the least I can do for you. I owe you my life, after all. And I'll forgive the crack about an old lady; we're not so bad when you get to know us. The run to Carcassonne this time by train was faster than yours on the bus, and less intriguing, though beautiful enough over dark gold earth under a sky of dull lead. Across the aisle a middle-aged woman read *Harry Potter* in French; at Arles, a bearded man got on and immediately opened Tolkien's *Lord of the Rings*, also in French. Am I the only adult on board? In front of me a hyperactive mama, dark and pretty as a cat, is up and down, in and out of the carriage, opening and closing her bag, doling out drinks, then sandwiches to her two sons, sturdy boys of about ten and twelve, who shrug and exchange precocious smiles of tolerance, as grown men do over the antics of a pretty girl.

French railways are indisputably the most reliable and efficient in Europe. Passengers are required at the risk of stiff fines to frank their own tickets before boarding, and as it is possible to make entire journeys without once encountering a conductor or showing credentials, the only disadvantage to the system, some would say, is a democratic one that allows buskers and beggars to take their chances, too. Just beyond Nîmes, a young man wearing neat blue jeans and a dark swinging ponytail appeared at the door of the compartment. 'If you please, ladies and gentlemen, a short announcement,' he said in a clear strong voice. 'I have no food, no place to stay, no way even to wash or stay clean. Anything you give will help, a few pennies, anything at all.'

I gave him some coins; jumpy mama gave him a flirtatious smile and half a sandwich; he thanked us as a well-brought-up youngster would and as far as I could tell collected no more from anyone in the crowded carriage.

At the very next stop we were invaded by another beggar of a type I have encountered only in France. A smiling young-ish man, he passed through the carriage dropping off at each table or fold-down shelf, such as the one in front of me, small dolls and slips of paper printed with the message that he was a deaf mute, and if we found any beauty in the fluffy toy he was offering us, we could buy it to ensure our happiness and good fortune: price – twenty or twenty-five francs. What is peculiarly disconcerting about this ploy is the cost of our happiness being so precisely stipulated, though in this case it was not yet translated into euros; and also, the toy in which we are supposed to find beauty is a clown of such sinister aspect it could appeal only to minor league Satanists. As usual, I returned the ghastly gewgaw when the boy reappeared, admittedly, I slipped him a coin. Nobody else in the compartment gave him a crust or a penny.

'Behold the mendicant,' said I to you, young one, every bit as abstruse as I, 'who can't . . .'

309

There was a conductor on our train to Carcassonne, too, the first I had seen in a long time; he would have been rare under any circumstances. He was as handsome as the sun: broad-shouldered and bronzed, he could have been an American Indian from the age of his tribe's prime, only with bright-blue eyes. I was chagrined, not to say downright annoyed, when this young godling did not ask to see my passport or so much as question my entitlement to the senior discount his colleague in the ticket office at Marseilles had urged upon me.

The crenellated walls of the medieval city of Carcassonne are a presence felt even when hidden in mist and rain, their weight palpable from parts of the low town where it is not possible actually to see them, their defensive purpose bred into the very air of the place. Whether it is hidden in layers of floral paper or an invisible essence trapped in crevices of stone, walls built long ago to shut things out retain a patina, a smell almost, of the things they shut in. To live within an ancient walled city, as I did off and on for years in the Old Town of Boulogne sur Mer, is romantic, yes, and alluring, and suffocating. It is to be locked in with sheltered dust and something dank, too, left over from dark and superstitious ages. Sensitive and thin-skinned young I – you and I, I and I – we agree: Carcassonne remains oppressive to our way of thinking. There is just too much history, too much suffering, too much Inquisitorial righteousness locked into it for comfort. Judging from the numerous souvenir shops, most of them closed for the season, tourism in the summer must test surrounding walls and ramps from within, as countless sieges used to from without. On a rainy day off-season it was a desolate and melancholy setting for a piece of theatre that had played its last act.

'Carcassonne is beautiful,' I said to the stout, middle-aged woman behind me in the checkout queue at Monoprix in the low town and indeed, it is.

'Really?' she replied, surprised. 'You don't find it sad?'

'Yes, to be honest, I do. But sad is beautiful, too.'

We both looked at the purchases I had put down on the counter: an umbrella, for it continued to rain, and a bottle of Evian water. The combination amused us both simultaneously. Even as we were chuckling together I took note that Carcassonne is another of those places on earth where inhabitants are desperate for a laugh.

Next to my small table in the station coffee bar, a door gave on to Platform One where the train to Paris would soon be pulling out, not my train; I was going on a later train to spend the night in Perpignan where a London friend had taken a house and invited me to drop in. My seat was already reserved on one of the great TGV trains the following day to Lille from the droll and slightly alarming station in Perpignan, built in homage to Salvador Dali. After a night in Lille, it would be on to Calais. And home. With an hour to kill over milky coffee, I opened Schopenhauer's treatise *On Human Nature*, bought hopefully twenty years earlier in a second-hand bookshop. When, if not a rainy morning, would I ever in this life get around to reading Schopenhauer? Where if not in the station café at Carcassonne? '. . . there is joined more or less in every human breast', he wrote, 'a fund of hatred, anger, envy, rancour and malice . . .'

At that moment the departure for Paris was announced and a pair of well-dressed women about my own age jumped up to hurry out for it, leaving the door to the platform open behind them so a cruel wind blew through the café. The waitress, who had until then treated us dozen or so customers with even-handed indifference, propelled her sturdy self towards the flapping door; before slamming it shut she shouted out on to the platform, 'You stupid cows! Maybe in Paris doors close themselves! But in Carcassonne we have to do it!'

I heard myself humming the stripper's theme from *Pal Joey*. 'Zip!' she sings, 'I was reading Schopenhauer last night. Zip! And I think that Schopenhauer was right . . .'

As Anglophone expats steadily colonise south-western France, they bring to it a little of the look and feel of a greener and less heavily trafficked southern California. It seems to me as expatriates go, those who choose rural France are trying to put health and order into rackety lives; many of them have left, angry at their home states and fed up with the weather, not unlike a lot of Americans drawn to the suburbs of California. The swift transition from mountains to sea of the countryside around Perpignan reminded me of

312

Orange County too, enough to make the signposts to Barcelona an enticement; I found myself tempted to head for the exotic border fast, as I do for Mexico as soon as possible after my plane lands in Los Angeles. An evening of gossip with the London friend who has rented a house in the area and an intense flirtation with the shorter-haired of her two cats, a smart tortoiseshell still traumatised by the flight south, and in the morning, refreshed, I boarded the TGV from Perpignan straight to Lille.

As soon as my back was to the Spanish border and I was facing more or less towards London, my heart filled to bursting with thoughts of home until, moored far out beyond a stretch of marshland I saw a rusty old tramp steamer, a visitor from clean and perilous spaces. Instantly, the yearning to be at sea was as strong as the one to be home; I had to turn the other way until the seductive old boat would be out of sight before I lost my mind to it. Parallel to our tracks the road inland was lined with witty trees like puffs of green smoke.

Across the aisle a heavily pregnant woman was reading a book about the undersea world by the great diver, Jacques Cousteau. 'Waiting for her waters to break, you see,' I whispered to you, child and silly companion.

The man next to me was holding a magazine that dealt with the arts and issues of high intellect; he was not reading it, just holding it open to a small photograph of himself, whoever he was, taken when his hairline had receded much less.

* * *

'1954: Outside the bus is good, wholesome, solid, rolling country. Houses are square and stone. Fields are neat and bullocks pull the tractors. Women work in the fields alongside the men. The towns are cleaner than Italy and filled with flowers. Here people live in the backyard behind their houses, not so much in the street as the Italians do. There are many old people. The old women are grand; they wear long grey skirts and black aprons and white lace scarves. Some of them wear round, mannish, black straw hats. When the shutters are open I catch glimpses of clean parlours, a kettle and a cat, and scrubbed, shiny floors. In some peculiar way I envy them. I envy what I see but of course each town has its fears and scandals.'

Stuck on the rails, we saw none of your picturesque old ladies; they were already leftovers from another era back in the 1950s, and they are non-existent now except perhaps in themed cafés, or on postcards. As for bullocks pulling tractors, not very likely these days, my sweet, not west of Turkey or east of Thailand; you still called it Siam. No question about the pink question marks bobbing in marsh grasses, however; they really were flamingos. North of Montpellier streaky clouds gathered, chill returned, and low stone houses sat in the same neat fields you saw in the summer of 1954, only now they lay with their brown sides up like pancakes on a winter table.

It was fascinating to watch how France became perceptibly

more serious as we sped north; unfortunately, however, window-gazing is generally seen as nothing to do and the solitary woman across from me who had also boarded in Perpignan was itching to talk. Every time our eyes made contact she sent out a friendly message that I resisted for as long as I could. Schopenhauer was getting a run for his money, helping me look studious and utterly absorbed. The journey ahead was about six hours, admirably short for travelling practically the length of a great nation; too long, however, to open conversation with an unknown fellow passenger. Her face was lightly freckled, her wide-set eyes of Gallic not-quite-green, her hair fair and cut short. She was petite, dressed carefully and comfortably; she had the wholesome glow and compact build of a sportswoman. A stocky young man had seen her on board, their restrained but cordial farewell struck me as suitable to brother and visiting sister or sister-in-law; a weepy three-year-old miniature of daddy held his hand and waved from the platform until we pulled out.

Our train had been boarded at the same station by a solitary ancient fellow who was installed diagonally across the aisle from me. As we entered a northern region of storm clouds and heavy traffic and industry, he became suddenly agitated; appealing to the carriage at large, he told us that he realised in his haste to catch the train he had not franked his ticket. Neighbouring passengers tried to put him at ease, to assure him that even if a conductor should appear, a man of his apparent honesty and years would have no problem.

315

The little drama made it impossible for the woman across the way and me to continue in silence. 'My aunt', she said, 'is ninety-five, amazing woman, she lives alone, cooks for herself, gardens, keeps her accounts and shops. But now she has been thrown into despair. She simply cannot cope with the euro. It has put her into a terrible depression. After all these years, she can no longer shop or pay her bills or care for herself. The euro is a wonderful thing for travellers and business, but I fear it will be the end of her.'

'Schopenhauer says . . .' I told her eagerly, for who knew how long before another occasion to quote Schopenhauer would arise? '. . . Schopenhauer says that coins are merely counters. But I'm afraid these days they count for everything, for life itself.'

When the young man sitting next to her interrupted to ask if he could raise the armrest between them, there was a swift flirtatious frisson between them. While she helped him unnecessarily, I saw a faint pale outline round the finger where her wedding band ought to be. She told me then she had two children, two horses, two dogs; the little boy who saw her off was her younger son and the chap was, in fact, her husband. He had several times relocated his family for his job, she told me, always in France. Perpignan was fine except there was active racism against what she called the 'gypsies'; I took it to mean immigrants in general from Eastern Europe. Bordeaux, where they lived for a while, was full of snobs; Rennes was pleasant; her happiest time by far, however, was in Lille. She worked too, mostly at home, something to do with finance; mercifully she spared me details about this, my area of deepest darkness. Once a month when she makes the trek to Lille for business, her husband takes care of the home and children. That is where she is bound now, to stay overnight in a fine hotel and attend a formal business dinner in Lille. She described lovingly a black silk dress in her suitcase overhead. 'And two bottles of superb Muscadet, too,' she said.

Oops! The peculiar redundancy of carrying wine to a formal business dinner struck us both simultaneously. She blushed. With over two hours left to our destination, it was her turn now to avoid further conversation; the closer we got to Lille, the more difficult it became for her to pretend to nap or read. She fussed with her pale-pink lipstick once or twice and discreetly perfumed her wrists with tuberose essence. I remembered that kind of excitement; I remember it: racing from afar to meet the other who is hurrying to the same place – most trains must be carrying one or two like that, nuts and bolts racing across nations to meet and make celestial screws. Quicker than a whippet, she was up and off the train when we arrived, not out of the station fast enough, however, to prevent me seeing her in the steamy embrace of a tall, fair man on the platform.

Lille is a fine city with interesting architecture in the old quarter, good food and a sympathetic pace. Just before dawn the next day I left my hotel to walk to the station for the

317

train to Calais and on that very instant the street lights were switched off to make way for a rare emerald dawn, a municipal miracle. At the Calais station waited one taxi as if by arrangement to take me to the dock.

'I was born in a coal mine,' said my aged driver, pleasantly opening conversation; indeed, I had never known the French in general to be as congenial and chatty as on this lap of my journey. 'Mama was hiding from English bombs. No hard feelings. We people of the North have big mouths, and even bigger hearts.'

The French ferry pulled away from the windswept edge of France, a solemn, sweeping landscape where in the summer poppies bloom, incarnadine. Standing there alone on the empty deck with the tricolour flapping beside me, I thought I had never liked France more. Except, once upon a time: once upon a time, I had liked it more, had I not, young I? I had liked it more than anywhere on earth.

'1954: Paris! Paris! Paris! Tomorrow we're in Paris! Paris! Paris! I want to keep saying Paris! Paris! I'm a fool for Paris!'

Eighteen

'1954: Paris! Paris! We arrived late last night in a grey rain and suddenly someone shouted and there was the Eiffel Tower. The Eiffel Tower! How is a person supposed to feel when she sees something she has heard about, dreamed about, all her life? Disbelief! Me here and Paris here! Together at last! I nearly cried, not from happiness, from the effort of making it real. This is Paris! Paris! And I am really here. How I love it! I crossed to the Right Bank of the Seine and walked alone through the Tuileries up to the Place de la Concorde. This is me! I am walking in Paris! I bought a postcard of the Pont des Arts and sent it to Marjorie. She is my best friend and the only person who will understand how I feel. She must have felt the same way last year when she came to Paris with Study Abroad. All I could write on it was "Eureka! Paris!" Marjorie will know all I cannot say. I went back to the Left Bank and looked at bookstalls, prints and paintings and coins and books. A few artists perched precariously on the walls by the great river and dabbed at canvases. Are they trying to reproduce the beauty of this city? Or does this city make artists out of them? Out of everyone? Out of me too, perhaps? Too much to hope for! There were bearded bohemians, too, and I was happy to see them. I love Paris. This is the place.'

Burbling child, what made you so easily hooked? Was it a congenital weakness for glamour? All those late-night sessions in the dormitory over Edith Piaf and Jacques Trenet? Too many mesmerising words in a language barely under-stood? Yours was not the first generation of Americans – it was, however, probably the last – to ascribe all essential refinement and style to the French as wistfully as the Russian court used to do. In the 1950s Paris was once again and briefly the coolest place on earth; black-and-white photographs of the time made heaven of its silvery tone; fashionable ballerina skirts were designed for its flat-chested, gamine women and a constant aura of Gauloises was devilishly suited to men renowned for their amorous achievement. In the Fifties, youth everywhere, in cafés and classrooms and seedy bars, used to talk and talk and talk as enthusiastically as later generations were going to yowl over electric guitars and nobody, but nobody, did talking better than post-war Parisians. True enough, I cannot remember one word they said; the superior clarity of their delivery, however, was unforgettable. And your beloved bohemians, precocious bratling, had a smart, funny line in chat. You will follow the

320

bohemian spoor through Greenwich Village, the Left Bank and, eventually, into Soho, even though the poor darlings will already be gasping for air by the mid-1960s, when you finally find your place in London. It had to be bohemia for you and me. We grew up between the beatniks and the hippies. The beats had hit the road by the time you entered the university from which Jack Kerouac had graduated a few years earlier. And you were on your way to middle age when the hippies skipped out on their daisy-strewn path, which was not, in any case, our kind of thing: too flowery and un- productive, too smug and comfy and lazy, too bloody com- munal. In spite of the generous way that bohemianism allowed its followers to grow very, very old in its style without becoming any more or less ridiculous, they are all but extinct these days. The flouting of convention that set bohemians apart under a lower-case 'b', their casual promiscuity, their acceptance of sexual deviation long before it was either politi- cally correct or correct politics; their incidental drug-taking and hard drinking, and all the showy bohemian self- indulgences are common throughout society now. Even the outrageous cut and colour of their garb is available to week- end bohemians in every high-street shop.

'Alas!' I hear you cry, 'is nothing profane?'

Bohemian wit and cerebral daring, devotion to art for its own sweet sake and, most of all, contempt for money as worth not a penny more than the ephemera it buys, all that is a receding memory in the hearts of a few surviving exiles.

321

Bohemia has disintegrated into motes that dance in air everywhere and nowhere.

You have informed me, my baby parent; I cannot return the compliment; I cannot tell you or let you know and, even if I could pull you back from your delirious ascent to disappointment, I would not. How could I? I am who you are becoming. I am your creation. To go back and change you, my ardent prototype, would be to kill myself, and if I were suicidal by nature I would have drowned us both in the filthy Seine one dark day all those years ago when our faith in freedom and adventure was spluttering and fighting for its life. So go along, sweet child, make what you must of Paris and the bohemians. I will not stop you. I cannot stop you. Like a sailor without immunity to fever raging in port, a single breath in your avid young body would be the death of me now and it would destroy you, too, for I carry an infection hostile to your exuberance and your very life: I am infected with the debilitating and mortal condition of experience.

'1954: Handsome Frenchmen everywhere with lit cigarettes dangling from their lower lips. I am in the first flush of love. I hardly know Paris. But I know my feelings for Paris are real and they will deepen.'

Yes, dear, they will deepen, down, down and deep as a well. As in torch songs so popular at the time in the cabarets of

Montmartre, your impatient love, the romantic conviction
you were born to belong to Paris, your deep and utterly
unreciprocated longing will drag you down too into dissi-
pation of mind and body that would have done for you, my
girl, and for both of us, had you been half as helpless as you
believed yourself to be. Paris, upon my first return in the
late 1950s, was as stunning as it had been when seen from
the window of the Study Abroad coach, only now that I had
designs on Paris for permanence and the future, and now
that I was alone there, it became elusive and distant and
hurtful.

'You are not ready for it,' a waiter said one night, dismiss-
ing the request for steak tartare I had finally found nerve
enough to order at last from his menu. Perhaps he was right;
perhaps I was not ready for Paris. An idealistic Yank raised
on happy endings is hardly prepared for the rigid and sophisticated rules of an old, old game.

'Black is only worn during the day by old ladies in mourn-
ing,' chided one of the dimmest female students at the language school where I worked for a while, and I walked the
side streets back to my flophouse later, collar up, to hide my
faux pas.

Isolation, poverty, frustration, self-disgust; my twenties
were wasting away in disappointment and stalked by
depression, snarling and ruby-eyed, not the mangy old grey
thing that turns up sometimes these days. I cannot remember
now precisely how testing the Parisian episode turned out to

323

be, just that it was pure misery and very hard. And, honey, you passed the test. Yes, memory fails us as we grow old. But we fail memory, too. Only youth creates memories worth guarding and only youth can make them so painful and dangerous they must be sidestepped. Although I now spend a lot of time in France, its capital to this day is mined and perilous for me; I can turn any corner there and bang! A high helmeted window, a corner café or a stall piled with polished apples explodes into memories of failure and despair; memories that you, dear unclouded I, were soon to make.

The handsome young Frenchman next to me on the Eurostar out of Waterloo Station to Paris was dark and compact. Was he crazy about the English girlfriend he told me he had been visiting in London? Mad passion is hard to recognise in men unless they are writing songs or sonnets to its object, or making love, and even then the exhibitionist has been known to overtake the lunatic. When he told me he was a musician with a group, I knew the noise they made would not be music to my ears; nothing about younger generations irks older ones as much as the racket they make. His name was Jean-Philippe. Forty years ago, when I lived in Paris, they were almost all some kind of Jean: Jean-Yveses, Jean-Françoises, Jean-Jacqueses, Jean-Louises, countless Jean-Pierres and Jean-Michels, and a wide sprinkling of Jean-Charleses. I found myself sitting next to the one and only Jean-Paul once in La Coupole and I shivered to see how intently the philosopher gazed at me until I realised his lazy eye was turned my way; his active eye was fixed on the pretty girl opposite. Somewhere in London was a young woman warm and dreamy, smiling to herself a lot and boring her confidantes rigid as she analysed again and again every gesture, every word spoken by her own darling 'Jean' during their time together.

'It is very expensive,' he complained and I was a little sad to know he meant carrying on a trans-Channel affair.

Outside, England chugged along to an outer edge of what used to be watery isolation. You could never have guessed, antique I, you whose windswept crossings were made with affection for London, increasing on each departure, you could not have dreamed that one day trains would actually burrow under the awesome Channel and the tunnel that was once a mariner's joke, 'the chunnel', was going to landlock England to France, while bringing them barely an inch closer in points of view. Eurostar trains are relatively efficient, at least on the French side, though far too expensive, as characterless as air travel and almost as uncomfortable. For a long time after we left Waterloo Station a group of stout Midwestern Americans continued to wander up and down the half-empty coaches wondering aloud, in their oddly punctilious American way, whether it was OK to sit anywhere at all, or did you have to stay in your reserved seat? There was no conductor to ask, so they asked each other. Nobody had helped hoist luggage on board either, or offered us coffee where we sat. 'The only way to justify the inflated price of first-class travel', I said to Jean-Philippe before I realised he was dozing behind his dark glasses, 'is to make the lower classes as uncomfortable as possible.'

Merely another *pensée trouvée*, I asked myself? Or could it qualify as a Great Truth and the sort of thing groups of us – former soldiers on the GI Bill, a few hopeful Anglophone scribblers, a scattering of South Americans and Asians – used to sit around discussing endlessly in cafés with students from the Sorbonne, smoking and drinking, and letting rip in flawed French and English that met at a height where the long words know each other. Our marathon conversations were different from those in the dorms of Barnard College in the early Fifties when the thrust of budding cults in psychiatry and sociology was to abrogate personal responsibility, pretty much as biological genetics does now, and lay blame for all the world's troubles along with our own on daddy and mommy and the state we were born in. A more demanding standard of palaver prevailed in Paris, one that acknowledged conscience and choice and rebellion. As I walked back to my cheap digs after midnight from the Café Tournon, or the Old Navy, or any of the nameless coffee holes on Boulevard St-Michel, my head buzzed with new ideas while very often one of the talkers walked beside me and whispered the oldest idea into my ear. Looking back, I can see that the young Parisians, whatever their political colour, were beginning to be as mad for American culture derived from Hollywood as we were for their older one. It was only because in the late 1950s more and more Parisians were asking to be taught in an American accent that I was grudgingly offered my penny-ante job teaching English at a British-run language school.

Our train had barely come to a full stop in the Gare du Nord before young Jean-Philippe was off and running for the Métro to what he told me was the emergent arty quarter of Belleville, where he and his group had a gig that night: a paid appointment to raise somebody's roof. Outside the station, where street noises were pitched half an octave or so higher than in London, I walked straight into the gorgeous old stink: magnolias, sweat and bread – Paris. Paris! Paris! Pushed along by the crowd, I noticed a muttering old crone looking out at me from a passing window, her eyes narrowed in shock, revulsion almost. So fierce and sudden had been the old Parisian ache of yearning and exclusion that I was shocked to find me in the glass there instead of you, young I.

'1954: Time is passing too quickly. Paris frightens me. This passion is too much. I sit here in the Tuileries, all by myself. I don't know where the group has gone. I don't care. I've had enough of the group. After she came back from her summer with Study Abroad, Marjorie always had a smile on her face when she talked about Paris and now I know why. People in the park look like a Seurat painting, animated bits of colour. Couples are necking on benches; big women lead

327

dogs or children with equal nonchalance. The best spot is right here near the big fountain. Everyone is seated around it on folding chairs. Older boys and some men are setting little toy sailboats afloat on the green water and then racing madly round the fountain to catch them before they bump or sink. Little girls throw bread for fat brown fish that rise to the surface and nibble daintily. Sometimes a flashing orange fish snatches a crumb away from the lazy fellows who then flutter indifferently: there's always more where that came from. Children bounce on the edge of the pond and make their mamas cry: "*Attention! Fais attention!*" Here I am describing fish-feeding at the Tuileries and I haven't been to the Champs-Elysées yet. I feel no burning need to see the Champs-Elysées right now. No need to see anything but this. Ever. In a little while I will stroll over to the Left Bank and walk beside the fishermen along the Seine. I never want to go home. Never. I would not want to go home ever again, except for the family. I will come back here. I must come back here. I have never been so happy. Why am I sad?'

Voluntary expatriation is undertaken either in anger or in love and you, poor virgin child, are in love. You have found your bliss, and to follow it means abandoning your homeland and your home, all known company and most of the birthright that passes for destiny. Even in the delirium of the Tuileries you knew, I know you did, that to reject inheritance and uproot hope meant no primal homecoming ever again, and no roots deeper than where you happened to be standing. Expatriation entails disorientation. Home changes too while the traveller explores and it soon departs for ever from the point she holds in memory; thereafter, she travels with a faulty compass. Look at you now: look at me – not a European, how can I be? Inclination is not enough. And I am sure as hell not much of an American, either. It seems curious to me now that you cited your family as a reason for postponement. Was it an apology in advance for a decision already taken? Perhaps you suspected what I later learned was true, that your defection was to be construed – misconstrued – as your father's fault: for being a dentist, for staying close to his impoverished past, for his table manners, for his inability to pronounce certain words – Saturday, Beethoven, dandelion – and for disappointing the expectations of his wife. Also, you were bound to be turned into an object lesson for your little brother: the absurd and nutty sister, drat her! For whom he was born to compensate.

'1954: Tony left us this morning. He went home to dear old London and we went to the Louvre to see some of the most beautiful things in the world. I can talk about the world with a little more authority now. One thing is all I know for sure: we are born into the world, to the whole world, not just to a country. And it is a crime to sacrifice youth to old age. That's *two* things I know for sure, isn't it?'

*   *   *

And I continue to hold with them, though I pay the price for both. By the way, missy, what a faithless little bitch you were back then. The departure of Tony, quondam princeling of Albion, written off with barely a line in your journal. Why could you not have remained so fickle and flighty and cruel? If only you had, my heart might not now resemble a jigsaw in an old people's home, frayed and cracked, with bits missing from the cottage at the end of the lane. Why did you bother to develop a heart, if it was merely to hand it over carelessly? Oops! Forgive me, little flibbertigibbet, I forget myself, and you: irony has yet to root itself in your repertoire. Take my meaning as the opposite of my words. Except, of course, on those occasions when I mean precisely what I say.

'1954: A letter from Mom asks why I do not stay a week or so longer in Europe. First, how am I supposed to pay for it? I'm booked out with Study Abroad on the *Castel Felice*, I have paid for my berth and, if it sails without me, where do I find the fare home? Second, I would have to stay all alone. I have only been alone for short weekends in the past; I think I should learn how to do it better at home before I try it for longer abroad. And finally, if I stayed an extra week or a month, it still would not be enough. I would still be just an observer. I want to live here and make lasting connections in Europe. As tourist and part of a tour it is time to go home. I am going to live in Europe some day. I will live in Paris. But now, the tour is over.'

*   *   *

Eighteen was a less sophisticated, dewier age in your less sophisticated, dewy era than it has become today; you were already wise to know that you were not ready yet to be so much alone, especially not in penury and a land where the language was not your own. Solitude is a sport for the old and a kid like you has years of hard training ahead before she's out of shape for it. The lessons of loneliness were going to be nailed into us later over innumerable solitary cold meals, all by myself, in Parisian rented rooms the size of broom cupboards. Mind you, a romantic American girl would have trouble these days trying to feel adrift alone in Paris. Of all European capitals, Paris is the one your countrymen – our countrymen I mean, of course – like best and tour most conscientiously in big, noisy groups. Even in the chill of not-quite-spring I saw them everywhere, parodies of their kind, camera-heavy, never alone, fat knees grinning under unseasonable Bermuda shorts. In the breakfast room of my nondescript hotel near the Place d'Italie, a married couple of Yanks thanked God for the continental breakfast they were about to receive while the Algerian waitresses exchanged looks over their bowed heads.

Paris cannot ever again be seen as you saw it, shimmering and expansive and alive. These days it is gripped in a hideous setting of high-rise slums that encircle it, allow it nowhere to grow and make of it a luxury item, a cultivated pearl of rich surface but without the breadth and oceanic currents of London, say, or the daring verticality of New York. From the moment I joined the queue for taxis outside the Gare du Nord, swollen by publishers in town for a French-language book fair who had incidentally also booked every room in the fourth arrondissement hotels I prefer, Paris came across as pampered, introverted and provincial: a false lover from the past, handsome yet, to be sure, but shallow and conventional, and how could I have been so deluded as to have suffered so much for such a fop?

One striking change was in local temperament. Parisians used to be every bit as brusque as New Yorkers, their nasty temper altogether unredeemed by the mocking and self-mocking New York wit. This time not a taxi driver, not a fellow traveller in the Métro, not even the *garçons* at the big café near my hotel, snapped or snarled at me gratuitously, or gawped as if my French were a Venusian's dialect; only a few salesgirls in the big department stores near the Opéra showed traces of the old disdain and snippiness. Perhaps this new sweetness is because so many workaday jobs these days are taken by immigrants who are scared of giving offence as Parisians never were. Or perhaps the friendliness of the Parisians I encountered and their eagerness to please was just the luck of the draw. Certainly, it was inexplicably diminishing, like bumping into a famed and fatal bitch from the old days and seeing that she has lost her teeth, lost her bite. While a shopkeeper near the gardens of Palais Royal kept me pinned in place for ten minutes discussing pleasantly enough a possibility of rain before evening, the splendid surrounding architecture began to look downright bungaloid to my eyes. In your day, young *moi*, Parisians were never, never heard to knock their town, either, certainly not to an outsider. Does any other city on earth have so many songs sung in praise of its beauty, its bridges, its seasons and its very soul? This time, street moans about traffic, crime, cost of living and, especially, about immigration were almost as vociferous as in London, the most self-deprecating of capital cities.

Too many memories put a barrier between me and Paris. Roaming aimlessly in a city where I had once upon a time been purposeful was disconcerting, no matter that my purpose had been insubstantial: to become what I imagined a Parisian to be – worldly, artistic and loved for simply being what she was: a Parisian. I feel distracted in Paris these days, not all there, worried, on the edge of missing an important rendezvous, although I have never had one of any urgency in Paris, ever. Only my first great love affair with Douglas, the sailor, was essentially a long series of rendezvous and it finally ended there. My city of romance was muted around me this time, muffled and distant, until by perfect chance I found myself suddenly on the Boulevard Arago right in front of a door it hurt like fury to see again. There had I stood, shaking and wounded, forty years ago, on those very molecules of pavement.

My first assault on Paris and Europe after university had failed within a year or so because I lost my nerve. Back in

New York I worked for a couple of lean years to save enough for a second attempt, each day more convinced that, for good or ill, I belonged on the sunrise side of the Atlantic. Long weekly letters to my friends, Hank and Rhoda, who were living in Paris, lucky dogs, chronicled my progress and my do-or-die designs on making a European life. At last, one day in the late Fifties, the ship sailed on what was to be my last sea crossing of the Atlantic. Exultant to be back in Paris – Paris! Paris! – there I had stood, right there, on the pavement in front of my friends' building on the Boulevard Arago. It was the day and practically to the hour the time that I had gleefully written and written again and again to warn them I was going to be knocking at their door with a bottle of champagne in hand and claiming their sofa until I found a place of my own.

'Not here. Gone to Spain on holiday. No, you certainly cannot have the keys. They told me nothing about the arrival of a . . .' the shrivelled concierge looked me up and down '. . . a friend,' she said and, with a sneer at my suitcases, she slammed the door in my face.

On that spot, poor child, you learned the bitterest lesson: we are flawed – we cannot be the other. Friends, lovers, parents who are able to free themselves from their own plans and distractions, to disentangle from self-love and envy, to set aside their invidious theories and opinions of how things should be, people who can put themselves into another's skin for a pure celebration of the other's joy, or sorrow, are as rare in this life as feathers on a shark. There, on that wide boulevard not ten paces from the Santé prison, you and I learned in a flash to expect less of practically everyone save our self, and forgive more, only less our self.

'Can I help you?'

Beside me stood a white-haired man, a Parisian. A Parisian! Offering to help a stranger? Almighty time brings miracles to pass.

'Are you looking for something?'

'My memories,' I told him.

'Oh, Madame, never look for your memories; they will find you soon enough.'

To make a great and ancient university central to their capital instead of sticking it uptown or downtown or in a town all its own seemed to us in days of old to express a Gallic respect for intellect that pervaded social classes and generations. Surely now it is only the very rich, often as not also deeply under-educated, who can live near the Sorbonne. Everything in your beloved Latin Quarter, my I of yesteryear, has become showy and expensive. Not a sign of those restaurants where for pennies in the late Fifties we ate whatever the cook was eating that night. And where are the cheap long-stay hotels with glorious names? My own was Le Grand Hôtel de France. Students and prostitutes and a few temporary romantics like me lived there in squalor alleviated somewhat by steamy sessions in the local public baths, where our voices rose from the cubicles in a shaggy medley of songs from disparate faiths and nations. An afternoon coffee at the Café Tournon, my favourite local hang-out in the old days, costs as much now as a three-course meal cost back then. At least the decor remains neo-Impressionist, the toilet is still what used to be called 'Turkish' and the middle-aged woman behind the bar could be the daughter or granddaughter of the old Madame, a harridan with coal-black hair that was commonly rumoured to be a wig. It was whispered her hair failed to grow back after her head was shaved and she was run through the streets for collaborating with the Nazis during the war.

It never entered your mind, love-blinded beggar girl, that just as London in the Fifties and into the Sixties still carried pockmarks left by bombs, so must Paris have been scarred in other ways by enemy occupation and by treachery. What humiliation was hidden and how much shame defended by the humourless Parisian street temper of old? The sentimental aggrandising of their city – all those songs, paintings and photographs – as well as the stealthy exclusion of the poor and disaffected from its centre, was it all undertaken to raise the fame of a beauty uniquely unscathed on a continent disfigured by war? Was Paris cultivated and protected in the post-war years, and brought to a peak of loveliness that would defang and transcend accusations of collaboration and cowardice by generations that remembered?

A group of trim Parisiennes passed in front of the café terrace where I indulged my unfriendly musing. They were smoking and talking into mobile phones. At the table next to me a pair of their spitting images talked into their own phones, turned away from each other, cigarette smoke rising around them. On every last café table in Paris where there sits a young woman alone or with friends is laid out beside each of them a mobile and a pack of Marlboro Lights, high-fashion accessories this season for girls of the capital. I never have had a Parisienne as a close friend. Being a single American woman abroad in those days made me a sort of dime store exotic and a worrying sexual curiosity for their men. Perhaps now I am old and retired from active duty on the distaff side, women of Paris would like me better? Probably not. Friendship with a woman of Paris requires one to dress for it and I have never had chic. I have not had a Parisian man as a great friend, either, only a few in a less enduring role: lovers more epic than tender, as I recall, accomplished and proud and profligate in their *force de frappe*.

'1954: I admit it helps endear Europe to me that I am considered here quite beautiful, as I am not in New York. I can wander around in a polo shirt and blue jeans, and men turn to look at me here, which is flattering.'

In the margin of this page is scribbled a note to yourself, to me – 'Remember what happened in Place St Sulpice! Strange!'

You had yet again escaped the group. It was a clear and sunny morning, and you were all by yourself in Paris. Paris! You stopped to browse the windows of shops around the Place St Sulpice that used to supply liturgical regalia to clergy; some of them still do, mixed now with statuettes, postcards and fridge magnets for tourists. You were wondering if a non-believing female could go in off the street and buy a gorgeous mitre or a hand-stitched linen surplice. But you had neither nerve nor French enough to dare; you still don't. Smiling, you turned from the window and started across the square that in memory is more leafy and shaded than I found it this time. You wore jeans as usual and a blue-and-white tunic tied at the waist with a sash of the same fabric. A sudden gust of wind blew your long hair away from your face and groomed you roughly; and in that instant you saw him. He saw you, too, and with a surge of mutual delight you knew each other. He wasn't as tall as you had expected and his eyes were not supposed to be brown. Nevertheless, you knew him. Surprised hearts leapt towards each other while you both stood still. Then you turned, each your own way: what else could you do? You were strangers to each other, possibly dangerous strangers. Never mind. You will see each other twice more: once he will be looking out of the window of a Fifth Avenue bus passing in the opposite direction. And once again, years later, you will catch sight of each other in Mexico near Oaxaca, appropriately enough across a field of ruins. He will be a blue-eyed gringo that last time, taller than he was, and walking with a cane. You will lose each other then for ever. Again.

I strolled from the Place St Sulpice to the Ile St-Louis where I was struck by the number of twee shops that have sprung up there since the old days; one, for example, where if I recall correctly used to stand a really useful greengrocer, now sells objects for domestic and decorative purposes, all of them shaped as pussy cats. I imagine a childless couple of retirement age wondering what to do with life remaining. 'I know, Jean-Louis,' says Madame, who has for all their married life been in absolute control of household arrangements. 'I will open a little shop that sells teapots and toilet brushes and any other thing shaped like a cat. Everyone loves cats . . .'

'Except', grumbles her husband, formerly a public notary, 'those who don't.'

On the main street that makes the spine of probably Europe's most glamorous urban island I stood outside the house where I used to live. All three windows on the second floor belong to a single small studio now. Then, it was partitioned into three very, very small ones; my own was stage left, nearest the great chiming church clock that overhangs the street. The street door now requires a code; when I lived there, first with my sailor boy, Douglas, and soon alone, we did not even need a key. Most of my hang-outs on the island have pretty much been transmuted into sit-down restaurants and boutiques; the Café Louis XIV endures, however, unchanged on its corner. I used to take an occasional glass of wine there with my near neighbour, Lise Danziger. Lise lived with her mother next to the public baths in a small block of flats reserved for homecoming survivors of the concentration camps. Lise invited me back a few times for lemon tea under the gaze of her mother who always stood, smiling vaguely at us from a faraway silence, waiting for other words, listening out for expected sounds. She looked very old, older than I am now or most people ever are. It was Lise who returned from a holiday to Ibiza, still an adventurous and remote destination in the late Fifties and early Sixties, and it was right there in the Café Louis XIV at precisely the small round table where I sat alone again more than thirty years later, that Lise, watching me in the clinical way she used to watch her mother, told me she had bumped into Douglas. He was drifting around the Balearics with his new woman, an American lingerie model called Robin. Behind the bar now is a crumpled, aged version of the young barman who used to be. No, he did not remember me and as he was an old-fashioned Parisian, he did not give a damn that I used to come by decades earlier to dilute his good wine with tears.

The walk back to my hotel in the Place d'Italie via the rue Mouffetard is not a taxing urban stroll despite the admonitions of locals asked mischievously for directions in order to test my growing impression that Parisians hold a much bigger city in their hearts. I asked directions frequently – to Montparnasse, the Cluny Museum, the Panthéon, the Place d'Italie – and every time I was warned that my destination was too far to reach on foot, though it always turned out to be no such thing. 'The rue Mouffetard? Oh no, Madame, it is much too far . . .'

In my day the Mouffetard used to agitate perilously during frequent political demonstrations, and often late at night resound with bursts of police machine-gun fire and the roaring chant 'Paix en Algérie!' which my Anglo-ear heard as 'Pay in Algeria!'. The locale bustles as ever and is still redolent of cloves, though the installation of a chain-run hotel for tourists, cute boutiques and restaurants serving cuisine a lot more expensive than oily plates of couscous used to be, is shoving it well over the cusp of gentrification and making a hash of cheap, long-gone late nights.

'1954: Yesterday I walked and walked for four hours. *Quelle joie*! I rode the Métro, too. What fun! But tomorrow is the last day. The last day! I feel physical pain when I think about leaving Europe. I close my eyes and see the steps of castles and cathedrals. We do not know in our "New World" the thrill of stepping into grooves worn by centuries of soles. And souls. The grace that makes even simple things so good here! The beauty! Jesus, it went so fast! I have not seen Europe, only seen what it would be to see Europe. Somehow I will return. I must return. I cannot wait to return. I feel as if I have been waiting all my life to be here.'

*　*　*

The glassed-in enclosure of the big café near my hotel was sheltered and warm in the setting sun. As I waited for my glass of wine, I recollected just how you sat scribbling your hot little heart out at a café table in Paris that sad last day, having come to the conclusion that your journal, scrappy and giddy as it was, could not, after all, be read by your mother or anyone except you yourself. And me, of course, who will be you and is I. A new hunger for footloose adventure, a longing to see the world, the very cornerstone of your expatriation were too apparent in what you had written. Of course, these were not the first secrets you had to keep from your parents; they were the first important ones. Only Marjorie, flatmate and best friend, having been with Study Abroad the previous summer, might be able to understand what you were feeling. Otherwise, the intensity of your feelings, if not their object, would bring down disapproval and scorn at home. The history of your entire homeland was reversing itself in you, for pity's sake! You were eastward bound.

The waiter delivered my wine and I raised the glass to you, the infant, stubborn and irrepressible in your determination against the odds to grow up and be I. At the table next to mine were two women, one of them an exquisite dwarf, the high heels of her smart leather boots barely touching the floor; both women smoked and talked into their mobile phones. Across the wide boulevard our resident *clochard* shuffled back to his corner under a spindly urban tree. I had seen him return each of the three previous nights. He was grizzled and sinewy with remnants of a strong man's muscle; probably he had once been a manual labourer. Early every morning, when he went about God knows what business, he left his bag tucked inside a grating in the pavement; it was a grubby pillowcase closed with safety pins – not even the street sweepers touched it. I watched him rummage for the bottle of wine stashed among his possessions. A long time ago, when my teaching of English came to an ignominious conclusion, I found steady work writing feature articles for the weekly *American Army Times*. Working out of an office on the rue Cambon, it was my duty to fill page after page with bland, apolitical stories about Paris, aimed at army wives and laid out between agency handouts and ads. It was tacitly understood by the staff – our English editor-in-chief, Mr Watt, two French secretaries and me – that our publication existed as some sort of post-war Franco-American PR exercise: we were there to be seen by the top brass – we probably had no readers at all to speak of.

'Just stick to the local colour . . .' said Mr Watt.

'But never read,' said I.

Out of the unread reams I remembered a story I'd written on the *clochards* of Paris among whom I found two former lawyers, a lapsed priest and a few men, once of property, who had thrown it all up and moved into cardboard boxes under the bridges. Sometimes, late at night could also be seen among them the fattest urban rats in Europe. The man

343

across the street was leading a life of luxury compared with most of those old-timers. He leaned against the tree trunk, tipped his head back and set his Adam's apple to work on the booze. Lights had begun to go on in the big block of flats behind him, silhouetting wardrobes and bedheads here and there. Is there any other capital city where citizens regularly use their windows as walls? I am something of an expert on the nature and design of Parisian windows, oh yes. I used to look up at them all the time with endless and hopeless longing for a place: for my place.

Night was gathering; neon resisting. The *clochard* tipped back his bottle of red again and I raised my glass of white. He drew hard on the bottle, then he leaned it carefully against the tree, stood, turned and addressed a group of passers-by jovially, with verve, just as I had seen him do the previous nights, not begging, only craving a civilised exchange of views. Nobody paid him the least attention beyond quivers of distaste as they studied to ignore him. Finally, he gave up and shrugged, raising his empty hands to the sky, before he slumped back and took up his bottle again. I lifted my glass. I knew just how he felt.

Never before had I been as eager to leave Paris, incomparably pretty Paris. Had I ever been as eager to be gone from anywhere? My mind raced past the setting sun and through night to morning and the train home. London. Home. Home. Who can imagine how strenuous and obsessive is waiting until, suddenly, waiting ends? I remembered being swept into the wide blue gaze of my son the first time I held him in my arms. So this was love. You and I know at last what love is, don't we, errant girl? Love is an end to waiting.

Nineteen

'1954: The voyage has been long. Nearly eight days! We are two days late because we had to go hundreds of miles out of our way to avoid a hurricane. It was too hot to sleep in the cabin last night so I crept out on deck until a sudden rain drove me back inside. The cabin door had locked behind me and I didn't want to wake up Midge and Ev. The closer we get to New York the more they talk about things and people I do not know. What is the reverse of getting to know people? I am getting to not know Ev and Midge. I ended up spending the night on the floor of the bar. May this not be a portent of life to come! In three days I will be nineteen. A baby has to live for a whole year before she has a first birthday, so that really means I will be in my twentieth year. My twentieth year! And I have found a whole new way to be. I want to get back to New York and the family, yes, and the books, and Marjorie and my other friends. But it hurts when I think of Paris and the towns of Italy and the wrong-way traffic in the dignified streets of London. I never really believed it would end. I cannot bear to think of how long it is going to be until I can go back again. So much time to get through!'

Don't worry about getting through time, sweetheart. Strictly speaking, time will get through you. Time gets through us until it's through with us. Yes, yes, I am about to deliver another lecture, dear child, the last one, I promise, before we part company for half a century or so. Know that nothing changes more in a lifetime than the pace and very consistency of time. It starts as molasses time, thick and sometimes too slow for comfort melting through infancy and childhood; it then picks up speed faster and faster until by your mid-forties you will all but feel the days, months, years slithering down the length of your spine. In the normal course of things, shortly before time runs out altogether, it gradually subsides to a measure that hardly moves at all, not so much a pace as a remote and desolate place furnished only with bodily functions and scattered memories, a stealthy otherwhere that absorbs fading energy and leaves a husk behind. While this slow decline is happening, lucky old ones – or possibly not – have children whose respect or fear or brute expectation is changed to guilt and concern that fuels their journeys from far parts of the world back to the old home where they arrive, worried and subdued, in rehearsal for a funeral. Nothing to say, no issues, no answers and no question about it: they are next in the queue – no time to waste, no love to lose.

347

With the dust of Paris still on my heels, I flew to America over your week-long Atlantic in seven rough and stinking hours. I had arranged to meet my brother and his wife who were flying east from California so we could see for ourselves and judge how Mother was coping with the inexorable trials of extreme age. If I know Michael, in spite of the noise and discomfort on board he was reading a book, as he would contrive to read in all but pitch darkness and even in the 'unlikely event' of an emergency. Within moments of our meeting he was bound to be recommending to me a well-written biography of an obscure Confederate surgeon, say, or the secret life of Aaron Burr. We three met at our hotel, a convention centre near Mother's community. There is no room to spare for us in Mother's house now that my surrogate has been installed. Lidiya is Russian, as an increasing number of surrogates seem to be for those jobs New York capitalists have outgrown. She is intelligent and attractive; a mature woman, the mother of adult sons in the Ukraine. Lidiya is not squeamish or impatient; she has a genuine faith in fruit and green vegetables that accords with her New Age tendencies, and she is in every way the ideal daughter for a woman in her nineties. Her attentions are calm and genuinely affectionate to Mother, who can still be returned now and then from her planet of the blind and sedentary to fizz momentarily with worldly charm, and scorn, and the wicked fun of living.

We sat in front of Mother's big television. The sound

was turned off and the screen swam before Mother's nearly sightless eyes. My sister-in-law dozed in the high-backed chair my father used to prefer. Our silence was broken only by the turning of my brother's pages and Mother's occasional slight cough. I thought of you, I saw you, bright-eyed I, as you were in 1954 at the end of Study Abroad when the *Castel Felice* sailed back into home port. We had spent the previous night moored within sight of New York's haughty challenge to the stars until an hour or so past sunrise, when we upped anchor and made slowly for the city that never sleeps and was going to work in the rosy glow. You, on deck, strained to separate your family out of the small crowd waiting on the west-side jetty; you were jumpy as a freshly deflowered virgin, fearing they would note immediately on your face evidence of the illicit penetration of your heart and mind, and your transformation into a woman of the world. In the unwholesome silence of our aged mother's living room I felt you beside me, knew your precocious self-containment and utter ignorance of its effect on others; I could have touched your dishevelled hair as I had not quite been able to see or touch you even when I went back to the parks of Paris that you had loved so much.

Mother used to boast with perverse pride that she was a word person and had even less interest in decor than she had an ear for music. On the wall over the television are a score of African masks, some of them relatively rare and valuable, that I have collected for her over the years in an attempt to displace her excruciatingly tasteless taste for gruesome schlock: plastic skulls and shrunken heads and joke shop bones arranged to impress visitors with her feisty disregard for death, and her attraction to what she called her 'dark side'. Under the alien gaze of those wooden faces my brother, sweet and serious, finally put aside his book. He rose and disappeared into the back rooms. After a while I followed and found him sitting on the floor next to the cupboard where I had the previous year discovered the Study Abroad journal. All around him were papers and photographs; I saw some of my old college notebooks and a picture of myself when I was six or seven, holding a tennis racquet almost my own size.

He looked up at me from a yellowing diploma in his hand; his eyes were moist. 'Jeez, Irm,' he said, 'look at all this junk. My whole life is here.'

This is when siblings part company if they are not very, very careful: as they find themselves swamped by the deepening silence and piles of second-hand stuff that departing parents leave behind.

After a few days Michael and Rosario returned home, where he would continue to read even in the summery torpor of southern California. He left me with a brotherly hug and a recommendation of *The Founding Brothers* by Joseph J. Ellis, an entertaining and enlightening exposition of early American history I was able to read only a week later after my return to London. The interim was spent in New York and, being deficient in my brother's single-minded concentration, I found myself incapable of reading seriously against the bossy clamour of midtown Manhattan.

'Do you wish a non-smoking room?' asked the young woman behind the reception desk of my East Side hotel. 'Do you wish a subway map?'

'Do you wish wine with your dinner?' asked the waiter at a nearby restaurant. 'Do you wish coffee? Do you wish the check right away?'

Since when has 'to wish' been a transitive verb in my old home town? When did 'want' become a dirty word? Or is it the local idiom of service with which I have never really been familiar? In olden days I used to commute regularly from nearby Jersey; later, at Barnard, I lived on the upper West Side first with Marjorie, then with a pair called Cornelia Grunge and Carlotta Leif: naturally, I called them Lunge and Grief. Finally, I had my own modest flat for a while on an unfashionable street. But I could rarely afford to eat out in restaurants and I had never before known in Manhattan the peculiar anonymity of staying in a hotel, or needed to re-create myself every morning from scratch as a stranger in the city.

'Do you wish coffee?' asked the young counterwoman in the coffee shop; she was already plunking the steaming cup in front of me.

'I wish . . .' I said with a histrionic sigh to signal a joke '. . . it were a decent cuppa tea . . .'

Only a slow count of three before she smiled, not bad in

a nation where an outsize fear of giving offence and possibly being sued for it subjugates native wit regularly to propriety and sentimentality. In fact, the land of America in general is chock-full of genteel restrictions and rules not meant to be broken.

'No littering' said the bronze plaque on the first of three benches at the bus stop near my hotel; 'no loitering' said the second; 'no sleeping on the benches' said the third. What was there left to do, I wondered, on a park bench in Manhattan?

It was as a child with my father on the streets of New York that I discovered the pleasure I enjoy to this day of walking in a city, taking local rhythm into the blood and gathering ripe sights along the way as country folk do blackberries. New Yorkers walk fast and cross their streets obediently at corners, as Londoners do not; they hate waiting for lights, however, and inch forward into heavy traffic, shifting from foot to foot to show they mean business. Londoners stay safe on their streets by pretending not to see what is weird or unseemly; New Yorkers protect themselves from oddness or threat by making a crowd around it. The pretty girl emerging from the subway, an Aphrodite from foam, unremarkably pretty except for her hair rolling in a golden cloak all the way to her ankles; the old lady browsing oranges at a Korean convenience shop, smoking a cigar and dressed in layers of petticoats; the six-foot-tall transvestite a few blocks further on wearing a severe black-and-white suit, Cuban heels, a little black hat with a veil to his chin, indisputably styled after his mother: show stoppers that drew audiences in a city of exhibitionists and voyeurs. Nobody, but nobody, not even an ageing woman, walks unobserved among the alert and nervy New Yorkers, citizens of markedly feline temperament.

'Love the bag!' cried a skinny girl in designer jeans who planted herself rather menacingly in front of me on Fifth Avenue. She nodded to an ingenious carrier bag from Switzerland faced with see-through plastic pockets for post-cards I had filled with images from my recent journeys: the proud nobleman of Siena, Dufy's yellow violin, the in-terior of a sixteenth-century Venetian synagogue, Peggy Guggenheim's Calder bedhead, the magnificent depraved Caravaggio *Sleeping Cupid.*

'Weeuhdjageddit?' she squalled.

The noise of Manhattan streets is constant; it is the roar of the urban beast itself and it never stops – there is no silence on that little island. Inhabitants shout to make them-selves heard: to hear in Manhattan is to overhear.

'That really makes me crazy when you do that!' a man's voice carolled in the hotel hall outside my door. 'Do that!'

'So she is having the dog autopsied . . .' one woman in a department store Ladies Room shouted to another, 'because he loved that mutt and he will never believe it was an accident . . .'

'Just tell me, do you or do you not wish Japanese chicken nuggets,' a mother in a local restaurant screamed to her fretful child.

The subway that used to be the IRT is now the 'Number 1',

uptown to Columbia Heights. No complaints, however, about the loss of a drop of mundane poetry, not after I realised on that hot morning in early June that Manhattan's trains are also these days air-conditioned. What greater service can a municipality do its troglodytes? With a quick thump of my heart I saw for the first time in decades the words 'Columbia University' set in mosaic on the subway wall at the 116th Street stop. I had forgotten how much I had forgotten, and how many. I had forgotten the joys and hazards of friendships made in that place, for the first time as an independent creature without family to return to after dark.

The dormitories of Barnard College for Women are now coeducational. Evidently, newfangled political correctness has put an end to the fruity surmises and giggling virginal colloquies of olden days in Barnard's halls. Probably, it has put an end to virgins. Puzzling, then, that nowadays a guard, armed I imagine, has to be posted at the high strong grille that used to be not much more than a picket fence around the women's college.

'And', I told the handsome young man in uniform, 'see where that big new building stands? That used to be our tennis courts.'

'Oh, yeah?' he said. 'Barnard used to have its own tennis courts? No kidding?'

I thought he was humouring an old girl; I looked again and saw he was genuinely impressed.

The College has certainly grown in its enclave across from

the main body of the university; new buildings have reduced the central green space that we used to call 'The Jungle' to not much more than the size of an urban backyard. I was pleased to see that the cluster of remaining trees is infested still by descendants of the very squirrels we used to feed with popcorn left over from sessions of sighing during whatever arty French film we had just seen at the Thalia cinema down the road. Out of the familiar old branches fell a memory so demanding that I stopped on one of the benches to loiter and litter and, if not to sleep, to remember, which is very like dreaming.

My senior year, eighteen months after study abroad, and I was more than ever determined somehow to return to Paris. I was walking through 'The Jungle', in jeans as usual, and balancing a pile of books on the flat tray of a loose-leaf notebook, a rehearsal, though I did not know, for balancing plates out of the kitchen of Schrafft's Restaurant on 34th Street where, soon after graduation, I was going to be working as an over-educated waitress to earn my return to Europe. It was the day of Miss Tilton's weekly seminar on comparative literature and I was hurrying for a front seat. A few of us discriminating undergraduates loved Miss Tilton's upright style and New England vowels; we preferred her banked wit to the flamboyance of general favourites in the English Department. It was there, on the path next to where I now sat as an ageing alumna, that my erstwhile best friend and flatmate, Marjorie, had appeared suddenly, moving my way in a wedge of her new coterie, Fine Arty types wearing skirts and cashmere twinsets. It was too late to turn aside. Ought I to smile and greet her as if nothing had happened? As if she had not, one day not very long before, slipped from argumentative disapproval into a cold and frozen silence resembling hatred, and finally moved out of our shared apartment. Should I nod coolly to her? Or should I snub her? I was not sure I knew how. Before I could make up my mind what to do, Marjorie turned her eyes, her head, her very being away from me in the path and as she passed within inches, without so much as a glance my way, I heard her say, 'Everything she has, she got from me . . .'

Decades later in 'The Jungle' it stung me, as it was soon to do you, thin-skinned youngster, to hear in my mind's ear the tinkling, icicle laugh of a former best friend. And I wondered again, as you were to do all those years before, just what she meant. Was it the grey pullover I had borrowed and returned? Did she mean the Scarlatti sonatas I used to listen rapturously to her play on Daddy's piano? Or did she mean the tour she had recommended to me, Study Abroad, and the trip to Europe that so profoundly changed my direction? Finally, I rose and left 'The Jungle' with its unanswered questions. What the hell. Most of the lessons I learned at Barnard were beautiful. I read Eng. Lit. What could be more beautiful? And, as you were going to spend the next decades discovering, child of my past, contentment in life requires a telling degree of what the hell.

356

The best of the old Broadway bookstores was renamed but not much changed, still using what looked to be the very same library step, that had once raised me and my classmates to the upper shelves of the tumbling stacks. Down the street a bit I stood so long on the threshold of what used to be the West End Bar and Grill that the young blonde waitress, possibly a student making part-time money, came over to ask suspiciously what I wished. The name of the place has been changed, the interior is just as it was, however, when Don-Don, and Donald M, Richard J, Jack R, W. Duell, Ronalda W, Carole H and other ragged Columbia reprobates, many of them brilliant, encircled the kidney-shaped bar and occupied the booths like a vociferous invading army.

'Do you wish lunch?' asked the blonde, who really was becoming suspicious.

'My misspent youth,' I said, nodding towards the dark interior.

'Oh, that!' she said with a quick laugh. 'We get a lot of you guys here.'

I was coming down the steps of Butler Library at the heart of the university and planning to return on foot downtown to my hotel, when I saw a woman of my own age approaching. She was part of the milling crowd on the path, yet apart from them, too, because she walked briskly, importantly and alone, and the surrounding horde of students fell away from her on either side. Straighter than I thanks to years of yoga, though no more than my height, she appeared taller; she wore her long grey hair in a chignon smart enough to be compatible with logic and evident academic eminence. Her turnout was highly tailored and under her arm she carried a handsome dispatch case. No doubt about it, a professor on her way to deliver, say, a lecture on a definition of wit in seventeenth-century pamphlets; or, given that it was summer when the campus is host to short-term, less serious students, perhaps a comparison of the beatnik poets to the classic romantics. Word for word, she had published much less than I – she was paid by the concept and I by the word – but of infinitely greater gravity and not on a glossy page, bet on it: no interviews with vainglorious celebrities, or local-colour essays on the lifestyle of Paris *clochards*: she had met Foucault once at a seminar in Europe. This was not a woman to apply her intelligence to the heartbreak or domestic agony of any other women, not unless the pain was old and published, and it scanned. Nevertheless, she had a good sense of humour, she was scrupulously fair, kept expensive sherry, and some of her students adored her. As we closed in on each other, I was unable to see whether or not she wore a wedding ring. If she had ever been married, it was a cool union with another academic or a psychologist or a medical man, and there were no children. Probably, she was divorced. I would be. She passed, oblivious to me in her wake, where I was turning, stunned yet only half surprised. The scent she wore is called L'eau d'ambre and as far as I know it is available only at a few shops in France. I wear it, too.

My hotel room was on the fourteenth floor and looked out on soaring skyscrapers, the most spectacular view I have ever been able to afford in Manhattan. Here and there were balconies and penthouse terraces so lushly cultivated that the neighbourhood awakens to birdsong, hardly the usual alarm call in the middle of New York. On a flat rooftop a few stories lower than my vantage point two lopsided deckchairs, a broken office chair and a sofa showing its springs were drawn into a circle. And there you were again, ghost of my young self.

'Are they waiting', you asked me – I asked myself – 'for a convocation of office workers from below? Or a visitation of angels from above?'

On the dressing table beside me lay your old notebook that had become a traveller's talisman, my baby St Christopher.

'1954: They are tying us up to the pier. I can see them waiting now! Mom and Dad. Michael is with them. He loves ships, too. He has grown. This will be my last entry. I am breathless with excitement and love. For my family, yes, and for New York, but also for what I have seen and will see: love backwards and forwards.'

Looking out fifty years later at New York's walls and windows beginning to flare in the late setting sun, I felt breathtaking love again, for you and Europe, yes, and also love of fireflies and yellow mustard and columbine in the garden: cradle love that draws us home as sure as the grave. An Americanism I don't need very often these days came to my mind and, with your hand in mine – your hand is mine – we wrote on the window and set afloat on the glass between us and New York's radiant skyline phantom words that are never quite concluded – Round Trip.